# Education

# Resources for the Study of Anthropology

Edited by
## James A. Clifton

# Education:
## Readings in the Processes of Cultural Transmission

Edited by
## Harry M. Lindquist

Houghton Mifflin Company · Boston
New York · Atlanta · Geneva, Illinois · Dallas · Palo Alto

*To my parents*
*Elmo G. Lindquist*
*Doscia R. Lindquist*

# Contents

# Foreword

The topic of education, as it refers to the more formalized aspects of cultural transmission and to the potentially more deliberate facets of cultural growth and adaptation, has long been an important area of anthropological inquiry. Yet only in very recent years, as anthropologists have been caught up in efforts to facilitate and guide social change and development schemes, have we witnessed the growth of this area as a specialized field of anthropology. In this selection of key readings, Professor Lindquist employs the defining feature of anthropological research by adopting a comparative cross-cultural stance. He also examines the historical and philosophical roots of our own Western educational values and strategies together with those of other high civilizations. Here then the educational ideas and systems of highly developed, complex nation states are set beside those of non-Western and developing societies. Thus Professor Lindquist offers an important corrective to those who, in analyzing the educational practices of other societies, take the standards and practices of their own culture as accepted, unconscious givens.

James A. Clifton

# Preface

During a period of fieldwork in Taipei, Taiwan, I became convinced of the central importance of education in comprehending what is happening in the developing areas of the world. At the same time, I was struck with both how much and how little is known about the processes of education and their relationship to industrialization, modernization, and westernization. Formal educational curricula, structures, and planning have been outlined, analyzed, and described at great length. Discrepancies between aspirations induced in part by education and the possibilities of fulfillment of those hopes are apparent even to a casual observer. Careful and sympathetic description of what goes on in classrooms, where the systems of education and individual student meet, is only beginning. When we broaden the definition of education to include reform schools, night schools and other institutions of learning which receive little official or public attention or funds but which serve large numbers of young people, both data and interpretation are severely limited. This reader brings together selections which attempt to approach education in a broad sense through both description and analysis.

My indebtedness to teachers, colleagues, and informants is due to so many people as to preclude mentioning all of them. My own research and insights rest on two primary sources: teachers and informants. The latter must remain anonymous. As for the former, I can mention only the most prominent: Robert Squier, James A. Clifton, Murray and Rosalie Wax, and Felix Moos of the University of Kansas have guided me in graduate study and postgraduate career. I owe Felix Moos a particular expression of gratitude for encouraging me to break out of the more formal constraints of academic approaches to anthropology. To John King Fairbank, the progenitor of so many students of Asia through his books, lectures, and example, I wish to pay tribute. Finally, my wife, Yen Lu, has been both a most effective fellow fieldworker and a constant comfort. My parents, to whom this effort is dedicated, have always gone far beyond parental duty in their help and support.

# Introduction

## I.

Formal education structures are under severe strain in all parts of the world. This reader contains selections which examine some of the significant problems in important areas of the world. In Africa, new nations struggle to adapt school systems and concepts of education developed in their colonial periods to their present and future needs — both local and international. In the United States, the racial, economic, and social strains on school systems and higher education institutions are well-known. In Western Europe, there is a struggle going on between elitist and mass education. The complexity of the issues extends from great, structural questions with profound social and political implications, as in France, to limited but locally difficult matters, such as in the conflict between the English and Welsh languages in Welsh education.

Asia, which contains almost half of the world's population, presents a mixed picture of struggle. In Japan, a principal — perhaps *the* principal — question is how to alleviate the enormous emotional burden on the young which is put on them by the drive of many to the universities and the passage of only a few through the needle's eye of the various levels of requisite examinations. In the People's Republic of China the Cultural Revolution, aside from its function as a political power ploy, is also an attempt to reform an inherently elitist education system to meet the enormous needs of the Chinese masses. In a sense, that struggle began after World War I with the May Fourth Movement student demonstrations which supported the change in Chinese education from the abstruse classical language to the modern vernacular language. The effort to make the intellectuals relinquish their special position as well as their assumptions about status and prestige continues. Finally, in India, all reform, including educational change, must contend with the caste system — certainly one of the most formidable barriers against change among the many configurations of social and cultural structure.

## II.

The role of an anthropologist in studying education is partially the application of ethnographic fieldwork methods, and crosscultural reference points to some aspect of education. Basic fieldwork methods, in summary, include (1) the need for participation and observation; (2) maintenance of as value-free and "objective" an attitude as possible toward the group being studied; (3) constant attempts to place the data being collected into a holistic conception of the culture and society of the group or groups involved; (4) gaining an understanding, even in the absence of agreement, of the goals of the superordinate group, if there is one; (5) grasping the variant meanings of symbols which the groups involved are using, both within each group and in communication between groups.

Ideally, fieldwork data helps a social scientist proceed from the particular to the general. In order to fulfill such an ideal, an anthropologist looks at many areas similar to the one under examination in order to compare his findings and shed light on difficult general problems. Education involves so many problems common to Homo sapiens that in fieldwork one must draw limits upon what he will investigate. Limits include the type of educational institutions (public, private, primary, missionary, secondary, and so on), the age range of students, the degree of formality of the school (a recognized government school, an unofficial night school, "cramming" schools for prospective college students), and principal problems (areas such as cultural communication, initiation into puberty, power and role relationships among age-sets in the student group, problems of communication between often uneducated rural parents and more urban, upwardly mobile youth.

Part of the task of an anthropologist who studies education is to be aware of the problems in education which local authorities and, in some cases, national or colonial authorities see. In some areas, he must also be cognizant of the principal issues in indigenous educational circles. This requirement adds considerably to the burden of his intellectual preparation and execution of his fieldwork plans. He must stand with his feet in two different realms of knowledge and methods. The situation is complicated further by the general factor that education and politics are almost never separate. An anthropologist's observations or recommendations are always directed in part toward or against a particular power structure. Within the educational community involved there are power relationships which inevitably come under the scrutiny of the participant-observer. The day is gone when an anthropologist can write about a group of people with the idea that his informants' grandchildren may read his articles or books. Today when he studies educational processes and institutions, he is studying the very means by which his academic output will be read and accepted or criticized.

III.

Any collection of readings represents a selection from a vast corpus of data and commentaries in at least one field. This reader involved selecting articles from both anthropology and education. Both these fields have long, complicated histories with an almost infinite variety of articles from which to choose. It is therefore very important that the reader understand the criteria on which the selections have been made. I applied three criteria to each selection. First, the article had to deal with a major anthropo-educational issue. Second, the writer must have provided depth in both intellectual insight and emotional comprehension of the people and/or situation involved. Third, the social groups described and analyzed must be part of a nation-state which is geographically or demographically significant in terms of world social, cultural, and political development. The specific relationship of these criteria to the selections will be shown in the prefaces to each major section. I have chosen, primarily, analytical and descriptive writings by social scientists. There are also selections from creative writers who are indigenous to the areas focussed on. These latter readings provide a view of how sensitive and intelligent participants in the cultures and societies described see the ironies, contradictions, and values of education and its uses. Each section also includes a bibliography which may be used to acquire more basic background data and analytical interpretation than a selection of readings can provide.

There is an important distinction to be made between socialization and education. Socialization is the series of formal and informal processes by which families and societies enculturate infants, children, and young adults into full adulthood. Methods of socialization and even the periods of life are radically varied among human groups, ranging from strong emphasis on distinctions of behavior between periods of life, as in the phenomenon of "teens" in the United States, to an underemphasis of adolescence, as in traditional Chinese rural groups. Socialization is, of course, a fundamental basis of education; in this reader, however, we are concerned only tangentially with socialization. The primary focus is on formal educational settings, such as village schools, reform schools, and so forth. We are, in other words, looking at a process through which social groups organize learners into institutions that provide the means for learning in a formal and ordered manner.

Many of the classic anthropological studies have been based on African societies. Most of them, of course, have focused upon tribal groups which had recently been incorporated into a colonial relationship with a European power. While the theoretical and practical importance of those studies is beyond dispute, new approaches are necessary for postcolonial Africa where new nations are painfully forging African ways. The purposes, methods, and assumptions which operate in the various African educational networks are a primary source of data for the study of personality development, cultural change, and conflicts of values.

*PART ONE*

# AFRICA

Three general African social-political patterns emerge in the selected readings: West African (using Sierra Leone as the model), a large and ethnically complicated nation-state (Nigeria is the model), and a nation with superordination and subordination based strictly on racial lines (South Africa). All three areas are crucial in the future development of Africa.

Clignet and Foster confront one of the major issues of African education, in fact, of the educational priorities of all developing areas: what can the government or political structure do when young people select occupations in the humanities, social sciences, and other nonscientific professions at a time when national priorities lie in technical and scientific avenues of development. We see the dilemma from two points of view: first, the West African governments have limited resources and the support of universities is financially very demanding. Government leaders and planners, of course, want to see educational funds used in an economical and nationally useful manner. At times, it seems possible for the universities to solve the dilemma through admissions policies based on occupational choices, provision of financial aid geared to national technical needs, and elimination of support if a student shifts to a nonessential field. Aside from the question of individual rights versus national needs, the problem is that such policies have been ineffective. Further, the individual student may have intellectual or personality barriers to selecting a "priority" field and yet have the capacity to utilize higher education in a meaningful manner. Clignet and Foster clearly show that there are no "answers" to this problem which can satisfy the demands of individual choice and national need.

In South Africa the policies of apartheid (enforced separation of the races) have made the position of an African intellectual even more tenuous, as Kuper demonstrates. An African intellectual in South Africa is, even more than in African-dominated areas, a marginal man or one who stands between two cultures. His marginality is more extreme in degree because he is an easy target for the resentment felt by the oppressed nonwhite majority in South Africa. From the individual point of view, education has an open-ended effect on aspirations. No political structure has been completely successful in modeling patterns of aspiration which educational structures have helped develop. South Africa is no exception. The South African nonwhite educated man is therefore put into a Western pattern of educational aspirations, severely limited in the level which he can achieve and occupations he can enter, and, at the same time, he is expected to be a middleman between the superior and inferior groups. We see here, then, the purposeful use of education to reenforce official ideologies which are, in the world view of the white minority, based on the necessary and natural differences between human beings.

Chinua Achebe is a leading African novelist. Although Nigeria is his home, his satire is much more generally applicable. The selection is the first chapter of a novel which sharply characterizes the conflicts between three principal aspects of contemporary African life: village versus urban, traditional versus Westernized, and the limitations of actual political leaders versus the unlimited hopes of Western-inspired political idealism. The novel presents two levels of reality. On the one hand, it is the story of the coming of age of a young school teacher whose maturation emerges through rather painful experiences with corruption, human frailty, and contests for political power. On the other hand, Achebe comments on the structure of political power in contemporary Africa. An important element in that structure is education. The Minister is not a very well-educated man by Western standards, but he has combined some Western learning with a greater portion of acumen and has emerged as a national leader. The main character, Odili, has a series of bewildering contacts with various power groups which all have one common aspect: Western-type educational experience. In Achebe's novel in general, and in this selection in particular, the reader gets a glimpse of modern forces in Africa which a student of anthropology and education must take into account.

## II

Dr. Julius Nyerere, President of Tanzania, is one of the leading statesmen of modern Africa. The problems facing his nation are general in many parts of Africa. His article, "Education for Self-Reliance," approaches the needs of a rural, agrarian, and poor nation from economic, social, political, and philosophical viewpoints. Whether one agrees or disagrees with all the solutions of Tanzania's problems which he suggests, any disinterested student of contemporary Africa must agree with the almost brutal honesty of the President's presentation of the current situation.

Significant portions of Africa, ranging from Lesotho in the southeast to Chad in the northwest, share common characteristics: growing populations, inefficient agricultural techniques, little realistic possibility of rapid industrialization, meagre natural resources, increasing demands for education, rapidly rising aspirations, and no clearly correct path to solution of pressing problems. The special relevance of this selection is that it gives us a glimpse of the thoughts of a national leader facing the main issue of one Pan-African problem: how can education best serve actual national needs.

3

# 1 ................. ....

# The Intellectuals

LEO KUPER

The position of the African intellectual is highly ambigous, surrounded as he is by the ambivalent reactions of others, both African and White. Even the concept of African scholar is ambiguous, and there is little in his social and academic situation to encourage scholarship.

The professional intellectual, living legitimately by his wits, is a new category in African society. Wisdom was valued traditionally, but in an instrumental role, as, for example, the wisdom of the councillor in political, judicial, or ritual decisions. This instrumental evaluation of education and of intellect persists, especially among the traditionally oriented. Intellectual achievement is assessed in terms of occupational opportunity or of its contribution to the struggle of the African people. A candidate for the doctorate degree in anthropology describes his own difficulties as follows:

> A man may be very clever and they [the Zulus] admire it, but only in so far as it's an instrument to fight the other group. . . . When you say you

Reprinted from *An African Bourgeoisie* by Leo Kuper, Yale University Press (New Haven), by permission of the author and the publisher. Copyright © 1965 by Yale University.

are learning now to take an extra degree, and so on [they say], now what are you going to do with it, how will it help us? Here the Europeans have taken away our land, the Indians take all the money and are monopolizing all business, and so on, now how is your education going to help us there? And if you cannot really relate your education to the problem that must be dealt with, then they just won't understand you.

Learning for its own sake is not easily accepted, he points out. "People ask why I don't earn a living. When they ask me to attend a synod meeting and I say I can't they ask what is it to go on learning when you are a married man?" Purely intellectual pursuits, which would establish standards of scholarship within the African community, are little encouraged.

Even when viewed in instrumental terms there is ambivalence, because the highest education does not emancipate a son from the racially subordinate status he shares with his uneducated father. And there is frustration when education does not lead to good employment, or when it creates estrangement between illiterate parents and educated children, adding to the anguish of sacrifice for children's education. An African health educator traces the conflict between educated and uneducated partly to estrangement between the generations within the family:

> There are people of the low type who have no respect for educated. They will say that some educated people misuse their gift. They say the worst drunkards are educated. This is a remark given by most people. When educated, they think they're too wise and abuse. The higher the educated become, they don't think of their illiterate community. They say they look low on them. If you look back to the background of most educated people, you will find perhaps, his father and mother are not. There are others whose parents were educated. The first group become ashamed of their parents. They will not introduce them. They don't appreciate that these old mothers had starved themselves to give education. Some will have the mother to starve in the country. If we educate our children they say, they will look down on us. They won't even come down to our level. They won't even call us father and mother. That's why there is always a line between the two groups. They despise education, because the educated don't come and work amongst them.

Suspicion of the political role of the educated, expressed, for example, in the accusation that the educated African makes money from the uneducated or sells himself to the White man, adds further ambiguity. There is both a need for the leadership of the educated, and a fear of betrayal by them. The African economist, Selby Ngcobo, feels that this suspicion is deeply rooted historically, and explains it as follows:

> Very often White officialdom of the Smuts regime looked up to the educated man as the most useful lever to work through as far as African

interests were concerned. They would take you into the committee room as the sort of man they could talk to — which created doubt and suspicion. You can talk the type of English they don't understand which also affects the relationship. In Natal the missionaries established mission stations and produced an educated type of African whom they weaned away from the tribal societies. Subsequently, he was used as a kind of interpreter, policeman, clerk, and given letters of exemption. In times of war, he was used also for spies and levies so that we have the expressions *izifundiswa* and *amazemtiti* (the educated and the exempted). They both became terms of contempt and derision. These people were regarded as betrayers or likely to betray[1] because they cast their influence with the Whites. The Nationalists have exploited this historical situation to the full. It has always been the technique of Native Commissioners to maintain their position by exercising a divisive influence against the educated. The educated are regarded by them or spoken of by them as agitators, or in Minister de Wet Nel's phrase, as wolves. Native Commissioners in the time of General Smuts would say, "we have passed a law, it is good for you. Now people will come and say it is no good. Don't listen to them. ..." There is a tendency to accord the educated people high prestige and to want their help, but on the other hand there is fear and suspicion that they will let them down. . . . I think that we educated people are responsible for the suspicion. We were more ready to cast our lot with the White community without explaining ourselves and taking Africans into our confidence (personal interview).

An African graduate confirms these impressions of tensions between the educated and the uneducated. He comments that the attitude of the lower classes is uncertain, being in transition — in Durban though not in the rural areas — from respect to distrust. He comments on the contempt for the educated as spoilt persons removed from custom, and given to drunkenness:

> They say, you have taken your child to school, you have educated him, and he is not improved. They also complain of lack of respect. They also distrust the position the educated man occupies between the European and his own people. The educated man is often the interpreter, the liaison, and is easily bribed. They associate the educated with cunning, with people who swindle in organizations, with people who know how to manipulate books. This comes from experience. They feel that we are an appendage to the Whites and would go with the Whites.

Jordan Ngubane (1963:Chapter 12), a leading African journalist, comments on the different racial attitudes of the tribal and the educated. The tribal people, he suggests, hate the White man and would like to drive him into the sea from which he came, but they need the educated African and are uncertain how he would behave in a crisis. The educated, on the other hand distrust the tribal man, knowing that he will be the first to betray them to the Whites. In private discussion, he said that the domestic servants, who are very close to the tribal milieu, hate the educated African above all. His portrayal of the antagonism toward the educated recalls an observation by Goldthorpe (1961:156):

> It is noticeable that in times of stress such as Mau Mau in Kenya or the 1949 riots in Buganda the group most consistently under attack have been the most Westernized Africans, for whom a fury has been reserved distinctly reminiscent of that against Quislings in German-occupied Europe.

And Banton refers in *West African City* to attacks made by African rioters on anyone wearing a collar and tie (1960:120).

Against testimonies of antagonism, disapproval, and distrust must be set observations of the extreme deference accorded the educated by the uneducated (Kuper, 1965:Chapter 11). There is often an extravagant recognition of educational achievement, of university degrees, based perhaps on the perception that the book is the source of the White man's power. The general standard of African education is too low for a critical assessment of the degree, of the university which conferred it, or of the standard attained by the candidate. Consequently the educated African is denied a test by competitive standards and encouraged to an inflated image of his achievement. Mere attendance at a university and any degree, however lacking in distinction, receive acclaim amongst the general populace, though the educated may differentiate, notably with respect to degrees by correspondence. In contrast, however, to the naïve acceptance of intellectual achievement, Africans are very critical of the behavior of the educated, setting much higher standards of proper behavior for them than for the population at large. Being relatively few in number, the educated are visible and vulnerable. This explains, to some extent, the adverse criticism, the rejection on moral grounds, and the expressions of disillusionment. The great expectations of exemplary behavior, conceived as appropriate for the educated, reflect the high prestige of education.

It is in this context of ambivalence that quite contradictory observations may be equally valid. Thus, as showing hostility, one medical student comments that, "The illiterate do not like educated people. You often hear them derisively saying '*Bathini o B.A. namhlanje?*' (What are the B.A.'s saying today?')." On the other hand, another medical student, praising the versatility of the intellectual, who is able to adjust to his own world as well as to that of the backward people, thought the uneducated tended to be content with their inferiority. "The uneducated have the great quality of respect; to them a teacher is a teacher, a minister a minister. They take you as a God. They will say nothing bad about you." These observations either relate to different segments of the population, or to different situations, or reflect ambivalence and change. Hostility for the educated is not confined to the illiterate. It may be expressed also by the educated who have failed to achieve a secure occupation or by the semi-educated who have failed to attain the educational standard required for the professions. It is only the bourgeoisie among Africans that accords a relatively unambiguous prestige to education, diminished somewhat by the growing opportunities for wealth in commerce and the changing status of the teacher under Bantu Education.

Within White society, there is again ambiguity and impediment to scholarly achievement. The missionaries detached the Africans they educated from tribal society without, however, integrating them into White society. Instead, they created a new segregated milieu. They developed the educated African as an individual because they were concerned with the salvation of the individual soul and not of the ethnic soul, and they suspended him between the two societies. He could not be integrated into the tribal group, since his education and outlook were disruptive of tribal values, and he was not accepted into the society of Whites. He had therefore to maintain his individuality and seek social participation within a new Christian-educated African community, a process which the segregated mission stations encouraged.

Education qualified Africans for the occupations of priest, teacher, and interpreter. In these occupations, Africans functioned for African society, teaching and serving their own people. Their role was not unlike that of the switches in the telephone exchange, passing the word — religious, educational, and administrative — from Whites to Africans. Working in the new segregated structure, they were again denied the higher competitive standards of the dominant society. When later some African intellectuals were appointed to the academic staff of "White" universities, the same pattern persisted. Africans were generally employed as Bantu language teachers, channeling culture from one group to another, but this time in reverse. The occupational role, like that of the social role, was intermediate between the two societies, an instrumental role shaped by others and not independent or creative.

The educational policies of the missionaries introduced a further ambiguity. These policies varied with different missionary societies and changed over the years. At first, different standards of education were often accepted either as adequate or as a matter of inevitable temporary necessity, given the starting point of an illiterate populace. Some mission schools emphasized manual skills, others a literary humanistic education modeled on the good English schools. There was concern over character building, discipline, and obedience. In time, as educational standards were raised, the African school system drew closer to that of the Whites, and students were trained in increasing numbers for the same matriculation examination. Implicit in this educational policy was the concept that Africans would participate in the same society as Whites. Presumably there must have been some vision of ultimate integration. In other words, the schools were shaping Africans for a society which has not yet emerged in South Africa. The sheltered school environment did not prepare the student for discrimination and subordination in the outside world. He was imbued with European culture and with ideals of equality and of the sanctity of the human personality, and he was destined to live in a society which now subordinates his individuality to the group and defines the mode and level of his participation in racial and tribal terms. There was thus tension between the universal values of a humanistic education and the particular values of racial perspectives, and ambiguity because of the different definitions and expectations.

Racial perspectives impede scholarly achievements, most obviously and generally through discrimination, but with perhaps equally destructive effects through racial definitions of appropriate standards. By virtue of these racial perspectives, lettered Whites, in the same way as unlettered Africans, give exaggerated recognition to the university trained African. There is no critical assessment: it is enough that the African should move on roughly the level of the White intellectual, that his achievement should be comparable to that of a White man. The exaggerated acclaim in fact expresses sentiments of African inferiority. Much as the image of the petty African trader is established in the minds of many Whites, so too the corresponding image in the field of learning is that of the petty African intellectual, notwithstanding the high academic and professional attainments of Africans during the late nineteenth and early twentieth centuries. That an African should graduate with a university degree is in itself regarded by Whites as an achievement, irrespective of the standard attained, and there is special acclaim at the graduation ceremonies, partly, no doubt, in recognition of the obstacles which have been overcome.

The university teachers know the level of achievement, but their more critical judgement is sometimes clouded by a benevolent paternalism for the African intellectual, or it is suppressed out of anxiety not to seem racialist. Some teachers are exasperated by what they regard as indifferent application on the part of the African student, or lack of gratitude toward his teachers, or the impossibility of getting through to him, and they react with racialist rejection of the African intellect. All these circumstances again deprive the African intellectual of a balanced judgement of his achievements. If he should succeed in gaining an overseas scholarship, and thus entering a freely competitive academic world and a less ambiguous social situation, he is likely not to return to his country under present conditions. As a result, the community loses its most educated members.

Inevitably there was ambiguity in the university life of Africans, since the status of the African scholar was never fully institutionalized and is indeed somewhat anomalous in a context of extreme racial domination. The ambiguity was expressed internally in the administration of the universities and externally in the tension between university and other milieus. The effect was to cast the African student for a political rather than an academic role and to give political color to academic issues.

African intellectuals were trained mainly in the mission schools and universities of South Africa, the former segregated, the latter either racially open or racially exclusive. Some 2,200 Africans in South Africa hold university degrees (according to a report in the *Digest of South African Affairs*, February 17, 1961). The English universities of Cape Town and Witwatersrand admitted students of any race. All the Afrikaans universities (Stellenbosch, Pretoria, the Orange Free State, and Potchefstroom) limited their student bodies to members of the White group. They were not, in terms of student composition, exclusively ethnic universities, since they admitted English-speaking White students, but they were and are essentially centers of Afrikaner ethnocentrism. Rhodes University (the English university at Grahamstown) and the Pietermaritzburg section of the University of Natal were also racially exclusive though they admitted some non-White students to postgraduate courses (in the case of Pietermaritzburg, a very recent innovation). The University College of Fort Hare was open to students of all races, but since White students rarely applied, it was virtually a segregated college for non-Whites — predominantly African, as originally intended, with an admixture of Indian and Colored students. Alone of all the universities of South Africa admitting intramural students (excepting the correspondence and vacation school tuition of the University of South Africa), the Durban section of the University of Natal was racially open in its enrollment procedures, but racially exclusive in its academic education. It freely admitted non-White students, but on an internally segregated basis.

There were some ambiguities in the nonracialism of the open universities. The University of Cape Town did not accept Africans in the faculty of medicine, owing to the lack of suitable clinical facilities, and the University of the Witwatersrand excluded non-White students from its school of dental surgery on the same ground. Because of national policy, non-White medical students at the Witwatersrand University were restricted in their clinical training to wards for non-White patients and might not be present at the autopsy of a White corpse. Barriers on social intercourse were imposed at the level of intimate physical contact — sharing the same swimming bath, tennis court, ballroom, or hostel, though not the same cafeteria. Some students and members of the staff established close friendships across these barriers. At the academic level, students were selected and trained on the basis of merit. There was an implicit assumption that opportunity for achievement would also be based on merit in the larger society, and hence there was tension between the academic and other milieus.

The racial universities automatically introduced a basic status differentiation by closing the doors of their well-endowed colleges to non-Whites. For the elect, the predominantly English-speaking or Afrikaans-speaking White students, education proceeded on the basis of merit and of democratic values. There was, however, a further differentiating function in the Afrikaans universities. Here students were nurtured in Afrikaner nationalism and trained for the key positions in the Government. The racially exclusive English university can no longer serve this function for the English-speaking minority. In relation to Africans, there was little ambiguity, total exclusion from universities being quite consistent with many of the ideologies and patterns of South African life.

The University College of Fort Hare carried on the traditions of the mission school, emphasizing the Christian way of life, and envisaging presumably ultimate integration in a racially open society. Superficially it might seem that this was an environment in which internal ambiguities and tensions would be reduced to the minimum. In fact, though possibly not as a matter of inescapable necessity, internal tensions became so acute at one stage, in 1955, as to lead to the suspension of 330 students out of a total of 367, and the temporary closing of the college. The following extracts from the valuable but little known report of the Fort Hare Commission describe the politicoacademic aspects of this situation — the forms and consequences of an exaggerated paternalism; the interaction of university and other spheres in the wider society, so that university discipline is identified with political domination; and the quite political character of academic protest, which becomes the symbol, or indeed arena, of racial struggle.

A noticeable feature of student life is suspicion — suspicion of the College authorities, suspicion of many (not all) Europeans, suspicion of one another. (The last-named, a most distressing feature, would seem to be partly due to unwise encouragement of tale-bearing as a means of control.) The attitude towards the white man, though harmful to the students themselves, is understandable in South African conditions, and is part of the obsession with the struggle for liberation and with politics generally . . . it is difficult not to come to the conclusion that some at least of the student body are opposed to all authority as authority. We believe that this is partly due to the confusion of legitimate discipline with *baasskap*. This can be understood in view of political and racial controversies outside the College, but it is none the less harmful and dangerous. Neither Fort Hare nor any other university can exist without discipline, but it may be desirable to modernize the rules of the College, provided that such as are still necessary in present-day conditions must be enforced. Booing, catcalls, and other hostile and uncouth noises when the Principal is speaking are quite intolerable in a university institution and indeed should not be tolerated. Even worse, if possible, are the disgusting anonymous letters and lampoons that are posted up on notice-boards. The easy recourse to boycotts and other forms of direct action are also to be deprecated. Much of this sort of thing may be explained though not excused by the failure at times of the College authorities to recognise legitimate requests or their slowness in implementing those which are acceptable; and in recent weeks by errors of judgment such as the Circular asking students virtually to inform on one another. . . . The humourless correspondence between these two bodies [the Students' Representative Council and the Senate], which we have studied, reads like negotiations conducted between two "High Contracting Parties" of equal standing in an atmosphere of cold war. The exaggerated sense of self-importance of the students as indicated in this correspondence is perhaps due to the feeling that the College must be looked upon as being in the vanguard of the political and racial struggle . . . we would urge that those in authority should not lightly turn down student requests as unreasonable, and that the habitual attitude towards student requests should be "Why not?" rather than "Why?". . . . It does seem to have happened on occasion that students have been reprimanded by the authorities for extreme or unwise statements made in student meetings, and that in circumstances where the only kind of evidence available was the testimony of fellow students. We feel that no harm done by these statements can be so great as the bad feeling aroused by what seems like what unkind critics would call "snooping." It is an exaggerated paternalism, out of place with modern university conditions, which alone can explain this interference with an elementary right. . . . In student meetings those who take an unpopular line — and supporting the College authorities is often an unpopular line — tend to be shouted down; or, if they are given a hearing at the time, persecuted afterwards as "sell-outs," the most devasting term in the present-day vocabulary of Fort Hare. There is much intolerance among students, and unfortunately a considerable lack of moral courage on the part of the students generally; for many students come to Fort Hare quite ready to devote themselves to study and leave agitation alone, but they are easily swayed or intimidated by the ardent politicians who tend to lead the student body. Those who claim freedom of speech should . . . learn not to obtrude political and racial speeches into any and every kind of discussion. . . . There is a real need for encouraging self-help and student initiative. Too often students fail to take responsibility, while complaining that they cannot be trusted to manage their own affairs. This may well be a vicious circle, and more trust on the part of the authorities may gradually lead to a greater acceptance of responsibility, but there are responsibilities which students could and should have taken even in existing conditions. On the purely educational side the picture is brighter . . . We notice, however, a very strong tendency on the part of the students to place the emphasis on examinations and degrees, and what these will bring in the way of material advancement, to the exclusion of the social and cultural side of education. . . . We are given to understand that while there are few if any animosities between African and European Staff members, coolness amounting almost to ostracism exists sometimes between African members supporting different political groups . . . It may seem as if we have dealt at undue length and with unseemly frankness on the faults of the students; but we feel that the present atmosphere is not merely unpleasant but dangerous in the extreme. It struck us at times as being a spirit of evil so strong as to be almost visible and tangible — a foe to all that is normal, sane and creative, like the evil possessions recorded in the New Testament. . . . it is totally wrong that a university should come to be used as the vanguard in a party political struggle, or even to be regarded as an appropriate place in which to make propaganda for party political purposes. . . . In general the Report aims at the elimination of the relics of the Missionary High School past surviving at Fort Hare and its transformation into a modern university institution (*Report of the Fort Hare Commission*, 1955).

The conflict at the University of Natal was never as acute as at Fort Hare, and discipline was certainly not of the mission type. Nevertheless some elements of the Fort Hare situation were also present in the non-White humanities section of the University. There was paternalism, although less pervasive; there was political involvement of the students, perhaps equally intense; and there was a thorough-going penetration of the academic sphere by politics. The nature and action of these elements may be seen clearly in the final campaign waged by non-White students against segregation at the graduation ceremony. But first a distinction must be drawn between the non-White humanities section of the University of Natal (Marian Buildings) and its Medical School.

Permission for non-Whites to start courses in the humanities was given initially on the conditions that non-Whites should not use the existing buildings of the University nor be admitted to classes organized for Europeans: there was also a general understanding that they should be no financial burden on the University (memorandum by the late Dr. Mabel Palmer, the organizer, dated May 1, 1952). The establishment of the section in 1936 was a reluctant concession, not guided by any philosophy of education but reflecting the racial inequalities and the racial prejudices of the larger society. Discrimination persisted throughout, and though it was somewhat modified in later years, there was always a temporary, improvised character in the arrangements for non-White students. Discrimination was most marked in respect of the material facilities — analogous to the difference between a location dwelling and a mansion — and in the range of courses offered; commerce, social science, education, and law degrees were added to the arts degree, but training in science and engineering was withheld. The same lecturers taught at both the White and non-White centers, duplicating, triplicating, or indeed, quadruplicating lectures if necessary, and this shared resource mitigated the general discrimination. Some changes were proposed when it was too late to implement them, and, in the last period, as non-White students were being diverted to the new Government colleges, there was increasing integration of classes, not only at postgraduate levels as in the past, but also in undergraduate years, and more of the "White" facilities of the University were made available to non-White students. An Indian student has now been admitted to the course in electrical engineering by permission of the Minister of Indian Affairs, there being no facilities for training Indian electrical engineers at the University College for Indians (*Race Relations News*, April 1964).

The non-White Medical School, in contrast to Marian Buildings, is relatively free from discrimination, though problems of race relations enter into the academic and training situation, and medical students were also subject to segregatory regulation of hostels, graduation, and sporting and other social activities. The Medical School itself established at a cost of over half a million pounds (paid mostly by the State) is a notable exception to the general rule of inferior segregated facilities for non-Whites. There is an adequate teaching staff, almost entirely White, which devotes its time to the non-White students without any competing claims by separate bodies of other students, and the facilities of the Medical School are freely available to non-Whites without racial restriction. Indeed the restrictions operate in their favor. Complaints about food in the hostels are endemic, as indeed generally among Africans at their boarding schools and at the University College of Fort Hare. But for the rest, medical students seem fairly content with the academic situation, or at any rate their dissatisfactions have not yet developed into protracted strikes and demonstrations. In the boycott movements, leadership and solidarity came from the students at Marian Buildings.

Many factors account for this difference. As we have seen, the prospects for non-White medical students are much more favorable than for their fellow students in the humanities. High prestige and relatively high rewards are assured to them — in the case of Africans, they are graduating to the peak of non-White society. Students at Marian Buildings, on the other hand, are training for the most part as teachers, often spurning the occupation for its meager rewards and opportunities, its declining prestige, but driven to it by lack of means and the hope of some security. For Africans the situation is even more frustrating, with the introduction of Bantu Education. There is often a strong feeling that teaching is no longer a noble profession, bringing enlightenment to one's people, but a political device for the withholding of education and the indoctrination of inferiority. This creates a dilemma for the students. Many are already teaching and seeking to raise their qualifications by part-time study. It is only in recent years that any number of African students have begun to find an escape into law. Marian Buildings is a prelude to limited occupational openings for students already experiencing the frustration of their ambitions. Higher education often requires half a lifetime of sacrifice. Although there is now a nucleus of African students from comfortable homes, most are struggling to pay their way, assisted by fee remissions from the University: sometimes they cannot find the tuition or examination fees and are obliged to withdraw. At the Medical School, on the other hand, African students hold substantial bursaries: these may not be adequate for their needs but they live in an affluent society compared with many of their fellow students at Marian Buildings.

Also relevant to the different reactions of students in the medical and humanities sections is the fact that Indian students are in a large majority at Marian Buildings, while African students are in a small majority at the Medical School, the respective enrollments in June 1960 being as follows:

Marian Buildings — African students 81, Indian students 558,
Coloreds 47
Medical School — African students 108, Indian students 92,
others 10

The social distance between Indians and Whites being narrower than that between Africans and Whites, Indians may be expected to react more sharply against discrimination.

The crucial factor, however, is the difference in the academic situation itself, relatively free of discrimination for medical students and highly discriminatory for other non-White students. There is a deep sense of deprivation at Marian Buildings, made all the more painful by the extensive academic and occupational opportunities and the infinitely better educational facilities for White students at the same university. Objectively considered, Marian Buildings may be less segregated than the University College of Fort Hare. Subjectively, however, the student is made more keenly aware of segregation in an internally segregated university. The discrimination is visible, part of the structure of the situation; it was imposed by the University authorities, and hence sanctioned by them; and the fact of racial separation within a single institution compels invidious comparison. It is easier to support poverty when it is the common experience of life and appears to be in the nature of things.

The rejection of discrimination at Marian Buildings, most strongly voiced by Indian students, is expressed in political movements and in the public life of the University. Active supporters of the different Congresses, Africanists, and members of the Unity Movement are all to be found at Marian Buildings. It is probably no accident that a minor political movement, the Unity Movement, should have taken effective leadership in the student body on issues of academic segregation. The ideology of the Unity Movement is based on a concept of the inevitable motivation of human behavior by material interests, and its members express a cynical view of human nature, at any rate of the human nature of their opponents. Tortured by the humiliations of the discrimination practiced against non-Whites, they voice the deep frustrations of the student body in an extreme form. Their aggressive use of vituperation, and more particularly of the epithets "quisling," "stooge," and "sell-out," give them a domination over their fellow students disproportionate to their numbers. It is primarily, though not exclusively, this group which crystallizes the public demonstrations against the University authorities, such as the boycotts of graduation ceremonies and of jubilee celebrations.

Desegregation of the graduation ceremony had advanced slowly, and under continuous pressure, through minute and delicate variations. Graduation of White and non-White students in separate blocks had given way to the sandwich method of graduation — first White students from one center, then non-White students, then White students from the second center. This in turn had given way to alphabetic graduation with racial segregation in the seating of graduands, and finally to alphabetic graduation and seating. Meanwhile racial segregation was maintained in the seating of visitors and students. This was the last citadel of segregation at the graduation ceremony (not, of course, at the University), and its defence seemed to acquire symbolic significance for the University authorities. To force the surrender of this citadel, non-White students launched their campaign, using the essentially political technique of the boycott. Again the action was symbolic, in no way affecting the basic discrimination at the University. It was rather as if the University authorities and the non-White students were engaged in a trial of strength, playing out on the academic stage the major racial and political conflicts of South African society.

The University was vulnerable. It proclaimed an academic ethic in accord with the ideals of the great universities which its own practices partly belied. It was this ambiguity that gave the non-White students and their supporters in the wider community effective opportunities for embarrassing the University authorities. Appeal was made to the higher tribunals of the academic conscience, and the moral conflict publicly exposed. Thus an editorial in an Indian weekly, *The Graphic*, on February 6, 1959, commented that it is pathetic and inexplicable that the University, the highest pedestal of learning where good sense and understanding should be the guiding factors, should be riddled with discrimination on grounds of colour. It is a negation of the very principles for which a University is constituted and that people of enlightenment and education should be party to discrimination between man and man is definitely preposterous.

The African National Congress and the Natal Indian Congress issued a joint statement attacking the discriminatory treatment at the graduation ceremony as

an insult to the dignity and self-respect of non-White parents, friends and relatives of the successful graduates. . . . there can be no justification for the maintenance of racial prejudices at an institution where the main criteria is the pursuit of truth and learning (*The Leader*, February 6, 1959).

The Fifty Year Jubilee celebrations of the University of Natal in 1960 rendered the University even more vulnerable, by reason of the very public nature of its celebrations. Visitors from overseas, distinguished representatives of the highest university traditions, were invited to take part in a conference on education which was the culminating point in a great publicity program focused on the University of Natal. The spotlight for the University of Natal was also a spotlight for the grievances of non-White students. The Durban Students' Union, organ of the Unity Movement, issued a "clarion call" to students in February 1960, stressing the theme that education cannot be divorced from politics.

The ruling class, in its mad pursuit of maintaining White Supremacy is *systematically* down-trodding and enslaving the oppressed both physically and mentally. Obsessed with this fascistic madness, the apostles of apartheid have chained the Non-Whites with a mountain of oppressive laws. The tentacles of apartheid reach out and entwine the Non-White in every aspect of his life.

Then follows some reference to discriminatory laws:

Education, instead of being man's *birth right*, is miserly extended as a privilege to the Non-Whites in South Africa. Education instead of developing the latent abilities of man, is prostituted to produce mental inferiority. These "Seats of Learning" are to produce servile automotons. These so-called Universities are converted into racial breeding grounds. These institutions, instead of allowing the individual to think freely, are converted into grave-yards for the intellectuals. . . . It is the responsibility of every student to understand that *education cannot be divorced from politics. . . . students unite!!! Fight for a democratic education in a democratic south Africa.*

The attitude toward the University was embittered and hostile. In the issue, "The Jubilee of an Apartheid University," the Durban Students' Union called for a boycott of the celebrations.

This Jubilee, this festivity, is not for us, the oppressed. The only people who have reason to celebrate are those who bask in the rays of happiness and contentment. That obviously excludes the oppressed. For us there is nothing but gloom, a bleak future and years of struggles. Celebrations at present are grossly premature and out of order. . . . Of course, it is undeniably true that the Non-White students have been *part* of this institution for many years and therefore one *logically* expect the Non-Whites to participate. But to do that would amount to a superficial glance at the problem. The question to be asked is: — To what part of this institution have the Non-White students been assigned? Were they accepted as equal members in this "House of Learning?" We need not labour this question. It is common knowledge that the Non-White students were and are relegated to the backyard (Sastri College) and to the warehouse (Marian Buildings). Inferiority in facilities . . . limitations of Courses of study . . . restriction of faculties . . . the crumbs from the tables of those who *now* want to celebrate. Hence we find that the history of the Non-White students for the past so many years is dotted with complaints, attacks and boycotts. These acts constituted a condemnation of the apartheid nature of this university.

It is truly a divided house characterised by a "privileged-underprivileged" relationship. Therefore social, residential and sporting segregation have become crusted traditions of this "House of Learning." Once an attempt was made to have a cricket match between the "privileged" and "under-privileged." The very idea was an outrage and therefore evoked a stern reprimand from the patriarch of the Household.

Now, because "celebrated" guests from world over are to pour in for the Jubilee, a façade of a united household has to be presented. The public and the world must be misled into thinking that "all's well" in this University. The Non-White students and those whites who think and feel like us must have no part in the perpetration of this fraud. We must go even further in exposing the truth in all in its nakedness. It is not *our* duty to cover up the sins of the University authorities. We must show the people of South Africa and the world that the Jubilee is not an occasion of happiness for us. *We must define our position* and show in clear language that 50 years of Natal University is not something that we can be proud of.

The result was that students achieved an almost complete boycott of the celebrations. Guests in their finest clothes at the most fashionable event of the year — a segregated gala performance by the Royal Ballet — found themselves confronted with protest placards — "Remove Apartheid from our University," or "If gold rusts, what shall iron do?" The special graduation ceremony for the conferring of honorary degrees on distinguished visitors and the education conference were not picketed, presumably because they were not segregated. In desegregating the special graduation ceremony, the University had set a precedent which it could not readily reject in the future.

There was by no means unanimity among the students on the boycott issues. One cannot say that the opponents of the boycotts lacked moral courage, as the Fort Hare Commission suggested in the context of its inquiry into the domination of the student body by political interests. The students were all suffering under discrimination outside the University, quite apart from their experience within the University, and inevitably they reacted with sympathetic emotion to expressions of resentment. Moreover, it is difficult, at a time when educated non-Whites feel the political need for solidarity against apartheid, to face the charge of being a traitor to the cause, a "stooge," a "quisling," or a "sell-out."

The division between students on the graduation boycott was based largely on differences in opinion or principle, with an admixture of racialism. Some students felt that they were obliged to accept segregated education at the University of Natal, but that they were under no obligation to attend the graduation ceremony. Graduation was simply a formality where students paraded in gowns of different colors, "an elaborate exit out of the university, and ours is not a grand exit, because of the segregation we had experienced in our stay in this university." There was no need to expose oneself unnecessarily to humiliation. Or, more positively, the boycott of the graduation provided an appropriate occasion for a symbolic protest against segregated education. Others thought it pointless to boycott the culmination of segregated education after years of acceptance. A complicating factor was the attraction of the graduation ceremony itself. It is a brief moment of glory in which non-Whites have the rare opportunity of public recognition on a basis of equality. The student who is politically committed can derive strength from his group, and feel that he is working for something greater in boycotting the ceremony. For the uncommitted student, graduating in absentia may be a heavy sacrifice.

Inevitably, the conflict of views brought African-Indian antagonisms to the surface through the oblique issue of discrimination against Africans by Indian cinema and café proprietors. This issue became confounded with that of the graduation, and the refusal by Indian students to boycott the cinemas and cafés stimulated anti-Indian prejudice among some sections of the African student population. There were charges against Indians of opportunism, of insincerity, and of using Africans for their own ends; to some extent Indian students were held responsible for the discriminations of Indian entrepreneurs. No doubt racialism was partly a device to justify taking part in the graduation ceremony and partly an unconscious mechanism for displacing, if not resolving, tension. The graduation boycotts were largely successful. In 1959, of the 47 non-White graduands, 40, including all the doctors, graduated in absentia, with 26 giving as their reason the racial segregation of guests. Under pressure in the year of its Jubilee celebrations, the University introduced a system of "voluntary segregation." Graduands and staff were asked to state whether they wished their guests to be seated with members of their own race or members of any race: 83.4 percent of the graduands and 62.5 percent of the staff asked for segregated seating. Most of the non-White graduands (48 of the 66) stayed away from the ceremony, 47 specifically by way of protest. In the medical faculty, 14 of the African medical graduands presented themselves, while the seven Indian doctors all graduated in absentia. There was thus a cleavage between African and Indian medical students and between the humanities section and the medical school. In 1961 the ceremony was fully desegregated — peacefully and with dignity, contrary to the predictions of those who favored the segregation of guests.

Probably more non-White students would have graduated in person in 1959 and 1960 but for the paternalism of the University authorities. This characteristic form of race relations is sustained, perhaps aggravated, in a university by the educational function of teachers for students. The role of educator is readily cast in the form of paternalism: and the paternalism is nourished by the feeling of service rendered to the students. At the University of Natal, the authorities could feel some justifiable pride in the number of degrees awarded to non-Whites (423 by March 1960). Paternalism was not entirely inconsistent with the educational function, but it could not resolve tensions arising from the desire of students for equality of treatment.

Paternalism was expressed first in the argument that students should not embarrass their friends by irresponsible action, but leave the issue in the hands of those members of the University Council and Senate who had their true interests at heart. This has the effect of stripping all initiative from the students and vesting it in the "fathers." Then, secondly, there was the threatened withdrawal of love.

> The decision of the medical graduands to absent themselves from the Graduation Ceremony had come as a profound shock to the staff. It had completely changed the attitude of the staff towards the students of the future. Many felt that under these circumstances they might as well seek other employment as a feeling of the hopelessness of the situation had been engendered (statement by a professor at an informal meeting between representatives of the University Senate and the non-White Students' Representative Council, March 5, 1959).

The same sanction was applied by the principal in a letter to the Medical School graduates after the 1959 boycott.

What you as a group expected to achieve thereby, I cannot imagine, but what I feel I must let you know is that you have succeeded in alienating sympathy in the minds of many people, particularly in the medical profession, who had all along been well-disposed to the Non-Europeans and especially to you as students in our Medical School . . . Many people have said: "If that sort of conduct characterises the products of the Medical school, why bother to retain it in the University? Why not let the Government take the whole show, and then the Non-European students can have everything separate?" (April 2, 1959).

Thirdly, the issue was handled largely at the level of personal relations (almost the intimacy of the family group, with the shadow of ingratitude for the love lavished by the parents) and not entirely as an issue of principle. Paternalism involves the transmuting of ideals and moral values into personal, familial relationships, which take precedence over moral values.

You have refused to be presented for the award of your degree in person by your Dean . . . By this action you as a solid group have contrived to inflict a gratuitous insult in public on a man who had fought so hard and had sacrificed so much on your behalf. It was as if at the very culmination of the years of training lavished on you as medical students, you deliberately turned your backs on him and told him: "I won't come and get my certificate from you. You can send it by post." This is the impression your action left on the staff of the Medical School and on the public in general (principal's letter, April 2, 1959).

Apart from paternalism by the authorities, a major circumstance, which favored greater participation in the boycott, was that the manifest injustice of internal segregation and inequality encouraged dominance by the most embittered section of the student population. The Unity Movement exerted an influence out of proportion to the small number of its members not because it reflected the political views of the student body but because it crystallized in emotion and slogan the underlying resentment and intimidated the nonconformist.

The position of African university students is not such as to promote scholarly detachment. Whatever the educational environment, whether open or segregated, many do become involved in politics, and their political ideologies influence their lives as university students. Political leaders are drawn from all the universities that trained non-Whites, and it is difficult to say which environment was most conducive to political training and action or to the dominance of particular ideologies. Certainly there was intense political involvement at both of the segregated universities, Fort Hare and Natal, and this permeated student life, giving it some of the qualities of a political struggle. Presumably the open universities, with their large numbers of politically uncommitted White students, provided contact with more varied perspectives and a counterbalance to the obsessive intrusion of political ideologies into the academic milieu. At the same time, the greater freedom within the open universities may have stimulated a more intense resentment of discrimination outside.

In an internally segregated institution with unequal facilities the academic environment takes on a political color. The imposition of segregated inequality is a political decision, not in the sense that it has been taken by a political party, but rather that it expresses the political attitudes which have shaped racial discrimination in the wider society. Conversely, educated Africans were committed to a universal system of values — assessment of the individual on merit, and equality regardless of race. This was largely the ideology of African intellectuals, reflecting their material and ideal interests (but now undergoing change as a result of increasing racialism and the possibility, or probability, of African majority rule). Consequently, academic discrimination was interpreted not as an isolated element in the separate context of education but as a violation of universal norms affecting political, economic, and social life. Even the "purely academic" issues tended therefore to become political issues.

In the detached type of segregated unit such as the University College of Fort Hare, students are insulated from effective contact in a hothouse of embittered resentment. Political involvement is fostered by bringing together, in isolation, a population of students aggrieved by their deprivations in the wider society. The medical school of the University of Natal is also a detached, segregated, non-White unit. But it is not isolated: students are freely in contact with the outside world, and the nature of their studies, the intense concentration demanded, and the potentially high rewards and fulfillment on graduation all help to detach them from political preoccupation. The medical students seem less politically committed than their fellow students, although they respond to much the same appeals and reflect in their attitudes the same ideologies.

Location of the university has an influence on political ideology and participation. In Durban there was easy access to political leaders and political headquarters, and a strong Congress tradition. University students in Cape Town were exposed to the intellectuals of the Unity Movement, which was well-established in the Cape Western area. The Cape Eastern area had a long tradition of political struggle, and many students entering Fort Hare were already committed to the policies of the African National Congress or of the All-African Convention. The traditions of the universities are also relevant: the kind of student political groups established in them, and their fluctuating fortunes. And the racial composition of the student body exerts an influence — whether it is racially exclusive or provides the interracial contact and experience from which a more inclusive concept of the political struggle can be based. But the role of the universities in the political involvement of non-White students is probably subsidiary, affecting the content of their political ideologies and the manner of their participation rather than the fact of their involvement itself. This situation derives at the present time from the application of apartheid and the struggle for liberation in the wider society. National emergencies and protests have their immediate repercussions in the university community, particularly at the segregated universities, where sympathetic demonstrations by students have sometimes totally suspended academic activity. And the culling of political leaders by imprisonment, bans, and exile places responsibility on the university students, who become the second echelon leaders, so that there is a continuous preoccupation with politics, and the political perspective dominates the academic.

Anthony Ngubo, in an unpublished study of African intellectuals, argues that the opportunities are too restricted for Africans to establish themselves as members of an intellectual elite and that for them, education is purely an instrument for better employment opportunities and higher status. He suggests that scholarly detached academic intellectualism is a luxury which only a free people can attain and enjoy and that African intellectuals are in no position to engage in this luxury when they have not achieved demonstrable necessities. This seems a doubtful proposition in view of the intellectual preoccupations of the Jewish people in the ghettoes of Europe. Subordination and deprivation may even stimulate scholarly detachment. The lack of an intellectual tradition in the African community is obviously a significant factor in this connection, but so also is the acute stage of racial conflict in which the political leaders are the potential saviors. They constitute the prestige group, both for the urban masses and also for the students, and the latter attach or subordinate themselves to the political elite. Ngubo comments that very few Africans have made any contribution to the store of knowledge in academic fields available to them, their mental energy being spent in political thinking. He argues that the lack of a true intellectual elite seems to leave a vacuum in the African community. The intellectual elites of eastern and western Europe, plus a few West Africans make up the wise men. Non-African intellectuals fashion thinking, and hand it to the African educated elites, who in turn disseminate it among their people. He concludes that educated Africans form a potential educated political elite: scholarship will be a future development.

Political involvement has the effect of pushing many educated Africans back to the masses. In the past, the structure of African society might have been conceived crudely in terms of a great body of tribesmen and a small "class" or "community" of the educated, bound together by Westernization, civil privileges, and an opportunity for personal advancement. Today the Government seeks to return the intellectual to his tribal group. Increasing use is made of the chiefs as the channel for communication with the masses, bypassing the intellectuals. Definition of life chances by the authorities is essentially in group terms: individual mobility must be confined within the tribal or linguistic group. The intellectuals are too vulnerable to resist these pressures unaided. Most educated Africans must seek employment in organizations which are under White control: even the independent professionals — doctors and lawyers — can readily be deprived of a livelihood. Hence individual salvation for the intellectual is not readily achieved by personal advancement nor by the collective effort of the intellectuals, and the situation thus turns the intellectual toward the masses.

Changes in the structure of the African community assist identification with the masses. The large urban proletariat has been exposed to Westernization and shares in some measure the ideas and preoccupations of the educated. There has been an infusion of educated Africans into the ranks of the uneducated. In consequence of Bantu Education, some teachers have been obliged to seek manual employment. The schools have trained more young students than could be absorbed into the white-collar occupations, and many of these are also occupied manually. Sharing the aspirations of the educated elite, but denied the opportunities and material rewards, they form a middle group between the bourgeoisie and the stable urban proletariat. Embittered, frustrated, aggressive, nonconformist, suggestible, and prone to violence, they reject the polished behavior of the educated elite, the *os'tshuzana* ("excuse me") class. They are an important element in the growth of a mass movement, exerting pressure on the educated and providing a link with the masses.[2]

The Government has now taken the final step in segregation at the university level by establishing the racial or ethnic university as the only model. Ethnic exclusiveness is represented in the tribal university colleges for Africans — the University College of Zululand at Ngoye for Zulu and Swazi students, the University College of the North at Turfloop for Sotho-, Tsonga-, and Venda-speaking peoples, and the University College of Fort Hare for Xhosa — and in the ethnic University College of the Western Cape at Bellville for Coloreds and the University College at Durban for Indians. At the same time, the racial exclusiveness of the Afrikaans universities is now being imposed on the English universities, which can only admit new non-White students by special Government permission.

The ethnic colleges offer Africans opportunities for employment in academic fields, not limited to Bantu languages. They could, therefore, provide the occasion for scholarship. But they are essentially political institutions, part of the program for harnessing education to apartheid, and seem unlikely to attain university standards. Control is authoritarian. Members of the staff hold either State posts (that is to say they are civil servants), or Council posts, which are also controlled by the Minister, whose approval is required for appointment, promotion, or discharge. The incumbents of State posts are guilty of misconduct if they do, or cause or permit to be done, or connive at any act which is prejudicial to the administration discipline or efficiency of any department, office, or institution of the Government; or if they display insubordination by word or conduct, publicly comment upon the administration of any department, become a member of any political organization, take active part in political matters, or become pecuniarily embarrassed. In the case of a Council post, the Minister may instruct the Council of the University to institute an inquiry into the conduct of the staff member and direct the Council to take such steps against him as fall within the competence of the Council. The conscience clause, affording protection against exclusion on religious grounds, was deliberately omitted. The composition of the Council and Senate is controlled by the Minister, and Africans are relegated to subordinate roles in advisory councils and advisory senates. Academic salaries are also discriminatory.

The activities of students are carefully regulated. The Rector has power to control meetings, student organizations, the circulation of any publication for which students are responsible, the release of any statement to the press, and, indeed, all student contact with the outside world. Sanctions are heavy, since expulsion from his university college may have the effect of totally excluding the student from full-time university study in the Republic. This has not prevented African students from coming together across tribal and university bounds. In December 1961, at a conference of students drawn from the African ethnic universities, Natal, Roma, and many senior schools, the African Students' Association of South Africa was formed to unite African students to promote close contact with other students at home and abroad, and to stimulate interest in educational and cultural advancement. The conference declared its opposition to all forms of discrimination in education and to the use of education to further party political ends, as in Bantu Education, and pledged itself to strive for free, compulsory, and universal education (but not divorced from the demand for a democratic society). Because African students suffer disabilities peculiar to their group, the conference decided that the association should be composed of African students (*The Graphic*, December 22, 1961).

At the University College of Fort Hare there has been continuous friction. The new system was received with hostility, as reflected in the poster displayed during a demonstration in October, 1959: "Maree,

Verwoerd and Co., University Funeral Undertakers, Afrikanerdom Embalmers, Specialists in Cheap Intellectual Coffins." The demonstrations have continued, with expressions of extreme hostility against the Rector, the expulsion of the Secretary of the Students' Representative Council, the building up of police forces at a neighboring police station in September, 1960, and the temporary closing of the college in June, 1961, following a demonstration in which the buildings of the college were painted with slogans — "To hell with Verwoerd and his Republic," "Democracy not Boerocracy," and "Solidarity with our Masses." At the University College of the North, there have been reports of occasional hostility: only the University College of Zululand, among the African universities, seems peaceful.

In the circumstances, it seems unlikely that the ethnic colleges will provide either the academic skills or the environment for the training of African scholars. And as for experience relevant to political outlook, the colleges offer only the alternatives of tribal revivalism or exclusive nationalism.

## NOTES

1. Molema writes, in somewhat similar vein, of the reaction of the tribal people in the Cape to "their half-civilised and detribalised fellow-countrymen. . . . They call them Ama-Kumsha or Ma-Kgomocha; that is, literally — speakers of European languages, a word which, however, in the mind of a tribal Muntu, is always associated with something of deceit, and is almost synonymous with that meaning turn-coat, cheat, or trickster" (Molema, 1920: 319).

2. Based on an analysis by Ngubo. Gordon Wilson, in an article on "Mombasa — A Modern Colonial Municipality," in *Social Change in Modern Africa*, ed. A. Southall (London, Oxford University Press, 1961), p. 104, reports a somewhat similar development. For the first time in the history of East Africa, he writes, educated Africans, at least educated to the point where they can read and write in English and Swahili, are unable to secure employment in white-collar jobs. They are forced to work as laborers, and they are able to communicate with the illiterate group by reading to them political speeches and manifestos reported in the press.

# The Fortunate Few:
# Some Concluding Observations

REMI CLIGNET

PHILIP FOSTER

Perhaps of all "imported" institutions in contemporary Africa the school has struck the deepest roots. To be sure, in many areas people were suspicious of the early efforts of missions and government to create a minimal system of formal education and were reluctant to send their children to school. Even today in parts of Africa the school is regarded as an alien institution. Yet this attitude is rapidly disappearing. One of the most striking features of the last decade has been the growth of a mass demand for education, which has often far outstripped the ability of governments or voluntary agencies to supply it. It is on the school

Reprinted from *The Fortunate Few: A Study of Secondary Schools and Students in the Ivory Coast,* Northwestern University Press (Evanston), by permission of the authors, Remi Clignet and Philip Foster, and the publisher. Copyright © 1966 by Remi Clignet and Philip Foster.

that the mass of the African peoples place their highest hopes and aspirations for their children. It is also on the school that African governments rely in great measure for the rapid spread of modernization and accelerated economic growth.

Unfortunately this African preoccupation with education has not led to any substantial volume of scholarly research on how the schools actually function in Africa and what part they are playing in development. Perhaps more is known about traditional lineage organization in Africa than about an institution which is playing a major role in the transformation of African societies.

Current studies of African education frequently attempt to examine quantitatively how groups in different parts of the educational system can be adjusted to meet expected demands for skilled personnel on the basis of current manpower estimates. Whether available data are adequate for the purpose of making reasonable forecasts is beyond the scope of our present discussion. We may note, however, that most estimates are likely to be wildly inaccurate, even if African governments were in any position to carry out the planning required. Further, this approach leads to a greatly oversimplified view of the relationship between the occupational structures of African nations and their educational systems. If the schools are to assume the major responsibility for training skilled individuals, there is still a general reluctance to realize what this type of planning involves on the part of the state: far greater control of the quantity and content of schooling and far greater power in the direction of labor than any African government is likely to be able to have at its disposal. Even within total-command economies, the adaptation of educational systems to government-defined economic priorities has been extremely difficult, and no present African regime is so stable that it can directly bend the schools to its immediate purposes. Educational development in Africa has an autonomous quality, and any government which attempts direct qualitative and quantitative control of the schools may well find itself in conflict with the aspirations of the mass of the population. The plain fact is that although educational systems continue to grow very rapidly, the numerous plans made for the transformation of the schools have been largely ineffective.

A second focus of current controversy concerns the question of the Africanization of schools and their adaptation to African cultural traditions and society. One has an intuitive sympathy for some of these views, stemming as they do from the present climate of African nationalism and an understandable desire for that cultural self-respect which colonialism did much to erode. Yet an air of unreality and a peculiar mixture of sense and nonsense attend the whole discussion. Few persons would deny the need for the Africanization of schools in the sense that curricula should contain more African content. Indeed it would be desirable for those Africans who have been actively demanding Africanization of content to bend their immediate efforts to the development of new curricula and the preparation of new texts. Unfortunately most books ostensibly prepared to conform to African requirements are still written by Europeans.

However, the implications of the Africanization controversy go far deeper than this, and at bottom there is a vague notion that somehow the schools can be wholly integrated with African culture. This is a delusion which avoids the basic issue: If modernization and economic development are major goals, then a price will have to be paid in the destruction of certain cherished cultural traditions. The school in Africa is inevitably an agent of change. Through its role as a creator of new elites, through its diffusion of new ideas and skills, through its increasingly important function as a criterion of economic and social status, it inevitably erodes the foundations of traditional society and culture. Schools in Africa can never become agencies of simple cultural transmission facilitating consensus and stability, whether the content of instruction is African or European. In this sense the whole issue of adaptation is spurious. Even if one were sure what the term "adaptation" really means (and this point is rarely raised explicitly), it would be equally clear that in any changing society an educational system might be adapted to one institutional complex but not to another.

What we suggest here is that this kind of controversy tends to overlook the real educational issues confronting the new states. In colloquial terms, the school has come to stay, and its curricula will remain primarily Western. Our task is to see how it actually operates and what are its functional relationships with other aspects of the contemporary social and economic order of the African states. For example, only systematic studies of African educational systems and their clientele can enable us to avoid both the oversimplified approach of the manpower planner and the rather more diffuse and prescriptive statements of the educational ideologues. We can now turn to examine the implications of the findings of this study for both further research and planning.

## SECONDARY EDUCATION AND SOCIAL MOBILITY

Few observers of the African scene have failed to notice the extraordinarily humble origin of many contemporary leaders in politics and other realms of behavior. In reading the biographies of many of these individuals, one notes that the local mission or government school seems to have played a salient part in facilitating their upward mobility. Further, in those areas where adequate primary schooling is available, entry to secondary school is often crucial to later success.

Of course, all this does not imply that aggregate rates of mobility in African societies are high; quite the reverse is true. Only a tiny proportion of individuals will achieve any degree of upward mobility in view of the relatively small number of places available at the top and middle levels of the occupational structure. In many African nations contemporary economic growth has been relatively slow, with the result that occupational opportunities are limited — apart from those generated by the Africanization of formerly European-held positions (a feature not so evident in the Ivory Coast). Yet despite limited occupational outlets and the small size of the secondary school systems in most African countries, present-day elites are drawn from a very broad base. It can never be argued that they are self-recruiting and that their membership is restricted to a predetermined group.

In earlier chapters we have attempted to show that, in the Ivory Coast at least, the secondary schools have been extremely effective in facilitating occupational mobility and potential elite membership. Of course, studies of this nature are always subject to two kinds of interpretation, depending on the "ideological stance" of the investigator. Initially one can argue in terms of the *relative* chances that different subgroups within the population will have of entering secondary school. In this case it can be said that patterns of inequality are very marked in the Ivory Coast. A southern Agni is about ten times more likely to enter some form of secondary education than a northern Senoufo. The chances of the child of a managerial or clerical worker are about eleven times greater than those of the offspring of a farmer. Those of boys and girls in the great towns of Abidjan or Bouaké are three times greater than those of children in small communities.

Thus one can build up a picture of glaring inequality of opportunity, much of which has resulted from earlier patterns of colonial penetration and development. This is quite apart from the question of sex differentials and the fact that among girls inequalities are even more marked. Yet we would argue that anyone concerned with the role that schools play in facilitating mobility is misled by this kind of analysis. For it is evident that in *absolute* terms, recruitment patterns are still extremely open. Of Ivory Coast secondary school students (excluding African foreigners), almost 70 percent do not come from the more advanced Agni and Lagoon peoples, over two-thirds are the children of farmers, and well over one-half come from the smallest towns and villages.

Further, the influence of ethnic and social background actually tends to diminish as students move up through the educational system. We had expected (in view of much Western evidence) that there would be differences in the ethnic and social composition of the student body at the *troisième* and *Baccalaureat* levels, while the different streams in the system would cater to distinctive clienteles. But though slight variations are apparent they are not large enough to be significant for processes of elite recruitment.

Indeed internal movement of students between cycles and streams within the system seems generally to smooth out differentials. The doubling of classes, with consequent downward mobility, more characteristic of students with superior social backgrounds, enables others to remain within sectors higher in prestige. To be sure, cross-sectional studies like the present one have severe limitations. Inclusion of students within *sixième* classes would have given a clearer picture, while a longitudinal investigation would have shown whether dropping out of the system is significantly associated with ethnic and social background.

Notwithstanding these deficiencies, one major finding concerning recruitment is that the characteristics of students in different levels and streams do not vary greatly. Once within the system, the rural farm child's chances of entering the higher prestige streams are not overwhelmingly different from those of his urban counterpart with a superior social background.

All this, of course, applies to only about 2 percent of Ivory Coast children, the proportion who enter secondary school. But it suggests that openness of access and allocation is possible even when the size of the secondary school system is very small. Therefore our rejoinder to those critics who have so vociferously condemned French-type systems as "elitist" in orientation is that they are sometimes equivocal in their use of the term "elitist." If they imply that schools actually check mobility and confine secondary education to a socially exclusive minority, then this contention is totally untrue. On the other hand, if they imply that only a relatively small proportion of the child population enters secondary school, then they are obviously right. Quite clearly, even where African leadership is genuinely committed to the mass diffusion of education at the primary and secondary level, sheer limitation of financial and teaching resources makes any short-run expansion of secondary education very difficult.

In view of the peaked nature of the occupational structure of the Ivory Coast, it follows that only very few Africans will achieve elite status or enter high-level occupations; the important thing is that access to these positions remains relatively open. We would argue that the crucial issue in the new African states is not whether the number of persons occupying high- and middle-level occupations remains small, but whether people perceive that they or their offspring have some chance of gaining such positions. Men may be prepared to accept glaring economic and social inequalities so long as they believe that the existing arrangement is "just" or that they have an opportunity to improve their lot. Indeed it might be suggested that a significant difference between Western societies and contemporary Africa is that in some Western nations the "lower orders," until very recently, accepted their subordinate status. In Africa relative deprivation will be tolerable only if there is a visible chance for mobility.

The schools have certainly provided such opportunity. Will they continue to do so? Will the doors to secondary schools remain open and opportunities increase, or will places become increasingly monopolized by the offspring of existing elites?

This touches upon a more fundamental question: What kinds of social structure are emerging in contemporary Africa? It is almost inevitable that income, education, and occupation should become increasingly important as determinants of individual status. Does this imply the gradual emergence of social classes as we of the West understand this term? Some observers (including many Africans) have suggested that the persistence of lineage and affinal ties, which tend to cut across potential lines of stratification, has militated against the emergence of class subcultures. The resulting open and fluid society is reflected in patterns of recruitment into secondary education and in a relatively weak association between students' attitudes and values and their socio-economic background. In other words, objective inequalities in wealth, status, and education have so far not been paralleled by marked cultural differentiation along class lines.

Alternatively, the fluid character of contemporary African societies may be perceived as transitional. One might therefore expect increased social differentiation, with a corresponding emergence of rigid horizontal strata. This trend, it can be argued, will be particularly marked if rates of economic growth and the consequent expansion of opportunities are low. Under these circumstances existing elites will attempt to perpetuate themselves while at the same time cultural differences between the higher occupational groups and the mass of the people will become sharper. This development will be correlated with a corresponding deemphasis of lineage and affinal ties and higher level of endogamy between occupational groups. Thus over time we would see the emergence of a much more crystallized and rigid class structure. The secondary schools would become correspondingly less effective as a mobility mechanism, reflecting in greater measure the rigidities of the class structure and becoming more and more the preserve of privileged minorities. Not only this, but social differentiation of students in a multistream system would be likely to increase.

The prediction of future trends in African systems of social differentiation is a risky undertaking. Undoubtedly they will be heavily influenced by economic development, and a quickening in the tempo of economic growth will maintain or enhance opportunities for mobility. In Western societies where rapid development is still going on there has been no indication of a decrease in mobility opportunities or an increase in rigidification of the status structure. But at present contemporary Africa (including the Ivory Coast) faces rather gloomy prospects for rapid economic growth in the foreseeable future. Many development schemes depend on primary products whose world prices are subject to drastic variations.

On the other hand, the expansion of secondary schooling might also keep existing jobs open to talented persons from various segments of society. As the number of secondary school places increases, almost certainly the absolute representation of different subgroups will also expand. However, it does not follow that relative representation will change very much. For example, it is well documented in the case of England that the expansion of secondary grammar and higher education has had little effect on the opportunities of lower class people to enter these types of institution.[1] One must not expect, therefore, that merely enlarging the secondary school enterprise in African countries will lead to radical shifts in the character of the student population.

In this connection it is worthwhile comparing the Ivory Coast with neighboring Ghana. Both countries are extraordinarily prosperous by West African standards, yet Ghana is certainly the more highly developed of the two. Its occupational structure is more complex and broader at the summit and at intermediate levels. Even more striking, educational development in Ghana is at a far higher level. In 1963 that country, with a population about twice that of the Ivory Coast, had eleven times as many students in some form of postprimary school, excluding those in higher education. To be sure, about four-fifths of them were in four-year middle schools, but these institutions are, generally speaking, not too different from the *Cours Complémentaires*. Further, Ghana had 20,000 students just in secondary schools roughly equivalent to the *Lycées* — as many as there were in the whole postprimary system of the Ivory Coast.

These striking differences, however, cannot be attributed to the fact that the pattern of recruitment in Ghana is much more open than in the Ivory Coast.[2] When a comparison was made between male students in the fifth forms of Ghanaian secondary schools and those at roughly the same level in the first *Baccalauréat* classes in the Ivory Coast, differences were smaller than expected. Both systems were very open, though understandably more Ghanaian students came from urban areas and from educated families; this was inevitable in view of Ghana's higher level of development. But when differences in the characteristics of the general population were taken into account, the picture was rather similar.

In ethnic terms a student from the southern part of the Ivory Coast has between two and three times the chance of entering the *Baccalaureat* class as has a student from the north or the central area. The proportionate chances are almost identical in Ghana. Indeed a northern Ghanaian boy has even less chance of reaching the fifth form of a secondary school than has his Ivory Coast counterpart. Even more striking, rural-urban differentials are still greater in Ghana than they are in the Ivory Coast. A student living in Abidjan or Bouaké has about the same chance of entering the *Baccalaureat* class as a boy from a community with a population of less than 5,000. By contrast, a Ghanaian student living in one of the larger towns (including Accra, Kumasi, and Sekondi-Takoradi) has about fourteen times the chance of reaching the fifth form of secondary school as has a rural child.[3] The only case in which the Ivory Coast shows a sharper pattern of inequality than Ghana is in level of paternal occupation. In Ghana the child of a professional, higher technical, or managerial worker has over twenty-eight times the chance of entering a fifth form as has the offspring of a farmer. In the Ivory Coast the comparable figure is thirty-two. It could hardly be claimed that this difference is significant.

In summary, although the secondary school enterprise in the Ivory Coast is so much smaller in scope than that in Ghana, it is remarkable that recruitment ratios in the two countries are not very different. In other words, as educational systems expand, there is no reason to believe that differentials in opportunities will rapidly diminish. To be sure, comparisons between Ghana and the Ivory Coast are risky (as indeed are all comparisons). Only studies over time will tell us whether openness or rigidity will characterize recruitment patterns in the new African states. Nonetheless Western precedent leads us to believe that recruitment patterns will exhibit a degree of "stickiness" in the years to come.

Despite these caveats it is still clear that schools in both Ghana and the Ivory Coast succeed very well in drawing their clientele from a broad spectrum of the population. In one sense the openness of the system is a function of the socio-economic environment in which the schools operate. It could be postulated that whether or not recruitment patterns remain open will largely depend upon what happens outside the schools rather than on specific educational policies concerning entry to secondary education. There is much to be said for this view. However, the structure of the educational system can in some measure enhance or diminish talented students' opportunities to advance. No one can fail to be impressed by the current volume of literature which argues against early selection for secondary education combined with relatively rigid tracking of students. In Western Europe there is growing pressure to delay the selection of students for specific types of secondary education by creating a longer common secondary school experience. In some places (Sweden, for example) such pressure has led to an outright demand for comprehensive forms of secondary schooling.

The 1959 educational reforms in France reflect this preoccupation with loosening up the system of secondary schooling. The creation of a common *Cycle d'Observation* for all children up to the age of thirteen as well as attempts to create greater opportunities for students to change their course of study are moves in that direction.

We could argue that this kind of development is equally important in the Ivory Coast if an open policy is to be pursued and maximum use made of talent. Indeed the Ivory Coast has been experimenting with the development of a *Cycle d'Observation,* and, as we have noted, there is a good deal more informal movement of students within the system than is sometimes supposed. Although the secondary school system is likely to remain small in size for some time to come, there is no reason why a period of *common* secondary schooling for selected students should not precede specialized study, to enable a more effective final allocation of students. Beyond this, it can be asked whether the present system of multiple tracking performs any function other than to enhance the rigidity of the system. In practical terms, is there any real rationale in the separation of the *Cours Normaux* from the *Cours Complémentaires* or the lower long academic system? Can a substantial case be made for the development of a highly specialized lower vocational cycle — a cycle which thus far, as we have observed, has not effectively carried out the functions ascribed to it?

Of course, arguments in favor of more general secondary education, later selection, and less tracking run counter to a great deal of current observation concerning African educational policy. It is frequently argued that because of manpower needs the new states cannot afford the luxury of deferred selection and general studies. Efficient use of available talent, it is urged, presupposes early allocation of individuals and development of more highly specialized types of secondary schooling directly related to manpower needs. On the contrary, we would argue that this is just the kind of development that the African states cannot afford. Under such systems the chances of misallocating students are vastly increased, the rigidities of the structure are reinforced, and there is greater danger of mismatching secondary school training with the skills actually in demand. It would be unfortunate indeed if the Ivory Coast or other African countries simply duplicated earlier secondary education structures that most European nations are now striving to change. In view of the overwhelming importance of keeping access to secondary education open and minimizing social and ethnic differentials between low- and high-status types of schooling, every effort should be made to keep the structure of secondary education as loose as possible.

## STUDENT ATTITUDES AND ASPIRATIONS

Perhaps one of the greatest unknowns in the calculations of educational and manpower planners in the new states concerns the attitudes and dispositions of the students. Human beings are not merely pegs that can be moved at will to meet expected shortages of certain types of manpower. Usually they have notions of the kinds of occupation they wish to enter and are able in some measure to indicate the factors that influence their choice. Indeed their occupational decisions are often based on rational appraisals of actual opportunities and benefits. Unless there is compulsory labor drafting, recruitment into certain types of occupation considered necessary for national development requires that individuals see these jobs as offering advantages over other alternatives. Occupational attitude becomes, therefore, one of the major parameters within which educational and manpower planners must work.

A striking feature of the aspirations of secondary students in the Ivory Coast is how loosely linked they are to social or ethnic background. To be sure, the use of a combined index of acculturation does discriminate between groups, but sex quite obviously remains a stronger predictor of aspirations than does any other variable. The fact is that nearly all students have high vocational and educational aspirations, quite incommensurate with their actual chances of continuing their studies. Of course, levels of aspiration tend to be modified by previous academic record and experience, but this does not deter most individuals from holding far too optimistic hopes for their own prospects. This optimism is understandable in view of the historical importance of education in assuring access to remunerative occupations and the fact that independence might be assumed to offer Africans new opportunities. Unfortunately enrollments at higher levels of the secondary system diminish rapidly as a result of the systematic weeding out of students, while opportunities are not expanding rapidly except in certain specific occupations, such as teaching. Under these circumstances there is always the likelihood of frustration among students. Indeed the lack of adequate opportunity in the senior cadres seems to underlie the dialogue that has continued over the last few years between the President of the Republic of the Ivory Coast and the *Union Nationale des Etudiants de la Côte d'Ivoire en France* (U.N.E.C.I.F.).[4]

Actually the generally high level of aspirations and their loose association with social or ethnic variables points again to the openness of the present status structure in the Ivory Coast. The experience of secondary education seems to exert a homogenizing influence on students that far outweighs the impact of earlier ethnic and social experience. In our initial remarks we noted that the present study could not establish the fact that schooling per se exerts a causal influence on occupational attitudes. This does not prevent us from suggesting that secondary education sets the elite apart from the mass and results in a minimal differentiation of attitudes and values.

Regardless of this putative effect of education, the fact remains that occupational aspirations are variably influenced by social and educational factors. Whereas preferences for careers in the administration or in medicine, for example, seem to be correlated with higher social background, agriculture and teaching are more frequently chosen by students from rural farming areas. By contrast, the choice of technological and scientific careers is more significantly related to academic record. In this sense the field of science and technology appears to be the one most open to talented individuals. Further, the evidence does much to dispel the myth that secondary school graduates in general are little disposed to enter careers other than those in administration. Of all male students no less than 38 percent are interested in technical and agricultural careers.

However, a caution is necessary here. Students who choose the scientific and technical field, in particular, look toward high-level jobs. Relatively few would accept humbler types of technical work. In fact, there is a marked shift away from such careers when aspirations are contrasted with expectations. The reverse is the case with teaching; individuals who aspire to enter this occupation do not shift their pattern of preferences when asked what job they expect to enter with their present level of education. Indeed three-quarters of all students expect to enter primary school teaching or clerical work only if they are unable to continue their studies. There is, therefore, a very real difference in the degree of commitment to various types of occupation, and it can hardly be assumed that former secondary school students will be likely to enter subordinate technical jobs in any numbers.

It could well be that this pattern reflects a fairly realistic view of opportunities. Compared with teaching and clerical work, lower level technical jobs offer fewer opportunities and also fewer advantages. This is in part reflected in the very unfortunate position of *Centres d'Apprentissage* in the present secondary school system. Few students wish to remain in them, and, as far as we can tell, the rate of unemployment is higher among the graduates than among those from other types of school. Moreover, dissatisfaction with current employment is more marked in this group. Above all, the *Centres d'Apprentissage* provide few further job opportunities for their students. Ironically the *Lycée Technique*, which enjoys relatively high prestige, does not rely upon the lower technical system for the bulk of its recruits; it prefers to enroll students from the academic schools. There can be no doubt that the *Lycée Technique* is currently successful because it does enable access to higher studies. Yet its success seems to have been achieved at the expense of the *Centres d'Apprentissage*, which now constitute a sort of backwater in the educational system. Since these schools offer hardly any opportunity for further education and provide training that is frequently ill-adapted to market needs, it is no wonder that the short technical system enjoys such low repute. One may well ask whether specific vocational education for middle-level employment would be better carried out by industrial and commercial firms themselves.[5] Clearly their own needs could provide incentives for the development of on-the-job training, and tax remissions would probably do much to stimulate adequate programs.[6]

It is instructive, however, to compare the position of the *Centres d'Apprentissage* with that of the new agricultural schools. Just over 14 percent of all male students wish to enter agriculture in one form or another — a surprisingly high proportion. To be sure, virtually none of them want to become farmers; most aspire to jobs as agricultural demonstrators and technicians. Further, only about 3 percent expect to enter agriculture with their present level of education. The general picture seems rather similar to that in science and technology, but the attitudes of students in agricultural studies are quite distinctive. The overwhelming majority would prefer to stay in their present school, which over one-fifth of students derived from other types of institutions (mainly short cycle) would also like to enter if they had the chance. Moreover, nearly all former graduates of agricultural schools are employed in the jobs for which they have been trained. Unemployment is nonexistent among them, and levels of satisfaction are significantly higher than in most other occupations.

Although these conclusions are based on a study of a limited number of cases, it would seem that the government of the Ivory Coast has been initially successful in establishing a moderate program of agricultural education. There are, perhaps, three reasons for this: (1) Government demands for agricultural technicians and demonstrators are explicit, and clearly defined employment opportunities exist for graduates of the agricultural schools. (2) The system draws overwhelmingly from students with rural-farm backgrounds, which constitutes some guarantee of motivation. (3) A second cycle of agricultural studies has been created which makes it possible for individuals in the lower cycle to proceed further. Of course, the very newness of the system has meant that the academic schools have had to provide a proportion of recruits, but the essential fact is that agricultural instruction does not constitute a totally dead-end type of education. If present efforts to create an agricultural *Baccalaureat* are successful, it is likely that the desirability of agricultural studies will increase, as has been the case with the *Lycée Technique*. However, one must not expect that such a development could lead to a large-scale expansion of secondary school agricultural studies, with the aim of turning out "progressive" farmers. Farming still remains one of the occupations least desired by students, and under present conditions secondary schools will probably not make any contribution in this direction. Other strategies will be necessary if the productivity of the agricultural sector is to be raised. Yet the use of extension workers and agricultural technicians, working with practicing agriculturalists, is vital to agricultural development, and it is only in the production of such personnel that the secondary schools can be expected to make a limited contribution.

### PERSONAL PREFERENCE AND DEVELOPMENT POLICIES

Nonetheless there are other areas where conflicts are apparent between students' aspirations and certain overall social and economic goals of government. The first of these concerns the high levels of student preference for urban employment. One well-nigh universal feature of contemporary Africa is the drift of people to the large towns and cities — most marked among those individuals with some schooling. Of course, there are good reasons for this movement: the towns are frequently the major centers of development; job opportunities there, if not commensurate with hopes, are more frequent; and, at worst, urban areas offer diversions not present in smaller rural communities.

In terms of short-run economic considerations, a good case can be made for saying that the preference for urban employment is based on sound, objective reasons and that in early stages of national growth the economic gap between urban and rural areas will necessarily become greater. Unfortunately the situation is by no means so simple. African governments cannot afford to let this gap continue to widen. In such countries as the Ivory Coast it is the cash-crop farmer who provides the wealth necessary for development schemes, and rural areas are understandably pressing for their fair share of educational, medical, and other services. Any government which fails to recognize the legitimacy of these demands runs the risk of alienating rural support. At the same time it is hard to recruit the personnel required for rural work; people are reluctant to work in these areas. Since financial incentives, such as they are, tend to increase the desirability of urban employment and since conditions in rural areas are so patently inferior, it is useless to address hortatory appeals to individuals to work in "backward" sections on the basis of "service to the community." It is true that students expressing a desire to enter primary school teaching, some forms of medical work, and agriculture show a somewhat higher preference for work in rural areas. However, even here the figure falls far short of that required if some degree of parity is to be maintained between urban and rural services. A frequent solution to the problem is, of course, the compulsory drafting of personnel to rural districts, often immediately after they have qualified. But this is a relatively inefficient way of distributing manpower resources. It results not only in the allocation of the least experienced personnel to rural areas but in a rapid turnover, since most individuals, after their initial tour of duty, are anxious to move to more desirable areas. Because rural areas need a continuity of personnel with a lasting commitment to work there, extra incentives should be provided — for example, differential salary scales weighted in favor of rural employment and a housing policy aimed at the improvement of rural amenities. How far these and other measures would be successful is difficult to predict, but there seems to be no other way of attracting and keeping trained personnel.

A second feature in which personal aspirations are likely to clash with policy involves the high levels of commitment to government employment. This is inevitable in view of the pattern of development in the Ivory Coast. Government has always provided a substantial proportion of employment opportunities in the modern sector of the economy, while in the past it offered conditions of work usually superior to those in the private sector. But the situation is changing. Many of the larger private companies realize that their continued presence in the Ivory Coast will depend on the increased Africanization of their personnel and on better conditions of employment. At the same time official policy concerning the projected pattern of economic development has tended to be fairly pragmatic and nondoctrinaire. While exhibiting a vague commitment to planning and the enlargement of state activities, the government has not placed restrictions on foreign investment and has accepted the fact that a growing private sector is important to the economy. Thus new opportunities in the larger, foreign-controlled companies are likely to be available to individuals with secondary school training.

So far the majority of students have not been attracted by these opportunities, although from the government viewpoint it is desirable that their aspirations be more diversified; the public sector cannot constitute an unlimited source of employment for growing cohorts of secondary school graduates. Yet some interest in careers in the private sector seems to be present among a small minority, and this interest is markedly associated with social and educational background. Students who would prefer private employment are usually from superior socio-economic backgrounds, are more likely to be in the higher cycle of secondary school study, and are more frequently planning on technical careers. From this group, which seems to be more aware of new opportunities, private business will probably draw a substantial proportion of its middle- and upper-level personnel.

However, preference for careers in the private sector is not usually associated with a desire for self-employment or for work with African business firms. Students are overwhelmingly concerned with opportunities in the larger European-controlled enterprises, and the few who would prefer to see themselves as self-employed are interested in such professions as law and medicine. There is still no evidence of any interest in the possibilities of self-owned or other African commercial enterprises, which suffer from the historical stigma of being in the hands of women or poorly educated individuals. Further, these negative attitudes toward African enterprise are reinforced by a heavy preoccupation with security, prestige, and congenial conditions of employment.

It is also striking that students attach great importance to education as a means of gaining employment and stress job proficiency as being the main determinant of success. By contrast, they feel that starting and succeeding in a self-owned business depends far more on initial wealth and family connections than it does on ability and effort. Very few students, in fact, would dream of investing resources in commercial, industrial, or agricultural enterprises. Housing (often rental housing) still remains the most desirable form of investment, followed by discharge of lineage obligations, investment in further education, and savings accounts.

One cannot suggest, therefore, that people with a secondary education are likely to make much of a contribution to the African-owned portion of the private sector. That sector will continue to be dominated by European-owned enterprises, which, to be sure, may themselves contribute substantially to Ivory Coast development. Yet one might feel happier if the African-owned enterprises would increase and generate new employment opportunities for Africans. We would hazard a guess that future development will not occur solely through the efforts of government or large-scale, foreign-controlled companies. It will depend also on the growth of a multiplicity of small-scale developments, initiated by Africans themselves, in both commerce and agriculture. This kind of thinking is often uncongenial to African governments, even if they are not hostile to the development of a private sector, because it is often easier to deal with large European-controlled concerns than it is to show an interest in small African enterprises. The potential role of the African entrepreneur is habitually underestimated, and attitudes toward him are, to say the least, ambivalent. He tends to be the forgotten man in most development schemes, and efforts to stimulate the development of African business are often regarded as a waste of money.

Of course, there is some basis for this negative evaluation. Although in West Africa generally there is a multitude of small-scale African enterprises, their position is usually precarious. Few persist beyond the lifetime of their founder, while traditional kinship obligations tend to dissipate resources that could be ploughed back into the business. In short, new African businesses are always being created, but few of them grow.

It could be argued that one reason for this is that African business is so often controlled by illiterates or poorly educated individuals. Clearly the schools themselves cannot produce the innovators and the entrepreneurs, but perhaps if persons of this type could be trained at higher levels of formal schooling, they would be qualified to develop African business firms beyond a minimal level. Of all human resources, the innovator is the most valuable and also the most scarce. It is unfortunate that this potential resource seems so limited within the ranks of the educated themselves.

## THE IMPORTANCE OF COMPARATIVE STUDIES

One may well ask what relevance a specialized study of African students in one country may have for other new African states. Are we really considering a unique case here, the conclusions and findings of which have very limited applicability? We think not. We have been struck by the marked parallels between the findings of our study and those derived from an earlier, if more limited, survey in Ghana. Both show substantial similarities in student attitudes as these relate to occupational aspirations and perception of future roles. Ghanaian and Ivory Coast students are much alike in many respects. Of course, if a comparative study of political attitudes and values were undertaken, it could show marked differences between the two groups, particularly in attitudes toward the former metropole and its culture. However, differences are not apparent in economic and occupational attitudes. This is significant in that both Ghana and the Ivory Coast exhibit common economic characteristics that are far more important than any special differences resulting from particular patterns of colonial overrule. Both countries, in effect, share similar problems in the attempt to achieve development.

The crucial point about these two countries is that they are fairly prosperous by West African standards and their economies relatively developed. It might well be true that studies of African students in less fortunate territories, such as Mali, Senegal, or Northern Nigeria, would reveal variant configurations of student attitudes (though we suggest that the differences might be of degree rather than kind). In effect, we suggest that the axis of comparison is rather along level-of-development lines than on the basis of the particular colonial power that formerly controlled the area.

In another respect, both Ghana and the Ivory Coast are particularly important areas for study. Precisely because they are more economically and educationally developed than many African states, their present problems provide a foretaste of possible developments in other nations that have not yet been able to duplicate their achievements. Countries intending to embark on programs of educational expansion would do well to consider both the Ivory Coast and the Ghana experiences.

## NOTES

1. See, for example, the Committee on Higher Education (1963:52).
2. For a fuller discussion of the findings mentioned here, see Remi Clignet and Philip Foster (1964:349–62). The complete results of the Ghanaian survey are to be found in Philip Foster (1965).
3. Actually these figures are a trifle misleading, since we are not suggesting that there is no relationship between urban residence and recruitment into the *Baccalaureat* classes in the Ivory Coast. However, there is a peculiar downswing in the relationship when the largest towns are considered. In fact, an Ivory Coast child living in a medium-sized town with a population between 10,000 and 50,000 has about six times the chance of entering a *Baccalaureat* class as does a child from a village with a population of below 5,000. By contrast, in Ghana the relationship is quite linear; the larger the town, the greater the chances of entry. All this does not alter the fact that entry into the fifth form in Ghana is more closely associated with urban residence than is entry into the *Baccalaureat* class in the Ivory Coast.
4. See Victor Dubois (1965).
5. Some French businessmen in the Ivory Coast have expressed this view, which is also endorsed by many expatriate supervisors in Nigeria. See Alan Sokolski (1965:75).
6. Some companies in West Africa seem to be doing a very effective job in this respect. See, particularly, Sokolski (1965), pp. 75–76.

# 3

# A Man of the People

### CHINUA ACHEBE

No one can deny that Chief the Honourable M. A. Nanga, M. P., was the most approachable politician in the country. Whether you asked in the city or in his home village, Anata, they would tell you he was a man of the people. I have to admit this from the onset or else the story I'm going to tell will make no sense.

That afternoon he was due to address the staff and students of the Anata Grammar School where I was teaching at the time. But as usual in those highly political times the villagers moved in and virtually took over. The Assembly Hall must have carried well over thrice its capacity. Many villagers sat on the floor, right up to the foot of the dais. I took one look and decided it was just as well we had to stay outside — at least for the moment.

Five or six dancing groups were performing at different points in the compound. The popular "Ego Women's Party" wore a new uniform of expensive accra cloth. In spite of the din you could still hear as clear as a bird the high-powered voice of their soloist, whom they admiringly nicknamed "Grammar-phone." Personally I don't care too much for our women's dancing but you just had to listen whenever Grammar-phone sang. She was now praising Micah's handsomeness, which she likened to the perfect, sculpted beauty of a carved eagle, and his popularity which would be the envy of the proverbial traveller-to-distant-places who must not cultivate enmity on his route. Micah was of course Chief the Honourable M. A. Nanga, M.P.

The arrival of the memebers of the hunter's guild in full regalia caused a great stir. Even Grammar-phone stopped — at least for a while. These people never came out except at the funeral of one of their number, or during some very special and outstanding event. I could not remember when I last saw them. They wielded their loaded guns as though they were playthings. Now and again two of them would meet in warriors' salute and knock the barrel of their guns together from left to right and again from right to left. Mothers grabbed their children and hurriedly dragged them away. Occasionally a hunter would take aim at a distant palm branch and break its mid-rib. The crowd applauded. But there were very few such shots. Most of the hunters reserved their precious powder to greet the Minister's arrival — the price of gunpowder like everything else having doubled again and again in the four years since this government took control.

As I stood in one corner of that vast tumult waiting for the arrival of the Minister I felt intense bitterness welling up in my mouth. Here were silly, ignorant villagers dancing themselves lame and waiting to blow off their gunpowder in honour of one of those who had started the country off down the slopes of inflation. I wished for a miracle, for a voice of thunder, to hush this ridiculous festival and tell the poor contemptible people one or two truths. But of course it would be quite useless. They were not only ignorant but cynical. Tell them that this man had used his position to enrich himself and they would ask you — as my father did — if you thought that a sensible man would spit out the juicy morsel that good fortune placed in his mouth.

I had not always disliked Mr. Nanga. Sixteen years or so ago he had been my teacher in standard three and I something like his favourite pupil. I remember him then as a popular, young and handsome teacher, most impressive in his uniform as scoutmaster. There was on one of the walls of the school a painting of a faultlessly handsome scoutmaster wearing an impeccable uniform. I am not sure that the art teacher who painted the picture had Mr. Nanga in mind. There was no facial resemblance; still we called it the picture of Mr. Nanga. It was enough that they were both handsome and that they were both impressive scoutmasters. This picture stood with arms folded across its chest and its raised right foot resting neatly and lightly on a perfectly cut tree stump. Bright red hibiscus flowers decorated the four corners of the frame; and below were inscribed the memorable words: *Not what I have but what I do is my kingdom.* That was in 1948.

Nanga must have gone into politics soon afterwards and then won a seat in Parliament. (It was easy in those days — before we knew its cash price.) I used to read about him in the papers some years later and even took something like pride in him. At that time I had just entered the University and was very active in the Students' branch of the People's Organization Party. Then in 1960 something disgraceful happened in the Party and I was completely disillusioned.

At that time Mr. Nanga was an unknown back-bencher in the governing P.O.P. A general election was imminent. The P.O.P. was riding high in the country and there was no fear of its not being returned. Its opponent, the Progressive Alliance Party, was weak and disorganized.

Then came the slump in the international coffee market. Overnight (or so it seemed to us) the Government had a dangerous financial crisis on its hands. Coffee was the prop of our economy just as coffee farmers were the bulwark of the P.O.P.

The Minister of Finance at the time was a first-rate economist with a Ph.D. in public finance. He presented to the Cabinet a complete plan for dealing with the situation.

The Prime Minister said "No" to the plan. He was not going to risk losing the election by cutting down the price paid to coffee planters at that critical moment; the National Bank should be instructed to print fifteen million pounds. Two-thirds of the Cabinet supported the Minister. The next morning the Prime Minister sacked them and in the evening he broadcast to the nation. He said the dismissed ministers were conspirators and traitors who had teamed up with foreign saboteurs to destroy the new nation.

I remember this broadcast very well. Of course no one knew the truth at that time. The newspapers and the radio carried the Prime Minister's version of the story. We were very indignant. Our Students' Union met in emergency session and passed a vote of confidence in the leader and called for a detention law to deal with the miscreants. The whole country was behind the leader. Protest marches and demonstrations were staged up and down the land.

It was at this point that I first noticed a new, dangerous and sinister note in the universal outcry.

The *Daily Chronicle*, an official organ of the P.O.P., had pointed out in an editorial that the Miscreant Gang, as the dismissed ministers were now called, were all university people and highly educated professional men. (I have preserved a cutting of that editorial.)

Let us now and for all time extract from our body-politic as a dentist extracts a stinking tooth all those decadent stooges versed in text-book economics and aping the white man's mannerisms and way of speaking. We are proud to be Africans. Our true leaders are not those intoxicated with their Oxford, Cambridge or Harvard degrees but those who speak the language of the people. Away with the damnable and expensive university education which only alienates an African from his rich and ancient culture and puts him above his people. . . .

This cry was taken up on all sides. Other newspapers pointed out that even in Britain where the Miscreant Gang got its 'so-called education' a man need not be an economist to be Chancellor of the Exchequer or a doctor to be Minister of Health. What mattered was loyalty to the party.

I was in the public gallery the day the Prime Minister received his overwhelming vote of confidence. And that was the day the truth finally came out; only no one was listening. I remember the grief-stricken figure of the dismissed Minister of Finance as he led his team into the chamber and was loudly booed by members and the public. That week his car had been destroyed by angry mobs and his house stoned. Another dismissed minister had been pulled out of his car, beaten insensible, and dragged along the road for fifty yards, then tied hand and foot, gagged and left by the roadside. He was still in the orthopedic hospital when the house met.

That was my first — and last — visit to Parliament. It was also the only time I had set eyes on Mr. Nanga again since he taught me in 1948.

The Prime Minister spoke for three hours and his every other word was applauded. He was called the Tiger, the Lion, the One and Only, the Sky, the Ocean and many other names of praise. He said that the Miscreant Gang had been caught "red-handed in their nefarious plot to overthrow the Government of the people by the people and for the people with the help of enemies abroad."

"They deserve to be hanged," shouted Mr. Nanga from the back benches. This interruption was so loud and clear that it appeared later under his own name in the Hansard. Throughout the session he led the pack of back-bench hounds straining their leash to get at their victims. If anyone had cared to sum up Mr. Nanga's interruptions they would have made a good hour's continuous yelp. Perspiration poured down his face as he sprang up to interrupt or sat back to share in the derisive laughter of the hungry hyena.

When the Prime Minister said that he had been stabbed in the back by the very ingrates he had pulled out of oblivion some members were in tears.

"They have bitten the finger with which their mother fed them," said Mr. Nanga. This too was entered in the Hansard, a copy of which I have before me. It is impossible, however, to convey in cold print the electric atmosphere of that day.

I cannot now recall exactly what my feelings were at that point. I suppose I thought the whole performance rather peculiar. You must remember that at that point no one had any reason to think there might be another side to the story. The Prime Minister was still talking. Then he made the now famous (or infamous) solemn declaration: "From today we must watch and guard our hard-won freedom jealously. Never again must we entrust our destiny and the destiny of Africa to the hybrid class of Western-educated and snobbish intellectuals who will not hesitate to sell their mothers for a mess of pottage. . . ."

Mr. Nanga pronounced the death sentence at least twice more but this was not recorded, no doubt because his voice was lost in the general commotion.

I remember the figure of Dr. Makinde the ex-Minister of Finance as he got up to speak — tall, calm, sorrowful and superior. I strained my ears to catch his words. The entire house, including the Prime Minister tried to shout him down. It was a most unedifying spectacle. The Speaker broke his mallet ostensibly trying to maintain order, but you could see he was enjoying the commotion. The public gallery yelled down its abuses. "Traitor," "Coward," "Doctor of Fork your Mother." This last was contributed from the gallery by the editor of the *Daily Chronicle*, who sat close to me. Encouraged, no doubt, by the volume of laughter this piece of witticism had earned him in the gallery he proceeded the next morning to print it in his paper. The spelling is his.

Although Dr. Makinde read his speech, which was clearly prepared, the Hansard later carried a garbled version which made no sense at all. It said not a word about the plan to mint fifteen million pounds — which was perhaps to be expected — but why put into Dr. Makinde's mouth words that he could not have spoken? In short the Hansard boys wrote a completely new speech suitable to the boastful villain the ex-minister had become. For instance they made him say he was "a brilliant economist whose reputation was universally acclaimed in Europe." When I read this I was in tears — and I don't cry all that easily.

The reason I have gone into that shameful episode in such detail is to establish the fact that I had no reason to be enthusiastic about Chief the Honourable M. A. Nanga who, seeing the empty ministerial seats, had yapped and snarled so shamelessly for the meaty prize.

The Proprietor and Principal of the school was a thin, wiry fellow called Jonathan Nwege. He was very active in politics at the local council level and was always grumbling because his services to the P.O.P. had not been rewarded with the usual prize-appointment to some public corporation or other. But though disgruntled he had not despaired, as witness his elaborate arrangements for the present reception. Perhaps he was hoping for something in the proposed new corporation which would take over the disposal of all government unserviceable property (like old mattresses, chairs, electric fans, disused typewriters and other junk) which at present was auctioned by civil servants. I hope he gets appointed. It would have the merit of removing him from the school now and again.

He insisted that the students should mount a guard of honour stretching from the main road to the school door. And the teachers too were to stand in a line at the end of the student queue, to be introduced. Mr. Nwege who regularly read such literature as "Toasts — How to Propose Them" was very merticulous about this kind of thing. I had objected vehemently to this standing like school children at our staff meeting, thinking to rouse the other teachers. But the teachers in that school were all dead from the neck up. Mr friend and colleague Andrew Kadibe found it impossible to side with me because he and the Minister came from the same village. Primitive loyalty, I call it.

As soon as the Minister's Cadillac arrived at the head of a long motorcade the hunters dashed this way and that and let off their last shots, throwing their guns about with frightening freedom. The dancers capered and stamped, filling the dry-season air with dust. Not even Grammar-phone's voice could now be heard over the tumult. The Minister stepped out wearing damask and gold chains and acknowledging cheers with his ever-present fan of animal skin which they said fanned away all evil designs and shafts of malevolence thrown at him by the wicked.

The man was still as handsome and youthful-looking as ever — there was no doubt about that. The Proprietor was now introducing him to the teachers beginning with the Senior Tutor at the head of the line. Although I had not had time to scrutinize the Senior Tutor's person I had no doubt he had traces of snuff as usual in his nostrils. The Minister had a jovial word for everyone. You could never think — looking at him now — that his smile was anything but genuine. It seemed bloody-minded to be sceptical. Now it was my turn. I held out my hand somewhat stiffly. I did not have the slightest fear that he might remember me and had no intention of reminding him.

Our hands met. I looked him straight in the face. The smile slowly creased up into lines of thought. He waved his left hand impatiently to silence the loquacious Proprietor who had begun the parrot formula he had repeated at least fifteen times so far: "I have the honour, sir, to introduce . . ."

"That's right," said the Minister not to anyone in particular, but to some mechanism of memory inside his head. "You are Odili."

"Yes, sir." Before the words were out of my mouth he had thrown his arms round me smothering me in his voluminous damask. "You have a wonderful memory," I said. "It's at least fifteen years . . ." He had now partly released me although his left hand was resting on my shoulder. He turned slightly to the Proprietor and announced proudly:

"I taught him in . . ."

"Standard three," I said.

"That's right," he shouted. If he had just found his long-lost son he could not have been more excited.

"He is one of the pillars of this school," said the Proprietor, catching the infection and saying the first good word about me since I had joined his school.

"Odili, the great," said the Minister boyishly, and still out of breath. "Where have you been all this time?"

I told him I had been to the University, and had been teaching for the last eighteen months.

"Good boy!" he said. "I knew he would go to a university. I use to tell the other boys in my class that Odili will one day be a great man and they will be answering him sir, sir. Why did you not tell me when you left the University? That's very bad of you, you know."

"Well," I said happily — I'm ashamed to admit — "I know how busy a minister . . ."

"Busy? Nonsense. Don't you know that minister means servant? Busy or no busy he must see his master."

Everybody around applauded and laughed. He slapped me again on the back and said I must not fail to see him at the end of the reception.

"If you fail I will send my orderly to arrest you."

I became a hero in the eyes of the crowd. I was dazed. Everything around me became suddenly unreal; the voices receded to a vague border zone. I knew I ought to be angry with myself but I wasn't. I found myself wondering whether — perhaps — I had been applying to politics stringent standards that didn't belong to it. When I came back to the immediate present I heard the Minister saying to another teacher:

"That is very good. Sometimes I use to regret ever leaving the teaching field. Although I am a minister today I can swear to God that I am not as happy as when I was a teacher."

My memory is naturally good. That day it was perfect. I don't know how it happened, but I can recall every word the Minister said on that occasion. I can repeat the entire speech he made later.

"True to God who made me," he insisted. "I use to regret it. Teaching is a very noble profession."

At this point everybody just collapsed with laughter not least of all the Honourable Minister himself, nor me, for that matter. The man's assurance was simply unbelievable. Only he could make such a risky joke — or whatever he thought he was making — at that time, when teachers all over the country were in an ugly, rebellious mood. When the laughter died down, he put on a more serious face and confided to us: "You can rest assured that those of us in the Cabinet who were once teachers are in full sympathy with you."

"Once a teacher always a teacher," said the Senior Tutor, adjusting the sleeves of his faded "bottom-box" robes.

"Hear! hear!" I said. I like to think that I meant it to be sarcastic. The man's charism had to be felt to be believed. If I were superstitious I would say he had made a really potent charm of the variety called "sweet face."

Changing the subject slightly, the Minister said, "Only teachers can make this excellent arrangement." Then turning to the newspaper correspondent in his party he said, "It is a mammoth crowd."

The journalist whipped out his note-book and began to write.

"It is an unprecedented crowd in the annals of Anata," said Mr. Nwege.

"James, did you hear that?" the Minister asked the journalist.

"No, sir, what is it?"

"This gentleman says it is the most unprecedented crowd in the annals of Anata," I said. This time I clearly meant my tongue to be in my cheek.

"What is the gentleman's name?"

Mr. Nwege called his name and spelt it and gave his full title of "Principal and Proprietor of Anata Grammar School." Then he turned to the Minister in an effort to pin-point responsibility for the big crowds.

"I had to visit every section of the village personally to tell them of your — I mean to say of the Minister's — visit."

We had now entered the Assembly Hall and the Minister and his party were conducted to their seats on the dais. The crowd raised a deafening shout of welcome. He waved his fan to the different parts of the hall. Then he turned to Mr. Nwege and said:

"Thank you very much, thank you, sir."

A huge, tough-looking member of the Minister's entourage who stood with us at the back of the dais raised his voice and said:

"You see wetin I de talk. How many minister fit hanswer *sir* to any Tom, Dick and Harry wey senior them for age? I hask you how many?"

Everyone at the dais agreed that the Minister was quite exceptional in this respect — a man of high position who still gave age the respect due it. No doubt it was a measure of my changed — or shall we say changing? — attitude to the Minister that I found myself feeling a little embarrassed on his account for these fulsome praises flung at his face.

"Minister or no minister," he said, "a man who is my senior must still be my senior. Other ministers and other people may do otherwise but my motto is: *Do the right and shame the Devil.*"

Somehow I found myself admiring the man for his lack of modesty.

For what is modesty but inverted pride? We all think we are first-class people. Modesty forbids us from saying so ourselves though, presumably, not from wanting to hear it from others. Perhaps it was their impatience with this kind of hypocrisy that made men like Nanga successful politicians while starry-eyed idealists strove vaingloriously to bring into politics niceties and delicate refinements that belonged elsewhere.

While I thought about all this — perhaps not in these exact terms — the fulsome praises flowed all around the dais.

Mr. Nwege took the opportunity to mount his old hobbyhorse. The Minister's excellent behaviour, he said, was due to the sound education he had received when education *was* education.

"Yes," said the Minister, "I use to tell them that standard six in those days is more than Cambridge today."

"Cambridge?" asked Mr. Nwege who, like the Minister, had the good old standard six. "Cambridge? Who dash frog coat? You mean it is equal to B.A. today — if not more."

"With due apologies," said the Minister turning in my direction.

"Not at all, sir," I replied with equal good humour. "I am applying for a postgraduate scholarship to bring myself up to Mr. Nwege's expectation."

I remember that at that point the beautiful girl in the Minister's party turned round on her chair to look at me. My eyes met hers and she quickly turned round again. I think the Minister noticed it.

"My private secretary has B.A. from Oxford," he said. "He should have come with me on this tour but I had some office work for him to do. By the way, Odili, I think you are wasting your talent here. I want you to come to the capital and take up a strategic post in the civil service. We shouldn't leave everything to the highland tribes. My secretary is from there; our people must press for their fair share of the national cake."

The hackneyed phrase "national cake" was getting to some of us for the first time, and so it was greeted with applause.

"Owner of book!" cried one admirer, assigning in those three brief words the ownership of the white man's language to the Honourable Minister, who turned round and beamed on the speaker.

That was when my friend Andrew Kadibe committed the unpardonable indiscretion of calling the Minister the nickname he had worn as a teacher: "M.A. Minus Opportunity." It was particularly bad because Andrew and the Minister were from the same village.

The look he gave Andrew then reminded me of that other Nanga who had led the pack of hounds four years ago.

"Sorry, sir," said Andrew pitiably.

"Sorry for what?" snarled the Minister.

"Don't mind the *stupid* boy, sir," said Mr. Nwege, greatly upset. "This is what we were saying before."

"I think we better begin," said the Minister, still frowning.

Although Mr. Nwege had begun by saying that the distinguished guest needed no introduction he had gone on all the same to talk for well over twenty minutes — largely in praise of himself and all he had done for the Party in Anata "and environs."

The crowd became steadily more restive especially when they noticed that the Minister was looking at his watch. Loud grumbles began to reach the dais from the audience. Then clear voices telling Nwege to sit down and let the man they came to hear talk. Nwege ignored all these warning signs — a more insensitive man you never saw. Finally one of the tough young men of the village stood up ten feet or so away and shouted:

"It is enough or I shall push you down and take three pence."

This did the trick. The laughter that went up must have been heard a mile away. Mr. Nwege's concluding remarks were completely lost. In fact it was not until the Minister rose to his feet that the laughter stopped.

The story had it that many years ago when Mr. Nwege was a poor, hungry elementary school teacher — that is before he built his own grammar school and became rich but apparently still hungry — he had an old rickety bicycle of the kind the villagers gave the onomatopoeic name of *anikilija*. Needless to say the brakes were very faulty. One day as he was cascading down a steep slope that led to a narrow bridge at the bottom of the hill he saw a lorry — an unusual phenomenon in those days — coming down the opposite slope. It looked like a head-on meeting on the bridge. In his extremity Mr. Nwege had raised his voice and cried to passing pedestrians: "In the name of God push me down!" Apparently nobody did, and so he added an inducement: "Push me down and my three pence is yours!" From that day "Push me down and take my three pence" became a popular Anata joke.

The Minister's speech sounded spontaneous and was most effective. There was no election at hand, he said amid laughter. He had not come to beg for their votes; it was just "a family reunion — pure and simple." He would have preferred not to speak to his own kinsmen in English which was after all a foreign language, but he had learnt from experience that speeches made in vernacular were liable to be distorted and mis-quoted in the press. Also there were some strangers in that audience who did not speak our own tongue and he did not wish to exclude them. They were all citizens of our great country whether they came from the highlands or the lowlands, etc. etc.

The stranger he had in mind I think was Mrs. Eleanor John, an in-fluential party woman from the coast who had come in the Minister's party. She was heavily painted and perfumed and although no longer young seemed more than able to hold her own, if it came to that. She sat on the Minister's left, smoking and fanning herself. Next to her sat the beautiful young girl I have talked about. I didn't catch the two of them exchanging any words or even looks. I wondered what such a girl was doing in that tough crowd; it looked as though they had stopped by some convent on their way and offered to give her a lift to the next one.

At the end of his speech the Minister and his party were invited to the Proprietor's Lodge — as Mr. Nwege called his square, cement-block house. Outside, the dancers had all come alive again and the hunters — their last powder gone — were tamely waiting for the promised palm-wine. The Minister danced a few dignified steps to the music of each group and stuck red pound notes on the perspiring faces of the best dancers. To one group alone he gave away five pounds.

The same man who had drawn our attention to the Minister's humility was now pointing out yet another quality. I looked at him closely for the first time and noticed that he had one bad eye — what we call a cowrie-shell eye.

"You see how e de do as if to say money be san-san," he was saying. "People wey de jealous the money gorment de pay Minister no sabi say no be him one de chop am. Na so so troway."

Later on in the Proprietor's Lodge I said to the Minister: "You must have spent a fortune today."

He smiled at the glass of cold beer in his hand and said: "You call this spend? You never see some thing, my brother. I no de keep anini for myself, na so so troway. If some person come to you and say 'I wan' make you Minister' make you run like blazes comot. Na true word I tell you. To God who made me." He showed the tip of his tongue to the sky to confirm the oath. "Minister de sweet for eye but too much katakata de for inside. Believe me yours sincerely."

"Big man, big palaver," said the one-eyed man.

It was left to Josiah, owner of a nearby shop-and-bar to sound a discordant, if jovial, note.

"Me one," he said, "I no kuku mind the katakata wey de for inside. Make you put Minister money for my hand and all the wahala on top. I no mind at all."

Everyone laughed. Then Mrs. John said:

"No be so, my frien. When you done experience rich man's trouble you not fit talk like that again. My people get one proverb: they say that when poor man done see with him own eye how to make big man e go beg make e carry him poverty de go je-je."

They said this woman was a very close friend of the Minister's, and her proprietary air would seem to confirm it and the fact that she had come all the way from Pokoma, three hundred and fifty miles away. I knew of her from the newspapers; she was a member of the Library Commission, one of the statutory boards within the Minister's portfolio.

Her massive coral beads were worth hundreds of pounds according to the whisper circulating in the room while she talked. She was the "merchant princess" *par excellence.* Poor beginning — an orphan, I believe — no school education, plenty of good looks and an iron determination, both of which she put to good account; beginning as a street hawker, rising to a small trader, and then to a big one. At present, they said, she presided over the entire trade in imported second-hand clothing worth hundreds of thousands.

I edged quietly towards the journalist who seemed to know everyone in the party and whispered in his ear: "Who is the young lady?"

"Ah," he said, leaving his mouth wide open for a while as a danger signal. "Make you no go near am-o. My hand no de for inside."

I told him I wasn't going near am-o; I merely asked who she was.

"The Minister no de introduce-am to anybody. So I think say na im girl-friend, or im cousin.' Then he confided: "I done lookam, lookam, lookam sotay I tire. I no go tell you lie girls for this una part sabi fine-o. God Almighty!"

I had also noticed that the Minister had skipped her when he had introduced his party to the teachers.

I know it sounds silly, but I began to wonder what had happened to the Mrs. Nanga of the scoutmastering days. They were newly married then. I remembered her particularly because she was one of the very first women I knew to wear a white, ladies' helmet which in our ignorance we called *helment* and which was in those days the very acme of sophistication.

# Education for Self-Reliance

JULIUS K. NYERERE

Since long before Independence the people of this country, under the leadership of TANU, have been demanding more education for their children. But we have never really stopped to consider why we want education — what its purpose is. Therefore, although over time there have been various criticisms about the details of curricula provided in schools, we have not until now questioned the basic system of education which we took over at the time of independence. We have never done that because we have never thought about education except in terms of obtaining teachers, engineers, administrators, etc. Individually and collectively we have in practice thought of education as a training for the skills required to earn high salaries in the modern sector of our economy.

It is now time that we looked again at the justification for a poor society like ours spending almost 20 percent of its Government revenues on providing education for its children and young people, and began to consider what that education should be doing. For in our circumstances it is impossible to devote Shs. 147,330,000 every year on education for some of our children (while others go without) unless its result has a proportionate relevance to the society we are trying to create.

The educational systems in different kinds of societies in the world have been, and are, very different in organization and in content. They are different because the societies providing the education are different, and because education, whether it be formal or informal, has a purpose. That purpose is to transmit from one generation to the next the accumulated wisdom and knowledge of the society, and to prepare the young people for their future membership of the society and their active participation in its maintenance or development.

This is true, explicitly or implicitly, for all societies — the capitalist societies of the West, the communist societies of the East, and the precolonial African societies too.

The fact that precolonial Africa did not have "schools" — except for short periods of initiation in some tribes — did not mean that the children were not educated. They learned by living and doing. In the homes and on the farms they were taught the skills of the society, and the behaviour expected of its members. They learned the kind of grasses which were suitable for which purposes, the work which had to be done on the crops, or the care which had to be given to animals, by joining with their elders in this work. They learned the tribal history, and the tribe's relationship with other tribes and with the spirits, by listening to the stories of the elders. Through these means, and by the custom of sharing to which young people were taught to conform, the values of the society were transmitted. Education was thus "informal"; every adult was a teacher to a greater or lesser degree. But this lack of formality did not mean that there was no education, nor did it affect its importance to the society. Indeed, it may have made the education more directly relevant to the society in which the child was growing up.

In Europe education has been formalized for a very long time. An examination of its development will show, however, that it has always had similar objectives to those implicit in the traditional African system of education. That is to say, formal education in Europe was intended to reinforce the social ethics existing in the particular country, and to prepare the children and young people for the place they will have in that society. The same thing is true of communist countries now. The content of education is somewhat different from that of Western countries, but the purpose is the same — to prepare young people to live in and to serve the society, and to transmit the knowledge, skills, and values and attitudes of the society. Wherever education fails in any of these fields, then the society falters in its progress, or there is social unrest as people find that their education has prepared them for a future which is not open to them.

## COLONIAL EDUCATION IN TANZANIA AND THE INHERITANCE OF THE NEW STATE

The education provided by the colonial government in the two countries which now form Tanzania had a different purpose. It was not designed to prepare young people for the service of their own country; instead, it was motivated by a desire to inculcate the values of the colonial society and to train individuals for the service of the colonial state. In these countries the State interest in education therefore stemmed from the need for local clerks and junior officials; on top of that, various religious groups were interested in spreading literacy and other education as part of their evangelical work.

This statement of fact is not given as a criticism of the many individuals who worked hard, often under difficult conditions, in teaching and in organizing educational work. Nor does it imply that all the values these people transmitted in the schools were wrong or inappropriate. What it does mean, however, is that the educational system introduced into Tanzania by the colonialists was modelled on the British system, but with even heavier emphasis on subservient attitudes and on white-collar skills. Inevitably, too, it was based on the assumptions of a colonialist and capitalist society. It emphasized and encouraged the individualistic instincts of mankind, instead of his cooperative instincts. It led to the possession of individual material wealth being the major criterion of social merit and worth.

This meant that colonial education induced attitudes of human inequality, and in practice underpinned the domination of the weak by the strong, especally in the economic field. Colonial education in this country was therefore not transmitting the values and knowledge of Tanzanian society from one generation to the next; it was a deliberate attempt to change those values and to replace traditional knowledge by the knowledge from a different society. It was thus a part of a deliberate attempt to effect a revolution in the society; to make it into a colonial society which accepted its status and which was an efficient adjunct to the governing power. Its failure to achieve these ends does not mean that it was without an influence on the attitudes, ideas, and knowledge of the people who experienced it. Nor does that failure imply that the education provided in colonial days is automatically relevant for the purposes of a free people committed to the principle of equality.

The independent state of Tanzania in fact inherited a system of education which was in many respects both inadequate and inappropriate for the new state. It was, however, its inadequacy which was most immediately obvious. So little education had been provided that in December, 1961, we had too few people with the necessary educational qualifications even to man the administration of government as it was then, much less undertake the big economic and social development work which was essential. Neither was the school population in 1961 large enough to allow for any expectation that this situation would be speedily corrected. On top of that, education was based upon race, whereas the whole moral case of the independence movement had been based upon a rejection of racial distinctions.

### ACTION SINCE INDEPENDENCE

The three most glaring faults of the educational inheritance have already been tackled. First, the racial distinctions within education were abolished. Complete integration of the separate racial systems was introduced very soon after independence, and discrimination on grounds of religion was also brought to an end. A child in Tanzania can now secure admittance to any Government or Government-aided school in this country without regard to his race or religion and without fear that he will be subject to religious indoctrination as the price of learning.

Secondly, there has been a very big expansion of educational facilities available, especially at the secondary school and post-secondary school levels. In 1961 there were 490,000 children attending primary schools in Tanganyika, the majority of them only going up to Standard IV. In 1967 there were 825,000 children attending such schools, and increasingly these will be full seven-year primary schools. In 1961, too, there were 11,832 children in secondary schools, only 176 of whom were in Form VI. This year there are 25,000 and 830. This is certainly something for our young state to be proud of. It is worth reminding ourselves that our present problems (especially the so-called problem of the primary school leavers) are revealing themselves largely because of these successes.

The third action we have taken is to make the education provided in all our schools much more Tanzanian in content. No longer do our children simply learn British and European history. Faster than would have been thought possible, our University College and other institutions are providing materials on the history of Africa and making these available to our teachers. Our national songs and dances are once again being learned by our children; our national language has been given the importance in our curriculum which it needs and deserves. Also, civics classes taken by Tanzanians are beginning to give the secondary school pupils an understanding of the organization and aims of our young state. In these and other ways changes have been introduced to make our educational system more relevant to our needs. At this time, when there is so much general and justified questioning of what is being done, it is appropriate that we should pay tribute to the work of our teachers and those who support their work in the Ministry, in the Institute of Education, the University College and the District Councils.

Yet all these things I have mentioned are modifications of the system we have inherited. Their results have not yet been seen; it takes years for a change in education to have its effect. The events of 1966 do suggest, however, that a more thorough examination of the education we are providing must be made. It is now clearly time for us to think seriously about this question: "What is the educational system in Tanzania intended to do — what is its purpose?". Having decided that, we have to look at the relevance of the existing structure and content of Tanzanian education for the task it has to do. In the light of that examination we can consider whether, in our present circumstances, further modifications are required or whether we need a change in the whole approach.

## WHAT KIND OF SOCIETY ARE WE TRYING TO BUILD?

Only when we are clear about the kind of society we are trying to build can we design our educational service to serve our goals. But this is not now a problem in Tanzania. Although we do not claim to have drawn up a blueprint of the future, the values and objectives of our society have been stated many times. We have said that we want to create a socialist society which is based on three principles: equality and respect for human dignity; sharing of the resources which are produced by our efforts; work by everyone and exploitation by none. We have set out these ideas clearly in the National Ethic; and in the Arusha Declaration and earlier documents we have outlined the principles and policies we intend to follow. We have also said on many occasions that our objective is greater African unity, and that we shall work for this objective while in the meantime defending the absolute integrity and sovereignty of the United Republic. Most often of all, our Government and people have stressed the equality of all citizens, and our determination that economic, political, and social policies shall be deliberately designed to make a reality of that equality in all spheres of life. We are, in other words, committed to a socialist future and one in which the people will themselves determine the policies pursued by a Government which is responsible to them.

It is obvious, however, that if we are to make progress towards these goals, we in Tanzania must accept the realities of our present position, internally and externally, and then work to change these realities into something more in accord with our desires. And the truth is that our United Republic has at present a poor, undeveloped, and agricultural economy. We have very little capital to invest in big factories or modern machines; we are short of people with skill and experience. What we do have is land in abundance and people who are willing to work hard for their own improvement. It is the use of these latter resources which will decide whether we reach our total goals or not. If we use these resources in a spirit of self-reliance as the basis for development, then we shall make progress slowly but surely. And it will then be real progress, affecting the lives of the masses, not just having spectacular showpieces in the towns while the rest of the people of Tanzania live in their present poverty.

Pursuing this path means that Tanzania will continue to have a predominantly rural economy for a long time to come. And as it is in the rural areas that people live and work, so it is in the rural areas that life must be improved. This is not to say that we shall have no industries and factories in the near future. We have some now and they will continue to expand. But it would be grossly unrealistic to imagine that in the near future more than a small proportion of our people will live in towns and work in modern industrial enterprises. It is therefore the villages which must be made into places where people live a good life; it is in the rural areas that people must be able to find their material well-being and their satisfactions.

This improvement in village life will not, however, come automatically. It will come only if we pursue a deliberate policy of using the resources we have — our man-power and our land — to the best advantage. This means people working hard, intelligently, and together; in other words, working in co-operation. Our people in the rural areas, as well as their Government, must organize themselves co-operatively and work for themselves through working for the community of which they are members. Our village life, as well as our state organization, must be based on the principles of socialism and that equality in work and return which is part of it.

This is what our educational system has to encourage. It has to foster the social goals of living together, and working together, for the common good. It has to prepare our young people to play a dynamic and constructive part in the development of a society in which all members share fairly in the good or bad fortune of the group, and in which progress is measured in terms of human well-being, not prestige buildings, cars, or other such things, whether privately or publicly owned. Our education must therefore inculcate a sense of commitment to the total community, and help the pupils to accept the values appropriate to our kind of future, not those appropriate to our colonial past.

This means that the educational system of Tanzania must emphasize cooperative endeavour, not individual advancement; it must stress concepts of equality and the responsibility to give service which goes with any special ability, whether it be in carpentry, in animal husbandry, or in academic pursuits. And, in particular, our education must counteract the temptation to intellectual arrogance; for this leads to the well-educated despising those whose abilities are nonacademic or who have no special abilities but are just human beings. Such arrogance has no place in a society of equal citizens.

It is, however, not only in relation to social values that our educational system has a task to do. It must also prepare young people for the work they will be called upon to do in the society which exists in Tanzania — a rural society where improvement will depend largely upon the efforts of the people in agriculture and in village development. This does not mean that education in Tanzania should be designed just to produce passive agricultural workers of different levels of skill who simply carry out plans or directions received from above. It must produce good farmers; it has also to prepare people for their responsibilities as free workers and citizens in a free and democratic society, albeit a largely rural society. They have to be able to think for themselves, to make judgements on all the issues affecting them; they have to be able to interpret the decisions made through the democratic institutions of our society, and to implement them in the light of the peculiar local circumstances where they happen to live.

It would thus be a gross misinterpretation of our needs to suggest that the educational system should be designed to produce robots, who work hard but never question what the leaders in Government or TANU are doing and saying. For the people are, and must be, Government and TANU. Our Government and our Party must always be responsible to the people, and must always consist of representatives — spokesmen and servants of the people. The education provided must therefore encourage the development in each citizen of three things: an enquiring mind; an ability to learn from what others do, and reject or adapt it to his own needs; and a basic confidence in his own position as a free and equal member of the society, who values others and is valued by them for what he does and not for what he obtains.

These things are important for both the vocational and the social aspects of education. However much agriculture a young person learns, he will not find a book which will give him all the answers to all the detailed problems he will come across on his own farm. He will have to learn the basic principles of modern knowledge in agriculture and then adapt them to solve his own problems. Similarly, the free citizens of Tanzania will have to judge social issues for themselves; there neither is, nor will be, a political "holy book" which purports to give all the answers to all the social, political and economic problems which will face our country in the future. There will be philosophies and policies approved by our society which citizens should consider and apply in the light of their own thinking and experience. But the educational system of Tanzania would not be serving the interests of a democratic socialist society if it tried to stop people from thinking about the teachings, policies or the beliefs of leaders, either past or present. Only free people conscious of their worth and their equality can build a free society.

## SOME SALIENT FEATURES OF THE EXISTING EDUCATIONAL SYSTEM

These are very different purposes from those which are promoted by our existing educational arrangements. For there are four basic elements in the present system which prevent, or at least discourage, the integration of the pupils into the society they will enter, and which do encourage attitudes of inequality, intellectual arrogance and intense individualism among the young people who go through our schools.

First, the most central thing about the education we are at present providing is that it is basically an elitist education designed to meet the interests and needs of a very small proportion of those who enter the school system.

Although only about 13 percent of our primary school children will get a place in a secondary school, the basis of our primary school education is the preparation of pupils for secondary schools. Thus 87 percent of the children who finished primary school last year — and a similar proportion of those who will finish this year — do so with a sense of failure, of a legitimate aspiration having been denied them. Indeed we all speak in these terms, by referring to them as those who failed to enter secondary schools, instead of simply as those who have finished their primary education. On the other hand, the other 13 percent have a feeling of having deserved a prize — and the prize they and their parents now expect is high wages, comfortable employment in towns, and personal status in the society. The same process operates again at the next highest level, when entrance to university is the question at issue.

In other words, the education now provided is designed for the few who are intellectually stronger than their fellows; it induces among those who succeed a feeling of superiority, and leaves the majority of the others hankering after something they will never obtain. It induces a feeling of inferiority among the majority, and can thus not produce either the egalitarian society we should build, nor the attitudes of mind which are conducive to an egalitarian society. On the contrary, it induces the growth of a class structure in our country.

Equally important is the second point; the fact that Tanzania's education is such as to divorce its participants from the society it is supposed to be preparing them for. This is particularly true of secondary schools, which are inevitably almost entirely boarding schools; but to some extent, and despite recent modifications in the curriculum, it is true of primary schools too. We take children from their parents at the age of 7 years, and for up to 7½ hours a day we teach them certain basic academic skills. In recent years we have tried to relate these skills, at least in theory, to the life which the children see around them. But the school is always separate; it is not part of the society. It is a place children go to and which they and their parents hope will make it unnecessary for them to become farmers and continue living in the villages.

The few who go to secondary schools are taken many miles away from their homes; they live in an enclave, having permission to go into the town for recreation, but not relating the work of either town or country to their real life — which is lived in the school compound. Later a few people go to university. If they are lucky enough to enter Dar es Salaam University College they live in comfortable quarters, feed well, and study hard for their Degree. When they have been successful in obtaining it, they know immediately that they will receive a salary of something like £660 per annum. That is what they have been aiming for; it is what they have been encouraged to aim for. They may also have the desire to serve the community, but their idea of service is related to status and the salary which a university education is expected to confer upon its recipient. The salary and the status have become a right automatically conferred by the Degree.

It is wrong of us to critize the young people for these attitudes. The new university graduate has spent the larger part of his life separated and apart from the masses of Tanzania; his parents may be poor, but he has never fully shared that poverty. He does not really know what it is like to live as a poor peasant. He will be more at home in the world of the educated than he is among his own parents. Only during vacations has he spent time at home, and even then he will often find that his parents and relatives support his own conception of his difference, and regard it as wrong that he should live and work as the ordinary person he really is. For the truth is that many of the people in Tanzania have come to regard education as meaning that a man is too precious for the rough and hard life which the masses of our people still live.

The third point is that our present system encourages school pupils in the idea that all knowledge which is worth while is acquired from books or from "educated people" — meaning those who have been through a formal education. The knowledge and wisdom of other old people is despised, and they themselves regarded as being ignorant and of no account. Indeed it is not only the education system which at present has this effect. Government and Party themselves tend to judge people according to whether they have "passed school certificate," "have a Degree," etc. If a man has these qualifications we assume he can fill a post; we do not wait to find out about his attitudes, his character, or any other ability except the ability to pass examinations. If a man does not have these qualifications we assume he cannot do a job; we ignore his knowledge and experience. For example, I recently visited a very good tobacco-producing peasant. But if I tried to take him into Government as a Tobacco Extension Officer, I would run up against the system because he has no formal education. Everything we do stresses book learning, and underestimates the value to our society of traditional knowledge and the wisdom which is often acquired by intelligent men and women as they experience life, even without their being able to read at all.

This does not mean that any person can do any job simply because they are old and wise, nor that educational qualifications are not necessary. This is a mistake our people sometimes fall into as a reaction against the arrogance of the book-learned. A man is not necessarily wise because he is old; a man cannot necessarily run a factory because he has been working in it as a labourer or storekeeper for 20 years. But equally he may not be able to do so if he has a Doctorate in Commerce. The former may have honesty and ability to weigh up men; the latter may have the ability to initiate a transaction and work out the economics of it. But both qualifications are necessary in one man if the factory is to be a successful and modern enterprise serving our nation. It is as much a mistake to overvalue book learning as it is to undervalue it.

The same thing applies in relation to agricultural knowledge. Our farmers have been on the land for a long time. The methods they use are the result of long experience in the struggle with nature; even the rules and taboos they honour have a basis in reason. It is not enough to abuse a traditional farmer as old-fashioned; we must try to understand why he is doing certain things, and not just assume he is stupid. But this does not mean that his methods are sufficient for the future. The traditional systems may have been appropriate for the economy which existed when they were worked out and for the technical knowledge then available. But different tools and different land tenure systems are being used now; land should no longer be used for a year or two and then abandoned for up to 20 years to give time for natural regeneration to take place. The introduction of an ox-plough instead of a hoe — and, even more, the introduction of a tractor — means more than just a different way of turning over the land. It requires a change in the organization of work, both to see that the maximum advantage is taken of the new tool, and also to see that the new method does not simply lead to the rapid destruction of our land and the egalitarian basis of our society. Again, therefore, our young people have to learn both a practical respect for the knowledge of the old "uneducated" farmer, and an understanding of new methods and the reason for them.

Yet at present our pupils learn to despise even their own parents because they are old-fashioned and ignorant; there is nothing in our existing educational system which suggests to the pupil that he can learn important things about farming from his elders. The result is that he absorbs beliefs about witchcraft before he goes to school, but does not learn the properties of local grasses; he absorbs the taboos from his family but does not learn the methods of making nutritious traditional foods. And from school he acquires knowledge unrelated to agricultural life. He gets the worst of both systems!

Finally, and in some ways most importantly, our young and poor nation is taking out of productive work some of its healthiest and strongest young men and women. Not only do they fail to contribute to that increase in output which is so urgent for our nation; they themselves consume the output of the older and often weaker people. There are almost 25,000 students in secondary schools now; they do not learn as they work, they simply learn. What is more, they take it for granted that this should be so. Whereas in a wealthy country like the United States of America it is common for young people to work their way through high school and college, in Tanzania the structure of our education makes it impossible for them to do so. Even during the holidays we assume that these young men and women should be protected from rough work; neither they nor the community expect them to spend their time on hard physical labour or on jobs which are uncomfortable and unpleasant. This is not simply a reflection of the fact that there are many people looking for unskilled paid employment — pay is not the question at issue. It is a reflection of the attitude we have all adopted.

How many of our students spend their vacations doing a job which could improve people's lives but for which there is no money — jobs like digging an irrigation channel or a drainage ditch for a village, or demonstrating the construction and explaining the benefits of deep-pit latrines, and so on? A small number have done such work in the National Youth Camps or through school-organized, nation-building schemes, but they are the exception rather than the rule. The vast majority do not think of their knowledge or their strength as being related to the needs of the village community.

## CAN THESE FAULTS BE CORRECTED?

There are three major aspects which require attention if this situation is to change: — the content of the curriculum itself, the organization of the schools, and the entry age into primary schools. But although these aspects are in some ways separate, they are also interlocked. We cannot integrate the pupils and students into the future society simply by theoretical teaching, however well designed it is. Neither can the society fully benefit from an education system which is thoroughly integrated into local life but does not teach people the basic skills — for example, of literacy and arithmetic, or which fails to excite in them a curiosity about ideas. Nor can we expect those finishing primary schools to be useful young citizens if they are still only 12 or 13 years of age.

In considering changes in the present structure it is also essential that we face the facts of our present economic situation. Every penny spent on education is money taken away from some other needed activity — whether it is an investment in the future, better medical services, or just more food, clothing and comfort for our citizens at present. And the truth is that there is no possibility of Tanzania being able to increase the proportion of the national income which is spent on education; it ought to be decreased. Therefore we cannot solve our present problems by any solution which costs more than is at present spent; in particular we cannot solve the "problem of primary school leavers" by increasing the number of secondary school places.

This "problem of primary school leavers" is in fact a product of the present system. Increasingly children are starting school at six or even five years of age, so that they finish primary school when they are still too young to become responsible young workers and citizens. On top of that is the fact that the society and the type of education they have received both led them to expect wage employment — probably in an office. In other words, their education was not sufficiently related to the tasks which have to be done in our society. This problem therefore calls for a major change in the content of our primary education and for the raising of the primary school entry age so that the child is older when he leaves, and also able to learn more quickly while he is at school.

There is no other way in which this problem of primary school leavers can be solved. Unpleasant though it may be, the fact is that it is going to be a long time before we can provide universal primary education in Tanzania; for the vast majority of those who do get this opportunity, it will be only the equivalent of the present seven years' education. It is only a few who will have the chance of going on to secondary schools, and quite soon only a proportion of these who will have an opportunity of going on to university, even if they can benefit from doing so. These are the economic facts of life for our country. They are the practical meaning of our poverty. The only choice before us is how we allocate the educational opportunities, and whether we emphasize the individual interests of the few or whether we design our educational system to serve the community as a whole. And for a socialist state only the latter is really possible.

The implication of this is that the education given in our primary schools must be a complete education in itself. It must not continue to be simply a preparation for secondary school. Instead of the primary school activities being geared to the competitive examination which will select the few who go on to secondary school, they must be a preparation for the life which the majority of the children will lead. Similarly, secondary schools must not be simply a selection process for the university, teachers' colleges, and so on. They must prepare people for life and service in the villages and rural areas of this country. For in Tanzania the only true justification for secondary education is that it is needed by the few for service to the many. The teacher in a seven-year primary school system needs an education which goes beyond seven years; the extension officer who will help a population with a seven-years' education needs a lot more himself. Other essential services need higher education — for example, doctors and engineers need long and careful training. But publicly provided "education for education's sake" must be general education for the masses. Further education for a selected few must be education for service to the many. There can be no other justification for taxing the many to give education to only a few.

Yet it is easy to say that our primary and secondary schools must prepare young people for the realities and needs of Tanzania; to do it requires a radical change, not only in the education system but also in many existing community attitudes. In particular, it requires that examinations should be downgraded in Government and public esteem. We have to recognize that although they have certain advantages — for example, in reducing the dangers of nepotism and tribalism in a selection process — they also have severe disadvantages too. As a general rule they assess a person's ability to learn facts and present them on demand within a time period. They do not always succeed in assessing a power to reason, and they certainly do not assess character or willingness to serve.

Further, at the present time our curriculum and syllabus are geared to the examinations set — only to a very limited extent does the reverse situation apply. A teacher who is trying to help his pupils often studies the examination papers for past years and judges what questions are most likely to be asked next time; he then concentrates his teaching on those matters, knowing that by doing so he is giving his children the best chance of getting through to secondary school or university. And the examinations our children at present sit are themselves geared to an international standard and practice which has developed regardless of our particular problems and needs. What we need to do now is think first about the education we want to provide, and when that thinking is completed think about whether some form of examination is an appropriate way of closing an education phase. Then such an examination should be designed to fit the education which has been provided.

Most important of all is that we should change the things we demand of our schools. We should not determine the type of things children are taught in primary schools by the things a doctor, engineer, teacher, economist, or administrator need to know. Most of our pupils will never be any of these things. We should determine the type of things taught in the primary schools by the things which the boy or girl ought to know — that is, the skills he ought to acquire and the values he ought to cherish if he, or she, is to live happily and well in a socialist and predominantly rural society, and contribute to the improvement of life there. Our sights must be on the majority; it is they we must be aiming at in determining the curriculum and syllabus. Those most suitable for further education will still become obvious, and they will not suffer. For the purpose is not to provide an inferior education to that given at present. The purpose is to provide a different education — one realistically designed to fulfil the common purposes of education in the particular society of Tanzania. The same thing must be true at postprimary schools. The object of the teaching must be the provision of knowledge, skills and attitudes which will serve the student when he or she lives and works in a developing and changing socialist state; it must not be aimed at university entrance.

Alongside this change in the approach to the curriculum there must be a parallel and integrated change in the way our schools are run, so as to make them and their inhabitants a real part of our society and our economy. Schools must, in fact, become communities — and communities which practise the precept of self-reliance. The teachers, workers, and pupils together must be the members of a social unit in the same way as parents, relatives, and children are the family social unit. There must be the same kind of relationship between pupils and teachers within the school community as there is between children and parents in the village. And the former community must realize, just as the latter do, that their life and well-being depend upon the production of wealth — by farming or other activities. This means that all schools, but especially secondary schools and other forms of higher education, must contribute to their own upkeep; they must be economic communities as well as social and educational communities. Each school should have, as an integral part of it, a farm or workshop which provides the food eaten by the community, and makes some contribution to the total national income.

This is not a suggestion that a school farm or workshop should be attached to every school for training purposes. It is a suggestion that every school should also be a farm; that the school community should consist of people who are both teachers and farmers, and pupils and farmers. Obviously if there is a school farm, the pupils working on it should be learning the techniques and tasks of farming. But the farm would be an integral part of the school — and the welfare of the pupils would depend on its output, just as the welfare of a farmer depends on the output of his land. Thus, when this scheme is in operation, the revenue side of school accounts would not just read as at present — "Grant from Government . . . ; Grant from voluntary agency or other charity. . . ." They would read — "Income from sale of cotton (or whatever other cash crop was appropriate for the area) . . . ; Value of the food grown and consumed . . . ; Value of labour done by pupils on new building, repairs, equipment, etc. . . . ; Government subvention . . . ; Grant from . . . ."

This is a break with our educational tradition, and unless its purpose and its possibilities are fully understood by teachers and parents, it may be resented at the beginning. But the truth is that it is not a regressive measure, nor a punishment either for teachers or pupils. It is a recognition that we in Tanzania have to work our way out of poverty, and that we are all members of the one society, depending upon each other. There will be difficulties of implementation, especially at first. For example, we do not now have a host of experienced farm managers who could be used as planners and teachers on the new school farms. But this is not an insuperable difficulty; and certainly life will not halt in Tanzania until we get experienced farm managers. Life and farming will go on as we train. Indeed, by using good local farmers as supervisors and teachers of particular aspects of the work, and using the services of the agricultural officers and assistants, we shall be helping to break down the notion that only book learning is worthy of respect. This is an important element in our socialist development.

Neither does this concept of schools contributing to their own upkeep simply mean using our children as labourers who follow traditional methods. On the contrary, on a school farm pupils can learn by doing. The important place of the hoe and of other simple tools can be demonstrated; the advantages of improved seeds, of simple ox-ploughs, and of proper methods of animal husbandry can become obvious; and the pupils can learn by practice how to use these things to the best advantage. The farm work and products should be integrated into the school life; thus the properties of fertilizers can be explained in the science classes, and their use and limitations experienced by the pupils as they see them in use. The possibilities of proper grazing practices, and of terracing and soil conservation methods can all be taught theoretically, at the same time as they are put into practice; the students will then understand what they are doing and why, and will be able to analyse any failures and consider possibilities for greater improvement.

But the school farms must not be, and indeed could not be, highly mechanized demonstration farms. We do not have the capital which would be necessary for this to happen, and neither would it teach the pupils anything about the life they will be leading. The school farms must be created by the school community clearing their own bush, and so on — but doing it together. They must be used with no more capital assistance than is available to an ordinary, established, cooperative farm where the work can be supervised. By such means the students can learn the advantages of cooperative endeavour, even when outside capital is not available in any significant quantities. Again, the advantages of cooperation could be studied in the classroom, as well as being demonstrated on the farm.

The most important thing is that the school members should learn that it is their farm, and that their living standards depend on it. Pupils should be given an opportunity to make many of the decisions necessary — for example, whether to spend money they have earned on hiring a tractor to get land ready for planting, or whether to use that money for other purposes on the farm or in the school, and doing the hard work themselves by sheer physical labour. By this sort of practice and by this combination of classroom work and farm work, our educated young people will learn to realize that if they farm well they can eat well and have better facilities in the dormitories, recreation rooms, and so on. If they work badly, then they themselves will suffer. In this process Government should avoid laying down detailed and rigid rules; each school must have considerable flexibility. Only then can the potential of that particular area be utilized, and only then can the participants practice — and learn to value — direct democracy.

By such means our students will relate work to comfort. They will learn the meaning of living together and working together for the good of all, and also the value of working together with the local nonschool community. For they will learn that many things require more than school effort — that irrigation may be possible if they work with neighbouring farmers, that development requires a choice between present and future satisfaction, both for themselves and their village.

At the beginning it is probable that a good number of mistakes will be made, and it would certainly be wrong to give complete untrammelled choice to young pupils right from the start. But although guidance must be given by the school authorities and a certain amount of discipline exerted the pupils must be able to participate in decisions and learn by mistakes. For example, they can learn to keep a school farm log in which proper records are kept of the work done, the fertilizers applied, or food given to the animals, etc., and the results from different parts of the farm. Then they can be helped to see where changes are required, and why. For it is also important that the idea of planning be taught in the classroom and related to the farm; the whole school should join in the programming of a year's work, and the breakdown of responsibility and timing within that overall programme. Extra benefits to particular groups within the school might then well be related to the proper fulfillment of the tasks set, once all the members of the school have received the necessary minimum for healthy development. Again, this sort of planning can be part of the teaching of socialism.

Where schools are situated in the rural areas, and in relation to new schools built in the future, it should be possible for the school farm to be part of the school site. But in towns, and in some of the old-established schools in heavily populated areas, this will not be possible. In such cases a school might put more emphasis on other productive activities, or it may be that in boarding schools the pupils can spend part of the school year in the classroom and another part in camp on the school farm some distance away. The plan for each school will have to be worked out; it would certainly be wrong to exclude urban schools, even when they are day schools, from this new approach.

Many other activities now undertaken for pupils, especially in secondary schools, should be undertaken by the pupils themselves. After all, a child who starts school at 7 years of age is already 14 before he enters secondary school, and may be 20 or 21 when he leaves. Yet in many of our schools now we employ cleaners and gardeners, not just to supervise and teach but to do all that work. The pupils get used to the idea of having their food prepared by servants, their plates washed up for them, their rooms cleaned, and the school garden kept attractive. If they are asked to participate in these tasks, they even feel aggrieved and do as little as possible, depending on the strictness of the teacher's supervision. This is because they have not learned to take a pride in having clean rooms and nice gardens, in the way that they have learned to take a pride in a good essay or a good mathematics paper. But is it impossible for these tasks to be incorporated into the total teaching task of the school? Is it necessary for head teachers and their secretaries to spend hours working out travel warrants for school holidays, and so on? Can none of these things be incorporated into classroom teaching so that pupils learn how to do these things for themselves by doing them? Is it impossible, in other words, for secondary schools at least to become reasonably self-sufficient communities, where the teaching and supervisory skills are imported from outside, but where other tasks are either done by the community or paid for by its productive efforts? It is true that, to the pupils, the school is only a temporary community, but for up to seven years this is the group to which they really belong.

Obviously such a position could not be reached overnight. It requires a basic change in both organization and teaching, and will therefore have to be introduced gradually, with the schools taking an increasing responsibility for their own well-being as the months pass. Neither would primary schools be able to do as much for themselves — although it should be remembered that the older pupils will be thirteen and fourteen years of age, at which time children in many European countries are already at work.

But, although primary schools cannot accept the same responsibility for their own well-being as secondary schools, it is absolutely vital that they, and their pupils, should be thoroughly integrated into the village life. The pupils must remain an integral part of the family (or community) economic unit. The children must be made part of the community by having responsibilities to the community, and having the community involved in school activities. The school work-terms, times, and so on — must be so arranged that the children can participate, as members of the family, in the family farms, or as junior members of the community on community farms. At present children who do not go to school work on the family or community farm, or look after cattle, as a matter of course. It must be equally a matter of course that the children who do attend school should participate in the family work — not as a favour when they feel like it, but as a normal part of their up-bringing. The present attitudes whereby the school is regarded as something separate, and the pupils as people who do not have to contribute to the work, must be abandoned. In this, of course, parents have a special duty; but the schools can contribute a great deal to the development of this attitude.

There are many different ways in which this integration can be achieved. But it will have to be done deliberately, and with the conscious intention of making the children realize that they are being educated by the community in order that they shall become intelligent and active members of the community. One possible way of achieving this would combine for primary school pupils the same advantages of learning by doing as the secondary school pupils will have. If the primary school children work on a village communal farm — perhaps having special responsibility for a given number of acres — they can learn new techniques and take a pride in a school community achievement. If there is no communal farm, then the school can start a small one of their own by appealing to the older members to help in the bush-clearing in return for a school contribution in labour to some existing community project.

Again, if development work — new buildings or other things — are needed in the school, then the children and the local villagers should work on it together, allocating responsibility according to comparative health and strength. The children should certainly do their own cleaning (boys as well as girls should be involved in this), and should learn the value of working together and of planning for the future. Thus for example, if they have their own *shamba* the children should be involved not only in the work, but also in the allocation of any food or cash crop produced. They should participate in the choice between benefit to the school

directly, or to the village as a whole, and between present or future benefit. By these and other appropriate means the children must learn from
the beginning to the end of their school life that education does not set
them apart, but is designed to help them be effective members of the
community — for their own benefit as well as that of their country and
their neighbours.

One difficulty in the way of this kind of reorganization is the present
examination system; if pupils spend more of their time on learning to do
practical work, and on contributing to their own upkeep in the development of the community, they will not be able to take the present kind of
examinations — at least within the same time period. It is, however, difficult to see why the present examination system should be regarded as
sacrosanct. Other countries are moving away from this method of selection, and either abandoning examinations altogether at the lowest levels,
or combining them with other assessments. There is no reason why Tanzania should not combine an examination, which is based on the things
we teach, with a teacher and pupil assessment of work done for the school
and community. This would be a more appropriate method of selecting
entrants for secondary schools and for university, teacher training colleges,
and so on, than the present purely academic procedure. Once a more
detailed outline of this new approach to education is worked out, the
question of selection procedure should be looked at again.

This new form of working in our schools will require some considerable
organizational change. It may be also that the present division of the
school year into rigid terms with long holidays would have to be reexamined; animals cannot be left alone for part of the year, nor can a
school farm support the students if everyone is on holiday when the crops
need planting, weeding or harvesting. But it should not be impossible for
school holidays to be staggered so that different forms go at different
periods or, in double-stream secondary schools, for part of a form to go
at one time and the rest at another. It would take a considerable amount
of organization and administration, but there is no reason why it could
not be done if we once make up our minds to it.

It will probably be suggested that if the children are working as well as
learning they will therefore be able to learn less academically, and that
this will affect standards of administration, in the professions and so on,
throughout our nation in time to come. In fact it is doubtful whether this
is necessarily so; the recent tendency to admit children to primary schools
at ages of five and six years has almost certainly meant that less can be
taught at the early stages. The reversion to seven or eight years entrance
will allow the pace to be increased somewhat; the older children inevitably learn a little faster. A child is unlikely to learn less academically if his
studies are related to the life he sees around him.

But even if this suggestion were based on provable fact, it could not be allowed to over-ride the need for change in the direction of educational integration with our national life. For the majority of our people the thing which matters is that they should be able to read and write fluently in Swahili, that they should have an ability to do arithmetic, and that they should know something of the history, values, and workings of their country and their Government, and that they should acquire the skills necessary to earn their living. (It is important to stress that in Tanzania most people will earn their living by working on their own or on a communal *shamba*, and only a few will do so by working for wages which they have to spend on buying things the farmer produces for himself). Things like health science, geography, and the beginning of English, are also important, especially so that the people who wish may be able to learn more by themselves in later life. But most important of all is that our primary school graduates should be able to fit into, and to serve, the communities from which they come.

The same principles of integration into the community, and applicability to its needs, must also be followed at post-secondary levels, but young people who have been through such an integrated system of education as that outlined are unlikely to forget their debt to the community by an intense period of study at the end of their formal educational life. Yet even at University, Medical School, or other post-secondary levels, there is no reason why students should continue to have all their washing up and cleaning done for them. Nor is there any reason why students at such institutions should not be required as part of their degree or professional training, to spend at least part of their vacations contributing to the society in a manner related to their studies. At present some undergraduates spend their vacations working in Government offices — getting paid at normal employee rates for doing so. It would be more appropriate (once the organization had been set up efficiently) for them to undertake projects needed by the community, even if there is insufficient money for them to constitute paid employment. For example, the collection of local history, work on the census, participation in adult education activities, work in dispensaries, etc., would give the students practical experience in their own fields. For this they could receive the equivalent of the minimum wage, and any balance of money due for work which would otherwise have been done for higher wages could be paid to the College or Institution and go towards welfare or sports equipment. Such work should earn credits for the student which count towards his examination result; a student who shirks such work — or fails to do it properly — would then find that two things follow. First, his fellow students might be blaming him for shortfalls in proposed welfare or other improvements; and second, his degree would be down-graded accordingly.

## CONCLUSION

The education provided by Tanzania for the students of Tanzania must serve the purposes of Tanzania. It must encourage the growth of the socialist values we aspire to. It must encourage the development of a proud, independent, and free citizenry which relies upon itself for its own development, and which knows the advantages and the problems of co-operation. It must ensure that the educated know themselves to be an integral part of the nation and recognize the responsibility to give greater service the greater the opportunities they have had.

This is not only a matter of school organization and curriculum. Social values are formed by family, school, and society — by the total environment in which a child develops. But it is no use our educational system stressing values and knowledge appropriate to the past or to the citizens in other countries; it is wrong if it even contributes to the continuation of those inequalities and privileges which still exist in our society because of our inheritance. Let our students be educated to be members and servants of the kind of just and egalitarian future to which this country aspires.

## SUGGESTED READINGS FOR PART ONE

### General

ASHBY, ERIC
  1964    African universities and western tradition. The Godkin lectures at
          Harvard University. Cambridge: Harvard University Press. vi+
          113 pp., index.
          Useful for discussions of the conflicts arising from the use of West-
          ern models to solve African problems

BURNS, DONALD G.
  1965    African education: An introductory survey of education in common-
          wealth countries. London: Oxford University Press. vi+215 pp.,
          bibliography.
          Presents an overall view of educational developments in former
          British colonial areas in Africa

HANSON, JOHN W. AND GEOFFREY W. GIBSON
  1966    African education and development since 1960: A select and an-
          notated bibliography. East Lansing: Institute for International
          Studies in Education and African Studies Center, Michigan State
          University. vii+327 pp.
          Useful for in-depth research

RUTH SLOAN ASSOCIATES
  1962   The educated African: A country-by-country survey of educational development in Africa. New York: F. A. Praeger. xvii+542 pp.

  Provides a brief overview of educational facilities in individual African countries in the late 1950's

## Applied Anthropology

BROKENSHA, DAVID
  1966   Applied anthropology in English-speaking Africa. Lexington: Society for Applied Anthropology, University of Kentucky. 31 pp., bibliography.

  Good discussion of types of research and programs in applied anthropology

## Nigeria

AJAYI, J. F. ADE
  1965   Christian missions in Nigeria 1841–1891: The making of a new elite. Evanston: Northwestern University Press. xvi+317 pp., maps, illustrations, appendixes, index, bibliography.

  Interesting in its analysis of missionary influences on an important African nation

NDUKA, OTONTI
  1964   Western education and the Nigerian cultural background. Ibadan: Oxford University Press. viii+168 pp., bibliography.

  An African's view of the conflicts between Western models and African realities

## Tanzania

CAMERON, JOHN
  1967   The integration of education in Tanganyika. *Comparative Education Review,* Vol. XI, no. 1: 38–56.

  Discussion of the multinational, multiracial, multilingual problems of education in Tanzania (formerly Tanganyika)

DODD, WILLIAM
  1968   Centralization in education in mainland Tanzania. *Comparative Education Review,* Vol. XII, No. 3:268–280.

  Discussion of the breakdown of schools segregated on the basis of race or class

Three nations dominate Asia today: Japan, China, and India. While these nations are always described as "Asian," the use of that term should not prevent one's comprehension of the basic differences present among the three. Western education has fundamentally altered all three, but the outcome of the processes of change in each shows that only the catalyst — the presence and demands of Westerners — is the same for each, and even that has differed in degree and historical structure in each.

## PART TWO

# ASIA

India was a British colony. China bore the weight of "unequal treaties" for a century ("unequal" in the sense that Western nations received certain rights, such as the power to regulate Chinese tariffs, which China did not receive vis-à-vis the Western nations). Yet, despite the weakness of the Ch'ing dynasty, only a tiny portion of Chinese territory was occupied as a colony by a Western power. The largest colony in China was created by Japan in the 1930's when the latter made occupied Manchuria into "Manchukuo" and restored the last Ch'ing emperor to the throne. The third nation, Japan, was entirely free of unequal treaty provisions by the early part of the twentieth century. And in 1905 when Japan defeated Russia, the Western world was made acutely aware of a basic shift in the Asian balance of power.

A basic factor in any discussion of India's development is the caste system. An important aspect of this system is the large number of untouchables. Harold Isaacs estimates that there are about 65,000,000 untouchables or one out of every nine Indians. That figure may mean more if it is put in American terms: if the same proportion of American citizens were "outcaste," then 25,000,000 Americans would be "untouchable." In his article Isaacs deals with three interrelated questions: has education permitted untouchables to improve their situation, has education encouraged other Indians who are not untouchable to reject their attitudes of discrimination toward the untouchables, and, given continuing discrimination and rejection, has education helped successful untouchables to accept themselves as worthy persons whom an accident of birth has put into an unfortunate social condition. The answer to all three questions seems to be a qualified "yes." The principal problems in India are that the proportion of untouchables affected by educational progress remains very small while the patterns of discrimination and rejection are still strong. These factors combine to impede psychological self-acceptance.

It is well known that Chinese culture has placed a high value on education. However, it is important to bear in mind that traditional Chinese education was elitist and that the great majority of people during the 3,000 years that China has had a written language have remained illiterate. The traditional assumption was that education was intended for a small minority. In addition, the fact of being educated made one a special person with high prestige and status on the local scene. Literacy also enabled a man to prepare for the examinations which often led to a government position.

The school day in China was generally from sunrise to sunset and involved constant recitation. Memorization of texts and commentaries was the basic educational method. Such emphasis on exactness of memory reflected two factors in Chinese culture: the necessity to remember a large number of characters in order to read Chinese script and the high value put on the exact words of Confucius and interpreters of the Confucian tradition. The Classics and commentaries on them were thought to contain accurate guideposts to all human ethical and practical situations, and the educated man knew them so thoroughly that he could order all reality by reference to what he had committed to memory.

Civilization was identified in the Chinese tradition with being educated in the Confucian manner. Anyone who had not been so educated lacked civilization and was therefore a "barbarian." From the late 1830's on, these traditional assumptions faced increasing challenges from outside sources. The great majority of the intelligentsia remained committed to the traditional assumptions. The downfall of the imperial system in 1911 symbolized the undermining of confidence in the traditional system of education which had for so long inculcated the social, ethical, political, and normative assumptions of Confucianism. In the cities, especially after World War I, university students pushed for basic educational reforms: education of females; use of the modern spoken language in place of ancient Chinese, which had to be learned much as Latin had had to be learned in medieval Europe; the removal of political pressures on the universities, and so forth. Martin Yang's description of the traditional and modern schools in Taitou village in the province of Shantung shows that the changes in education had begun to filter to the village level by the 1930's. However, the school described in Yang's article reflected many traditional factors as well, such as the denial of education to females, a strong class element which served to maintain the elitist tradition, and clan sponsorship of educational facilities.

In the autobiographical account of a school teacher in Jan Myrdal's description of village life in the People's Republic of China, the basic changes begun in the first part of this century are shown coming to fruition. At the same time, some traditional attitudes toward education prevail. "Character," for example, in the sense of the basic structure of the "inner" man, is still closely related to education. The desirable qualities of character have, of course, been substantially modified by the Communist regime. Other traditional qualities remain, though in different form as in the case of group loyalty. Formerly, primary group loyalty was one's patrilineal kin group — the clan. Now the ideal is to identify with the social rather than the kin group. Under both systems individualism, as exemplified in personal competition, is played down. The national goal of making intellectuals familiar with the rigors and experiences of manual labor is evident in Liu Ling. Gardening and physical education are becoming basic parts of a person's education in present-day China. This is a real departure from the traditional assumption of a strict division between men of learning and men of labor. One important factor in the recent Cultural Revolution was the desire of the regime to prevent continuation of the old Chinese distinction between intellectual and worker which had led to classes being formed along those lines.

The three readings about China provide a perspective on the changes which Chinese education has undergone in the last fifty years. Western learning caused great emotional and intellectual conflicts in the generation which has provided the leadership in China for much of the twentieth century. In Taitou, the village school which Martin Yang describes reflected both change and conservatism, a combination often present during the Republican (Nationalist Chinese) period of rule, 1912–1949. Now, a generation beyond the establishment of the Communist regime on the Chinese Mainland, the Liu Ling village school provides an example of the dual purpose of education in China: for the mass education (i.e., literacy) of the younger segment of the population and for the inculcation of an official ideology in the entire population. The first purpose is a radical departure from traditional China, where the masses were illiterate and formal education was elitist, being limited to a very small proportion of the population. The second purpose, however, seems to represent a continuation of past traditions, in which education and Confucian ideology were closely intertwined. Finally, the autobiographical selection, based on research in Taiwan, shows the influence of non-Chinese, nontraditional education in an area moving toward modernization yet still culturally conservative.

The most spectacular economic and educational success in Asia is Japan. The three selections on Japan are intended to provide historical, rural, and urban perspectives on Japanese education. The selection from John Whitney Hall's article describes the educational system and methods during the Tokugawa period (1644–1868), which is often said to have been "feudal" in its social structure. The Japanese had possessed a system of writing for a thousand years before the Tokugawa period. The initial system was borrowed from the Chinese and then two systems which indicate pronounciation were later adopted. Those two systems are, in fact, functionally similar to the English alphabet. However, since Chinese characters continue to be used, a Japanese student still faces the same tasks of memory as his Chinese counterpart.

The Meiji Restoration (1868) ended the Tokugawa period and nominally made the Emperor (Meiji) the ruler of Japan in the place of the Tokugawa family military regime. While there is much historical dispute about the actual extent of the Emperor's power and the part the Emperor played in the government, there is no doubt that the shift brought to power a group of leaders who devoted themselves to making Japan a modern and powerful state by Western standards. The government dispossessed the *samurai,* the military class under the Tokugawa, and replaced it with a modern military organization. The ruling authorities stressed industrialization, efficient agriculture, mass education, and military prowess.

Embree's discussion of education in Suye Mura shows how far-reaching mass education efforts were in the period before World War II.

Japan, alone in Asia, had general literacy by the end of the nineteenth century.

Any comparison of Japan and China must, of course, take several quantitative factors into account: China's population is between six and seven times greater than Japan's; Japan is about equivalent to the state of California in land area while China is larger than the entire continental United States. At the same time, there is little doubt that a difference in adaptability exists between the two cultures. One key to understanding that difference is study of their respective educational methods, systems, and philosophies.

China remains a predominantly rural and agricultural nation. Since World War II, Japan has become an urban society. Dore's analysis of the school system serving Shitayama-cho presents many contrasts with Suye Mura. Those contrasts reflect postwar changes in the status and role of women, a rapid shift of the population (especially the younger people) to cities, the rise of Japan to its present position as one of the foremost industrial nations in the world, and the transformation of Tokyo from a city to that phenomenon of the twentieth century — a megalopolis. In the selection from Dore, it is evident that there is more uncertainty about what is to be taught and how it is to be taught than there was before Japan's defeat in 1945. There are also greater areas for individual decision-making, and, despite the risks involved, such decision-making is encouraged. Opposite trends have been promoted in the People's Republic of China. Central control and national coordination have replaced traditional conditions of local village or clan sponsorship and management of education. It is important to bear in mind in any comparative discussion of Japan and China the great differences in economic, technological, and demographic conditions between the two nations. To regard both as "Asian" and therefore similiar in development, problems, and solutions to internal problems can lead only to confusion. The need for such distinctions in analysis is even more acute when India is brought into discussion. Even a brief glimpse, as follows here, of education in India, China, and Japan points more to differences than to similarities.

# 5

# India's Ex-Untouchables

HAROLD R. ISAACS

### THE FATHERS: EARLY EDUCATION

Until well into the 1930's, it plainly took some special circumstance or special person to bring an Untouchable child to school and to keep him there. As I met some of these individuals and began to listen to their stories of how they had gotten started, I became aware that this special person was very often a father, and the special circumstances some impulse, some drive, that had moved him to defy fate by sending his son to school. Some of these fathers were men who had gotten started themselves on the road to education — indeed, in general the rule seems to hold that the higher-achieving the sons, the better educated the fathers. But others were quite illiterate and yet had been moved in some way to put a son's small foot on the path that led to complete rejection of the fate which for so many centuries had been accepted without question. These fathers played their parts in this story of human change and, dimly as they may appear in this misty gallery, they are not to be passed by.

Around the turn of the century thousands of laborers used to go each year from the east coast of India for spells of work on the docks at Rangoon in Burma. One of these migrant laborers, a member of the Untouchable Mala caste of cowherds from an Andhra village, decided not to return with the others when their contract was up but to stay in Rangoon, where he managed to get himself apprenticed to a tailor and to learn this new trade. "He decided to change things, and to become another kind of man," his son told me. "He wanted me to be like him and not like all the others who went just to labor and come back. So he took me to Rangoon the year I was seven and for some years I learned how to be a tailor." In Rangoon the son went to school, later returned to India to go to high school and then on to the university and a career in politics inspired by Gandhi in the early 1920's. This was the story of the father of B. S. Murthy, a self-assured man now close to sixty, who became Deputy Minister of Community Development in the Nehru cabinet.

B. N. Kureel, who is forty-three and occupies a Congress Party seat in the Lok Sabha, or lower house of Parliament, from Uttar Pradesh, came of a family that was entirely illiterate. Kureel was the first in his family ever to go to school and when I asked him why his father had sent him, he said:

> I wondered about this and only a few years ago I asked him. He is still there in the village, about eighty years old now. He told me that at that time he was feeling harassed by the zamindars [landlords] who were pressing the men of the village, including my father, for forced labor for them. One day, he said, it suddenly came to his mind: "If a son of my family were educated, this might not happen. It would never happen to *him*. So I decided to send you to school." That's what he said, and I went to school in a village a mile away.

B. P. Maurya, a Republican Party Member of Parliament, a Chamar from Uttar Pradesh, was also the son of a farm laborer, but his father was a man who had received the beginnings of an education. This came about because one day when he was a youth — it was back in the 1890's — an English Roman Catholic priest came to his village and offered to teach reading and writing to anyone who came. Three young Chamars, of all in the village, went to him, all three of them, Maurya said, from the families that were relatively the best off among the Untouchables of the place. He learned to read and write a little Hindi in the time that the priest came. Maurya went on:

> My father had strong feelings about education. "Only education will solve our problem," he would say. This is what he learned from that padre and he used to say it to us all the time. He used to say Untouch-

ability would vanish when all people got educated. In his day Untouchables were treated like animals, and this is much changed now. He did not embrace Christianity with the padre and he did not embrace Buddhism although he followed Ambedkar in politics. He is still a Scheduled Caste Hindu. He is eighty-eight years old, and what he wants is to cease being a victim of Untouchability.

The story of a man who at forty is an M.A., and a Lecturer in History, presented a three-generation pattern with some rather special features. In his case, the early impetus came not from his father but from his grandfather, who quit the village early, went to work on the railroad and rose to be a fireman. "So long as my grandfather was there," he said, "we were in a good position." His father, however, took off on his own way, possibly getting some pleasure or satisfaction out of it but hardly becoming much of a help or spur to his son.

My father grew up a jolly person with an aptitude for singing. So long as my grandfather was there it was all right. I was the only child because my mother died when I was seven months old. My grandmother looked after me. The family was in Bombay and I went to primary school here. My father became a kind of wandering singer or poet, a composer of *lawani,* or songs in praise of old warriors. Such people were called *tamasgir,* or entertainers of soldiers in old times. A *tamasgir* is one who follows the profession of *tamasha,* being part of an entertainer group consisting of a dancer, a comic, somebody who could play a noble person, and a singer; and they also could all play instruments. They would wander from place to place, making up songs, entertaining, singing ballads.

We have *tamasha* of various castes, Brahmin *tamasha,* Mahratta *tamasha.* My father learned *tamasha* at the feet of a Brahmin. He never worked except at his singing profession which did not pay very well. He didn't really earn anything. It is really a begging profession, well, maybe not exactly begging, but having to depend on whatever the public might feel like giving. The money my father spent was earned by my grandfather. My father wanted me to follow his profession of *tamasha.* But I went to school without support from my father. I got a freeship as a Scheduled Caste person and worked as a teacher when I was in high school, teaching first and second standard,[1] for which I got five rupees a month. This was in the British time. I passed my matric in 1940.

There is a glimpse of another father who had come to the city and found work as a laborer. Turning to one of the universal solaces of the frustrated poor, he nourished some deeply glimmering impulses of his own. His son told me:

My father's pleasures were to drink wine and to have us read to him from two books of the Mahabarata. He used to come home in a drinking condition and ask us to read to him from these books. This was when he would love his children most, when he would come home after drinking at the wineshop and ask us to read or sing. That is the way his day would finish — work, wine, home, and work again. That was his life.

From some of the younger men, we begin to discover fathers who had some slightly greater chance to change their lives if they would reach out to do so, and perhaps the most striking story of this kind came from a cool and self-confident man of thirty whose name is Sonavane and who is one of the small number of ex-Untouchables to pass the Class 1 civil service examination. He told me this story about his father:

My father's father died when he was only seven years old and my father worked as a laborer in the field. Another young man of the village, a relative of my father's, got an education with the help of the Maharajah of Kholapur. My father decided that he too would get an education. He was twenty-three years old when he made this decision. I was already in school, in the second standard at that time. People laughed at him, but he had determination in his mind and he was not deterred. The principal of the school helped him, and he did 11 years' work in four years, moving from vernacular first grade to matric (matriculation) which he passed in 1943. He now works in the Central Excise in Bombay, a Class 3 post, and he earns R429 a month.

In the accounts of men in their thirties and down into the twenties, we come on fathers who are still laboring in the villages, but by now they are often men who had one or two grades of primary school in the vernacular and this was often true of the mothers as well. We also begin to come on fathers, who migrated at some point to the city and, in some cases, moved out of their traditionally menial occupations into some new and better kind of work. A Siddarth graduate who took a degree in chemistry and now works in the government meteorological service was the son of a man who came to Bombay as a youth and became a motor mechanic, and a mother who went as far as the 7th standard vernacular. Another rising young academic told me how his father came to the city from their Gujerat village and became a sign painter, eventually setting up a little sign-painting business of his own. The Registrar of the Siddarth College of Commerce is the son of a Mahar who was a Grade C fireman on the railway, worked all his life to put his eight children through school, and at fifty "began to read a little himself." A lecturer in mathematics at Siddarth is the grandson of a well-digger and the son of a man who learned to read and write from some Catholic priests who came to their village. This father went on to primary school and became a teacher, and has lived to see his sons win university degrees. Of the youngest undergraduates I met, around twenty years old, almost all had started from some slightly raised parental threshold. Several had parents who had finished primary school and become teachers. One father had become an inspector in the telephone company; another a truck driver in the same company; and a third had gone up to matriculation and become an employee in a large department store.

As some of these stories have shown, the initial impetus, usually from a father, also came sometimes from others in this gallery of men — the occasional foreign Christians who came with the offer of literacy, and more often, the caste Hindu teachers who accepted Untouchable children with a kind, helping spirit, and did what they could to move them along to some chance of a better life. Indeed, like so many other unique particulars in Indian life, even this impulse to help Untouchables was, in a few of the cases mentioned, the product of tradition, in this case the particular tradition of a Kshatriya caste called "CKP" (Chandraseniya Kayastha Prabhu). This group, described as an intellectual community, came into conflict with the Brahmins at least 300 years ago over their right to be teachers and scholars. As an act of special defiance of the Brahmins, CKPs of that distant day began helping Untouchables and as a consequence, as one ex-Untouchable told me, "they have had a soft feeling for Untouchables ever since." For this man it had been a CKP school principal who had given him his main chance to advance in school.

It not only took some rather special impetus to put these individuals on the road to an education, but it also took a special kind of persistence and courage to stay on this road. The lonely little boys who made their way to schools in many scattered places in India during the first 30 years of this century had to accept the bluntest kind of rejection and exclusion and had to be able to persist in the face of it year after year to get through. They could go *to* school, for example, but very rarely could they go *in.* Despite long-standing official policies of nondiscrimination, the Untouchable child almost invariably was made to sit outside in the dirt near the door or under a window, sometimes on the verandah if there was one, and take his lessons by listening from there. Where they were allowed to enter the classroom, they had to sit on separate benches or on the floor. Since so many of these individuals were "firsts" in their village or district, they usually sat out there in the dirt or apart in the classroom quite alone. One or two went to Christian mission schools set up especially for Untouchables and therefore did not have to face the problem of contact with caste Hindus until they reached the 5th standard in middle school. Some Christian schools, especially in the south where they were attended by caste Hindu children, also maintained some form of separation for the rare Untouchable child who came. Since schools were often quite a distance from home, it was frequently not only a matter of suffering exclusion from the classroom but also of finding a place to board. Untouchables would not be allowed to stay at school hostels or special arrangements had to be made for them to eat and sleep apart. Here is a typical account:

> When I came to the school to which my father sent me, I was the first boy ever to come there from the Scheduled Castes. I had to sit separate, out on the verandah, and listen from the outside, and that is where I sat every day for three years. In the third year one day an inspector of schools came and put questions to the class and found me to be the best. He asked me why I was sitting outside. The teacher answered for me and said I belonged to the Chamars, that I was Untouchable, that the other boys wouldn't touch me. The inspector said that according to government rules, Untouchability could not be observed to such an extent and that some other arrangement would have to be made. So the teacher had me come inside and sit in a chair behind his chair, and that is where I spent the whole fourth year, sitting behind the teacher, facing the entire class. That was in 1928.

At age ten he was sent to a middle school, nine miles from his home. At the school hostel three boys ordinarily shared a room, but no one would share with him although the teacher in charge, "a kindhearted Brahmin, a Gandhian who wore khadi [homespun], tried to persuade the other boys," but failed. The problem was solved for a time by bringing in two other Untouchable boys whom the teacher agreed to take although they were at a much lower level.

An older man who went to school in Travancore early in the 1920's remembered:

> I was able to go inside, although to sit on a separate seat. I was the only Scheduled Caste boy in the class and I had a seat in the corner. The teacher would not come near me. I would write on my slate and put it on the floor and he would come and look at it. Sometimes he would beat me and would do this by throwing his cane against my outstretched hand. It would hit my hand and then fall to the floor and he would pick it up and throw it again against my hand. He was an old man. I met him years later and reminded him how he beat me. He only smiled.

What made this example notable was that the school where it happened was a Catholic school, located in what is now the state of Kerala. In the south, Christians had for many generations simply continued the customary caste practices, with ex-caste Hindu Christians excluding ex-Untouchable Christians just as though nothing else had changed. This practice, long common among Catholics,[2] was also common among Anglicans of more recent date. The fact that the boy in this case had been allowed to enter the classroom at all was a recent and quite radical innovation at the time he attended, part of the post-1919 reforms encouraged by the Maharajah of Travancore. "This was better," he explained, "than in communities where the Nairs [a local upper caste group] were in control because they previously would not allow Untouchables to go to school at all, whereas the Christians allowed us to come and stand outside and, by the time I went, to come inside."

By the 1930's, signs of change multiplied. There were scholarships (maintenance stipends) being offered in some states for Untouchable children going to school, and various central government programs also offered help and encouragement. In Uttar Pradesh a lad of ten received six rupees a month to keep himself at a middle school. It was still early in the decade and he still prepared his food all by himself each day and sat outside in the dirt at the school. But a new era began one day when a new teacher appeared.

> I was in the 5th standard when he came along and asked me why I was sitting outside. When I explained, he said: "Never mind, come in and sit on the bench." The other boys objected. Each bench was for six boys but they would not sit with me. They crowded onto other benches and I had a bench all to myself. That teacher was a Shudra (i.e., of low but touchable caste) and was quite bold. He wanted to eradicate these evils, he said, and he told the other boys: "If you don't want to sit here, you can leave." By the next year in the 7th standard we were all sitting together.

In the last prewar years, there was rapid expansion of school facilities, partly under the impetus of the new Congress governments in the states, popularly elected for the first time in 1937. This brought correspondingly broader opportunity for Untouchables, especially in the cities. But it still called for a strong drive and grim persistence for a youngster to make his way ahead.

> At high school I was a good student. I read my books under the street lamps at night. The principal gave me a place to study in the school building. The school was two miles from where I lived. After school I would walk home and take food and then go back to school to study for as long as I could. Then I would sleep there on the floor. Early in the morning I went back home to eat and then came back to school in time for the first class. There were three or four of us doing this.

Great events heralded greater changes. The onset of war in Europe and then in Asia itself brought on a major political crisis in India. The quickening of the coming of change was felt at every level of life. The youngest of the ex-Untouchable undergraduates who told me about their fathers were born in 1940 or 1941, and were just about at school-starting age themselves in 1947 when the government of newly independent India proclaimed the goal of free primary education for all.

## NOTES

1. "Standards" in India are equivalent to American "grades." Secondary schooling ends with the eleventh standard, one year sooner than in the American system. The usual arrangement provides for four years in primary school, three in middle school, and four in high school. The successful matriculate or "matric" goes on to higher education, four years for a bachelor's degree in arts (somtimes divided between a "preuniversity" year and a three-year degree course), or five years for a degree in science or technology.

2. Sanctioned by a special papal bull issued by Pope Gregory XV, says Ghurye, quoting the *Encyclopaedia Britannica*, 11th ed., V:468.

# 6

# Traditional Education and Untraditional Demands: Autobiographical Case Studies from Contemporary Taiwan

HARRY M. LINDQUIST

## INTRODUCTION

### Taiwan: A Description

Taiwan is an island off the southern coast of China. It has a total area of 13,844 square miles and a population of about 13,000,000. Since only one-third of the island is arable, population density poses a serious problem. If we can accept late nineteenth-century estimates as accurate, the population of Taiwan has increased almost 600 percent in less than a century. Population density has increased from 226.03 per square mile in 1952 to 361.30 per square mile in 1966. Most of that increase has been the result of local growth and not of migration.

The author gratefully acknowledges support for fieldwork from the U.S. Public Health Service, National Institute of Mental Health, through postdoctoral fellowship no. 1–F2–MH–36,943–01. The author alone is responsible for the statements in this article.

The government of the Republic of China, often called Nationalist China, is now resident in Taiwan and is recognized as the legitimate government of China by the United States and other noncommunist nations. Taiwan is regarded as a province of China in which the government of the Republic of China is forced to reside because of the Communist seizure of power on the Mainland. A canon of the Nationalist government is that Mainland China will be recovered in due time, and the Communist regime in power will be deposed. Although twenty years have passed since the Nationalists fled from the Mainland (1949), its recovery is a basic and undebatable policy of the Taipei authorities.

The population trend described above is complicated further by the increasing tendency, common in all of Asia, for people to move from rural to urban areas. In addition, the remarkable agricultural revolution in Taiwan, based on land reform, fertilizers, improved seeds, and partial mechanization, has rapidly reduced the numbers of people required for agriculture. As a result young men and women often have no choice but to go to the cities.

There are three segments of Taiwan's population: aboriginal, Taiwanese, and Mainlander. In terms of urban research, the aboriginals are quite peripheral. Mainlanders are persons who were born on the Mainland of China, or their children, who consider their native home to be the Mainland. The Taiwanese are Chinese whose parents consider themselves to be natives of the province of Taiwan.

### Education in Taiwan

In 1968 the government of Taiwan decreed that compulsory education would be extended from six years to nine years; that is, both primary and middle schools are now included. Thus, only upper middle schools and the universities remain selective. This formal education system logically and structurally leads to completion of college education. Yet, the proportion of the total school population who achieve that end is very small at the present time. Nevertheless, public literacy and general education are on the rise. Increasing education and the movement toward urbanization have led to the familiar pattern of rising personal aspirations. Other social changes such as acceptance both of the need to educate women and of the necessity for wives to work outside the home coincide with rapid changes to neolocal residence after marriage and the decline of arranged marriages. Perhaps the greatest change is that literacy no longer means automatic employment.

During a sixteenth-month period in 1967–68 I conducted research in Taiwan and Hong Kong on a postdoctoral fellowship through the National Institute of Mental Health under the sponsorship of Dr. Murray Wax.

My principal question was:

> How do literate young people with a formal education equivalent to upper middle school or less utilize their literacy?

That question led me to a study of night schools where English is taught. The great majority of Taiwan's school population enters the labor market with few skills or special characteristics to set them off from the large number of men and women in competition for jobs. Underemployment is so common that gaining a skill is requisite. For many learning English represents an opportunity to get a job and be connected, in some way, with the wealth, economic growth, and mobility which foreign enterprise seems to offer.

There are three main categories of night schools in Taipei. First, there are the so-called "sweat-shops" which are set up by enterprising merchants of knowledge, sometimes in conjunction with equally enterprising Americans. These one- or two-man operations usually function like a Chinese store: instruction in front and living quarters for the Chinese in back. I avoided this type because it usually draws on one small area and stresses the profit motive so strongly that student cooperation would have been difficult to get. The second type are the large institutions which offer instruction on a mass basis to several thousand students. Finally, there are service organizations such as churches and social service groups which offer instruction either to proselytize or fulfill their social service ideals. The government maintains what can best be described as a *laissez-faire* attitude toward all the night schools. There are no official standards for the teachers.

I approached the samples I desired through working as a night school teacher both in a large institution and in a social service, nonchurch-affiliated night school. My role as an anthropologist was known to the administration, other teachers, and, of course, to the students.

Foreign teachers of English are in very short supply in Taiwan. English instruction in the official school network is uniformly bad, from middle school through college. Oral-aural instruction is, in practical terms, almost absent.

Three types of students, in general, attend night schools. First, there are great numbers of college students who are preparing for the dreaded TOEFL (Test of English as a Foreign Language). This examination must be passed in order to obtain a visa to study in the United States — the most persistent and widespread goal of college students.[1] Second, there are older professional people who see English as a means of adjustment to the local situation and whose age and/or marital status prevent immigration. The third and largest group is made up of those who look to the night school as a source of a skill which will separate them from the masses of literate, unskilled, and undereducated people of Taiwan.

## AUTOBIOGRAPHIES

### Background

These autobiographies were written at my request in return for free English instruction. Though I provided an outline in Chinese of what general topics I wanted included, I also stressed that I was interested in any detail or aspect of the life of the respondent that he or she considered relevant.

I have taken every precaution to protect the anonymity of the respondents. I have eliminated any reference to specific time or place and have provided a general statement in place of any particular which could identify the respondent. Otherwise, the autobiographies contain all the details originally included.

In translating the handwritten autobiographies great attention has been paid to preserving the original spirit and style of the language used. Each autobiography represents a considerable emotional effort on the part of the writer in what is essentially an act of self-examination. Often, the writers used metaphors (the Chinese language being rich with them), to express their emotions, and we have tried to provide a faithful, though sometimes literal, translation of each metaphor so that the *feelings* expressed stand a better chance of glimmering through a foreign language.

These autobiographies form a selection from our wider sample. Each is interesting in itself, but these particular ones represent especially well four general trends and situations in contemporary Taiwan. Mr. A is an excellent example of two factors. First, as was described earlier, there is considerable movement in Taiwan toward the cities and urban areas because they are more exciting and interesting, arable land is so limited, and economic opportunities for advancement seem to lie in the cities. Second, Mr. A's generation of young Taiwanese has gained economically, educationally, and socially. He has, of course, participated fully in the upward movement and intends to use his English to complete that cycle: to go abroad.

Miss B is also a native Taiwanese. Her education level is quite low, and, if she were an average person, her future would be limited to menial work or hand labor. She also represents a less positive factor of present-day Taiwan: capable people who, for reasons of poverty, are unable to utilize their talents. Miss B intends to use her English training to try to escape from the dilemma in which her lack of education has placed her.

Miss C represents the Mainlander whose life has been disrupted by the shift in the late 1940's from Mainland China to Taiwan. Many members of the Chinese elite left with the Kuomintang in the belief that their return was imminent. Now, twenty years later, we know that their hopes were baseless. She also represents another trend: the movement of the children of Mainlanders to the United States. Miss C, like all four persons in this section, is exceptional: she gained an education despite the loss of both parents. Usually, the death or material absence of a father seriously jeopardizes chances for advanced education. The loss of both parents presents almost incalculable odds. But, as with Mr. A, Miss C became independent at a very early age.

Finally, Miss D's autobiography is similar to that of Mr. A. In both, there was family disruption caused by the father. Both were talented in school, and both were native Taiwanese. But, in Miss D's case, there was no local teacher to help persuade her parents. Miss D, then, also represents the increasing impersonalization in an area where the forces of urbanization are becoming stronger and consequently the competition fiercer.

These autobiographies are intended to give the reader a general and personal glimpse into the life patterns of four types of students in English night schools who are attempting to use their training, in the midst of social and economic change, to improve their opportunities for advancement.

## Mr. A

Mr. A is about 30 years old. A native Taiwanese, he is about 5'4" tall, of slight build, and has an intense, single-minded manner about everything he does. At a very early age he saw education as the tool for advancement in Taiwan society, and acted accordingly.

> . . . My father is a farmer. In my home there were my grandmother, who lived to be ninty years old before she died, four younger brothers, two younger sisters and my parents. My childhood was happy and carefree.
>
> My father and mother worked all day in the fields and did not pay much attention to the upbringing of their children. The children did not go to kindergarten or nursery school. Everyday they either played with neighborhood children or helped with the farmwork.
>
> When I was four, there was a disruption in my parents' feelings for each other. My parents often quarreled about the fact that my father went with his friends to the wine parlors to play with wine-girls. My father spent a lot of money and sold a lot of property to pay for the wine-girls. As a result, my family became poor. But, after a while, my father came back to my mother, and they were reconciled. In my small heart, at that time, I hated "women," who had ruined my family and destroyed our property. The loss of our family's property later influenced my education.
>
> My paternal grandmother loved me the most. She always gave me lots of things to eat; so, sometimes, I had stomach trouble. Love in a poor family in a village is most truthful and most touching. Parents sometimes pretend that they do not like to eat this and that so that the children can eat a little bit more.

I went to school when I was seven years old. The primary school was very far from my home. The round trip took three hours to walk. For grown-ups it required two hours. When I came home at night, there was no light to do my homework by. During the holidays, I had to help my father till the land. From grade one through grade six, I always graduated first in my class.

My teacher helped me persuade my father to let me continue in a *hsien* middle school. I, therefore, left home to go to the city . . . where I rented a house and learned to do my own cooking. [Mr. A was 13 years old at that time.] At graduation from middle school I was third in the class. After graduation my father wanted me to go home and continue with farming, but I wanted to continue with my education. At that time, I was aware of the difference between living in the city and living in the country. I wanted to study more so that I could live in the city. Finally, my father permitted me to go to commercial-technical school so that, after I graduated, I could find a job and start earning money.

After I started to study at the commercial-technical college, my desire for learning became even stronger. I worked harder than other people to try to prepare for the entrance examinations. In the end, among the three graduating classes in the whole school, I was the only one to be accepted to a college. I studied in the business administration section . . . I finished my college education by studying halftime and working halftime. During this period, I worked as an accountant in a shop, a family tutor, and in a shop. Of course, I also received scholarships. The second year, when I passed the higher level of examinations, it was regarded as a most glorious event in my village. In a farmer's heart, it is like passing the imperial examinations in the period of the emperors. In my village, there is no one else who both graduated from college and at the same time passed the higher examinations. My parents, therefore, also received great honor. My mother was selected as model mother.

After serving in the armed forces for one year, I returned to my alma mater as a teacher. But the salary was too low. The next year, I passed the examination to take a job in ——. Among the 450 contestants, only 10 were selected. I was among the lucky 10. After serving for —— years, I again felt the need to continue research, and the United States is the haven for business administration studies. I hope that one day I can fulfill my last desire for knowledge.

As for my feelings about religion, when I was young, my mother would take us to the temples to pray. I then felt that the images of the gods were terrible and fearsome. Although prayers came from the deepest feelings of our hearts, those who are fortunate are still fortunate; those who are poor are still poor. The images of the gods give no reaction whatsoever. When I grew up, I knew that the images of the gods were carved from wood. After being educated, I learned about natural phenomena and the reasons behind their changes. The fairy tales which were in my heart before then became like pure rubbish. But, those fairy tales and prayers are the stabilizing forces in Chinese rural society.

As for marriage, a wholesome marriage is like a pair of scissors. It takes both the husband and wife to complete it. As a rule, before marriage, love comes before duty. Frequently, at that time, we use a microscope to see the opposite's good points. After marriage, we use a magnifying glass to look at the shortcomings of our opposite partner. That's why a pair of lovers, after marriage, have disruptions of feelings and sometimes even a divorce. Perhaps what I have just described is the reason.

I was married in ———. My marriage is a typical Chinese-style marriage. I was introduced to my wife through a good friend. We met only once and were engaged. Judged by American standards, it must seem very strange. But my marriage is very successful and happy. Before our engagement, we fully realized each other's personality characteristics and family backgrounds. From our engagement to our marriage, we had one long year. We were in love to the utmost before we were married.

A successful marriage, other than fully recognizing one's responsibility, should have the following: first, patience and the ability to give, to let the other person be first. Second, frankness: whenever there is some kind of doubt, one should mention it so that whatever is bothering him can be frankly discussed. There should not be a moment of doubt. Three, one should, at an appropriate place and time, really pray and be sincerely thankful. These three points my wife and I have been capable of putting into practice. That is why our marriage has been successful.

As for divorce, in such an instance one person must be "smuggling" his feelings. Or maybe one person's shortcomings are being magnified. In a divorce, the child is always the first person to suffer, because he cannot fully receive the love of his parents. He will most often develop psychological trouble and perhaps even sociological problems.

. . . my views on the education of children. I already have two daughters. One is three years old and the other is two years old. I let them go about quite freely under ordinary circumstances. Once they have done something wrong, however, I must correct them in a very serious manner so that they can acquire good habits of living. I use as educational tools the things that they most like and dislike in daily life. If you want a child to do something or not to do something, you must see what she likes and what she hates. I avoid fairy tales or childish tales. I try to give them directly all kinds of knowledge. And I try to take every opportunity to teach them the common knowledge which has to do with their daily lives.

During the holidays, I take them out to the suburbs, to the countryside, to expand their knowledge of nature, to stimulate their desire for knowledge of nature, and also to stimulate their desire for general knowledge.

As for language, I teach them two dialects, Mandarin and Taiwanese. In this way, I can develop their abilities to pronounce and enunciate. After they are eight, I will teach them English.

The upbringing of children, their daily habits, their languages, have great relationships to one's wife. There is a direct influence on everything from her. The psychology of a child changes in a thousand ways. Those who are parents must use different methods to suit different periods.

*Comment.* Mr. A's story and analysis of himself and his background indicate several important trends in Taiwan life. First, the city, with its attractions and opportunities, is the goal of more and more people. Second, a sceptical attitude toward religion by educated Chinese has a very long tradition in Chinese history, starting with Confucius. My impression is that the higher the educational level, the more irrelevant religion becomes. Third, Mr. A's comment on the teaching profession is generally true. Taiwan faces a problem of getting well-qualified people to teach because of low pay. Fourth, and most relevant for our purposes, his autobiography shows a direct relationship between his education and his own separation from the mores and beliefs of his native, rural home. And the effect of that education is extending into the next generation, his children, whom he is raising to look at natural phenomena in a scientific manner and whom he wants to prepare to meet the needs of the modern world. His education has enabled a jump in two generations from a world-view largely dominated by a village and its immediate surroundings to a world-view increasingly shaped by influences from outside Taiwan. The problem for Taiwan is whether the people of Taiwan like Mr. A, whose world-view and practical knowledge have become international, will take one more step and permanently leave their home, Taiwan.

### Miss B

Miss B, a native Taiwanese, is in her twenties. Both her parents had a primary education, and she is one of a rapidly diminishing minority in Taiwan: young people whose education level has not exceeded their parents' level, if their parents had a primary school education or less.

Her employment prospects without English training would have been very bleak. About average in height and weight by Taiwan standards, her manner is self-effacing, and she gives the impression of a person very much aware of what she feels is her inferiority. During an interview she admitted that she often felt very depressed and, judging by her face when we alluded to suicide, we felt that she had had many thoughts about it. At the same time, her autobiography clearly shows that she has not given up.

The daughter of a washerwoman, she spent much of her childhood helping her mother wash clothing. After she had to stop school, she began to exchange washing university students' clothing for assistance in English. She loves her mother, but she is also deeply ashamed of her mother's profession. In our interview, this ambivalence was evident and the pain her own feelings caused her is very great.

First, my family background . . . I was born in the spring in Taiwan. In my family there are my father, mother, elder brothers, younger brothers, elder sisters, and younger sisters. Altogether, there are twelve. My father works in the area of technical help in an agricultural agency. His income is very low, only enough for his own livelihood. My mother is kind and great. The whole family depends upon her personal savings and effort.

I could not stand to see my mother's worry and hard work and still not help her. Therefore, I willingly sacrificed my education and, after graduation from primary school, I did not try for middle school. I stayed home and helped my mother, to create a little happiness for my family.

Second is my education. Ever since my eldest brother graduated from technical college and found a job, he has been able to contribute a little to the expenses at home and has lessened my responsibility. When he started to do this, I became determined to learn English. I went to the —— to study English. I started with the alphabet and studied three hours every day. Every term has three months. I have studied sixteen terms in a period of five years, and I have not missed one class. Now I am graduating. Although I did not receive the titles and courses of most universities, in actuality, I did finish university equivalent in English.

I have never entered into any kind of work in society. I do not understand a lot about social relationships. As for work experience, that is something I cannot speak of either. Other than going to school in the evening, I worked all day at home. I get up at 5 o'clock in the morning and stay up until midnight. Every second is filled with work. Although this has been a very difficult and busy period, I have also thought a little and have a basic philosophy.

I have often thought that in society, matters are very complicated, and the work load is heavy. But, if a person can treat other people with sincerity and do things in a responsible manner, if one is careful, no matter who he is, these attitudes are useful.

Because I lack a proper education, I do not have enough time to find much amusement for myself. I often feel that, at this time, in the complicated nature of society, I dare not raise my head and must suit myself to the things which other people like. So, most of the time, if I have free time, I try to read books, newspapers, and magazines. To overcome my feelings of emptiness, I also go to movies which are rich in educational or literary value. As for sports, because I work so hard everyday and am so tired at the end of the day, I am very lazy. So, my only hobby really is going to the countryside; because it is like another world, and it can enable a person who is sensitive and a little bit on the pessimistic side to forget about many things. At the same time, the fresh air and sunlight are also there.

My hopes . . . I am very much interested in English typing, even though I feel that my English foundation is very poor. Because of my family environment and my own lack of time, I could not choose courses, which required a lot of outside work. Now that I have finished my courses, I hope to have an opportunity to find a job that fits a little more into my hopes. Then I would like to continue my study so that I can fulfill my other courses.

Although I do not have deep knowledge or much experience in working, I have a very sincere and responsible heart; and, judging from what I have described above, I believe that, no matter how difficult or how much struggle I face in working, I must do my best to fulfill the requirements of the work. Because of the rapid progress, industrialization, and modernization in Taiwan, I feel that my position in my family is not very secure. I also feel insecure about the lag in my own thought and the decline of the productivity of my work.

As for work or profession, in this society in every corner those who are hired must have a diploma or certificate. If you do not have one, no matter what the circumstances are, it is most bothersome and distressing. So, I am very distressed. I hope that Teacher will perhaps point out a way for me. What shall I do with my future? How will it affect me? Is there any way that I can save myself?

Divorce was once regarded as most immoral here in Taiwan, because marriages, in former times, were closely bound. In other words, when a man and woman were married, they usually had never seen one another beforehand. So, they did not know the character of the other party. That is why situations where marriages were not successful were very often created. So, both sides had to have patience. If the husband would want to have a divorce, for example, then he must pay the girl's family and it was a great insult and injury to the girl.

Today, when society is becoming more modernized and prosperous, everything is following the trend of free choice of mate. Both parties can have an opportunity to understand and observe the other's personality and interests. In this sense, divorces have decreased. But, Western countries have concepts of free choice and marriage. This has also influenced us quite a bit.

My own personal view is that I feel that Free China, with its three thousand years of history, should put more emphasis on moral conduct than on material wealth. That's why I hope that, though we go on the road to industrialization and modernization, we also lessen the number of divorces. If we do not, then it will be a great loss and a hindrance for the future of women. It is also my hope that every couple, before they are married, will have a period of reflection and therefore have a base before they talk about marriage.

Because I am not very learned, and what I can express and understand is just the above, I hope, dear sir, that you will not be bothered. You make me feel most honored to be able to help you and to help you finish your work. I will try my best to come and help you.

*Comment.* Through sheer determination and dogged effort, Miss B did finally find a position as an English secretary. After getting her job, she improved her physical appearance, which formerly had been quite mousy. Miss B became more stylish in her hair style, clothing, and began to use some make-up. Her greatest hope remained her own determination, because the existing educational structure offers her no further alternatives.

## Miss C

Miss C, now in her 20's, was born in the southern part of China during a period of increasing chaos. She comes from a "good" family, which in China means a combination of education and wealth. The shift to Taiwan, however, was traumatic for several male members of her family and nearly resulted in the ruin of the entire family.

She is tall, extremely beautiful, and possesses a manner of intelligence and sensitivity. At the same time, she has an air of inner turmoil. Yet, she is self-confident without conceit.

Her autobiography was most expressive in the use of language, and we have striven to retain her metaphors.

In my family, there were six boys and four girls. I was the tenth. When I was born behind the lines [this refers, of course, to the military front lines maintained by the Chinese against the invasion of the Japanese] on the Mainland, the boys had already left home to make a living on their own. After the Japanese occupation of that area, we followed the Government [Kuomintang] and went back to Nanking. Our footsteps and laughter were present in many scenic spots, but good things do not last . . . eight years of relative peace for China went away like the blessings of the *yun-hua* [a type of flower which takes several months to come into bloom and then it blooms in one night]. Once again we went on our wandering journey. We pushed into the tidal wave of refugees, we walked, we waited for busses, we were in boats. Although I was only five, I can still remember the hay which was made into a bed and the sad and sorrowful whining of the truck body. And in the pitch-black night the moon tried to shine its pitiful rays.

On the wharves children were screaming: "Where's my father" and "Mommy." This type of whining is like a coyote's sound.

We made our way onto the last military vessel leaving Canton. We escaped the firing of the bandits [Communists], and in the year 1949 came to Taiwan and settled in a little Chinese village in the northern part of the island.

My father, in his early 20's, was already a high-ranking official in the government. Our family background contains great wealth, but because both of my parents did not know how to manage money, together with eight years of constant running, we became as poor as water. So, the up-keep of the whole family was left to my second older brother, who served in the Air Force. My father could not take the extreme poverty and his drinking habits in his last years. He had a stroke and died and left us in this bitter rain.

My mother, after this blow, aged ten years. Sometimes she would sit in front of a window and sigh: "Do not blame your father. Do not blame him for playing around. This is the habit of his age. Just blame the fact that I was weak at that time and could not insist upon cultivating my older sons but let them lead very useless lives. Wealth and luxury have only given me loneliness and emptiness. The happiest part of my life were those few months when I was with your father."

So much bitterness, so much sadness, so much suffering, my dear mother. In that setting sun when you, with your sweet and serene smile, leaned against my father's side and waited for us to come home from school — that's like a picture, and that is the sweetest moment forever kept in your heart. It was such a short period, and you waited all your life for it, and in that one moment your life was filled by it. But, after that, you were again in loneliness and sadness.

Mother was an old-fashioned sort of girl. She never raised her voice, and did not go out of her own household. After my father's death, I almost became my mother's shadow. Whenever she would go to buy groceries, cook, wash, sleep, I kept close to her, except for going to school. When I would come home and not see my mother, I would cry and scream for her.

The heavy burden of living crushed my mother. When I was five years old, my mother had a severe illness. I took a week's leave from school and stayed home to help her. At night, I would humbly kneel in the courtyard, cold and quiet. I would pray to God to help my mother, to protect her. Finally, my mother's illness was over and I also dried my tears. But, a heavy, dark shadow crept over my little heart. I was afraid that my mother would leave suddenly like my father had. I dared not leave mother even for one step. But, just because I did not dare leave her, I wanted to leave home even more because that fear crushed me so that I could no longer breathe. I could not talk to anyone, because I was afraid that it would be whispered around, and people would take it as gossip. When I would go out to camp with my schoolmates or to school functions, I was so surprised that my friends would cry when they were homesick. I never understood this type of separation. All I had was fear.

I always did very well in school, ranking with the first in my class. I really felt that I did not deserve it. I really did not know rationally what I was doing. When I reached that point, I could not concentrate. The higher I got in my class, the more the praises poured in, the more I felt lacking. I always felt that I had not worked really, really hard. I wanted to discipline myself so that my actual level and my examination marks would match each other. But, I did not know where to start. Hesitation, indecision, this type of feeling became deeper. And I also had the feeling that I was not as good as anyone else. I lost all self-confidence in myself.

Maybe it was a sign. Maybe it was extrasensory perception. But, every moment I could see my mother's grave. I was afraid. I was tormented. I tried to do my mother's work in every possible way. I got water for her. I scrubbed the floor. On the days when I was home, I would wash clothing at the stream and lug the load back to dry. All the neighbors used to laugh at me. Who knew that I had limited strength? I was so tired that I could not wash any more. At the same time, my temper became worse and worse. At the slightest provocation, I would throw a temper tantrum at my mother. I would not eat. I would not talk. And once I went out into a downpour and caught pneumonia. In a high fever, I became more and more uncomfortable and passed a month in near hysteria. Because of my mother's day-and-night care, I gradually recovered, but my mother got sick. I took an oath that I would never again make my mother suffer.

Although my spirit was already at the point of breaking, I still did what I could. In the severe winter, in the dark, dark night, I would go by myself in the rain to look for my brother, who was bewitched by mah jong. [a game of chance, very popular among the Chinese — occasionally, in a way similar to persons addicted to gambling in the West, Chinese will get "hooked" to mah jong, which usually then involves gambling] At that time, I was so afraid of the dark. I was more quiet than before. But I did not tell my mother about what I was encountering in my life, because I did not want her to worry. I did not trust other people. My brother never asked me questions, because I was always a good student and did not go out very often. Who would know that in the heart of a girl like this, there were such serious questions. She longed for someone to care for her.

In the autumn, when I was in upper middle school, in the second year [Miss C was eighteen years old at the time], I kissed my mother good-bye in the morning. In the evening, when I came back, my mother had already shut both of her eyes and was breathing faintly. I was numb and followed people round and round and looked at my mother, who had left this world. I had no feeling, but I cried. From that night on, I was no longer afraid of the dark. I was no longer afraid.

Every day I went to class and came back to cook and do my homework. Days passed like the murky water in a dead pond. Nobody cared about me. Nobody kept me company at home. When I was lonesome, I would turn on a record or some songs, and I'd let it play for hours. When I walked, I would daydream. Every Saturday, maybe in the afternoon, I would go with my friends for a movie. That was my greatest pastime.

I was very fortunate. At the end of my upper middle school days, I was first in the whole school. In order not to disappoint my school and to save face for them, I studied very hard for one month and again was fortunate enough to enter a college I had never dreamt of.

Leaving the home where I had spent twelve years, I felt no sadness. Walking alone into a role that was new and totally strange to me also gave me no discomfort. I was still first in my school. My teachers and fellow students felt that I was not up to my standard. I wanted to work so hard that I did not know where to start. To be kind, warm, and work very hard — these were my goals. But, I walked alone, going and coming. I could never find peace. From the sunrise until the moon went down water could never wash away the deep depression in my heart. I was afraid of life and despised life.

In the spring of the third year of my university years, I met a person to whom I could trust my feelings. He also felt that I was no ideal person. I knew that I was rather strange, but I wanted him to understand the real, true, and sincere me. I tried to tell him about my life, my family, my experience, my feelings. I told everything to him, but sometimes I would not even comb my hair or dress up. I wanted him to know that I was not as beautiful as he thought. I did not want him to have half a second of unhappiness, but I was always stubborn and said many unkind and acid things to prove to him that I was not who he thought I was. I was not that good. In the long two years since then, I have realized that I did this to grind him down, because I had no self-confidence that I could be perfect, because I was afraid that one day he would be disappointed, and also because I could not forgive that dark depression in my heart. It was a very lovely kind of foolishness, a very bitter kind of foolheartiness.

I had tears in my eyes, and I tried to hide my suffering, tried to let go of this feeling, which had almost driven me to madness, almost driven me to distraction. Every time I dreamt about it, my heart would suddenly contract, and the only comfort I had was that today, maybe, he was very happy. This was the only way that I could feel a sigh of relief.

Following days and days of loss of heart, one day a friend gave me a book called *Streams in the Desert*, which saved me from the deep chasms of depression. In everything, if you try hard, it is those who love God who will receive benefits. Tears are the best makers of rainbows, and the Cross is the best ladder for mountain-climbing. Everything is like pure streams flowing over the valley. My heart began to open, and I found out that in my heart it is as if there is deep water holding immeasurable love. The sun is bright and shining. The grass and the flowers are fragrant. Life is full and beautiful. I feel that I am no longer just a skeleton, that I have a strong burning of life, and I believe, hope and love. My heart is full of sincerity and zeal. I once again returned to school.

The liveliness of the boys, the softness of the girls gave me a lot of excitement. Very often, when I stood on the podium and looked down at those childish, innocent, lovely faces, I sometimes wished that I could go down and kiss them. And now, in my work, I felt perhaps some struggle; or in life that there is difficulty. But no matter what, I am no longer doubting. I believe that there is a Father somewhere, looking after us. Before now, and in the future, it's all the same.

When I think back, I no longer feel only bitterness and suffering, but I believe that my mother really loved me, that my brothers and sisters cared for me, and *he* also once liked me — truly. All the people around me like to be near me because I truly love to be near them. I know how to enjoy and appreciate everything that is good and beautiful and can also deeply bless others' happiness and good fortune. Knowledge helps us to be good people. Love gives us strength. I hope and want to work very hard in order to go after what I would like to be and that is to be like a very small candle burning in the night, even though, whatever light it has, is very soft and weak.

About education, based on my experience when I was growing up, the fight and struggle, I think that a suitable education can prevent a lonely groping in the darkness — the kind of mistake which one makes under those conditions. You save a lot of unnecessary waste of energy and initiative. And we can also use our innate qualities to enjoy a good and beautiful life. But suitable education is very difficult to achieve. It must be changeable in terms of time, space, and individual material necessities and provisions. The only things which cannot be changed are love and care.

The following are the four stages of my outlook on education: First, womb education. In other words, in the ten months of pregnancy, we must help the fetus to develop in every aspect so that it will not have congenital disease. Second, infant education. From the moment he is born until his twelfth year, we must give the child the most serious, correct guidance and teaching so that he can have good habits and the basic capacity to distinguish between good and wrong. Most of all, we must not neglect to protect the child. Do no let him, at a tender age, come into direct contact with the jolts of the environment so that they feel lost and insecure. Third, adolescence. From thirteen to eighteen years of age, children have a high degree of self-respect. Other than giving them suitable guidance, do not neglect their opinions. We should reduce scolding and punishment and should try to bring up their self-respect and sense of achievement. Fourth, the adult. Self-education in the adult stage is constantly to acquire new knowledge and to maintain contact with society. The attitude of the educated toward other people is to use the example of one's self to influence other people, to use hints, to explain to people, and, most of all, not to hurt an adult's sensitivity and feeling.

Confucius said: "Everyone needs education." Those who are obstinate and bad need special attention. We should not neglect those who are quiet and good. We must try to lead those children, especially those who are sensitive, into a higher, more profound and wholesome direction. We must never allow them to use their oversensitive, bright, intelligent energy, to go up a unicorn [this last expression means to take one's whole self and enter a cul-de-sac].

My ideal of marriage — the responsibilities of the husband and wife. First, in bringing up their children, the outlook of both the husband and wife must be the same. The one who is more lenient and the one who is more harsh must be rightly matched. Punishment and encouragement, scolding and comfort are all important.

From my point of view, the most important points in marriage are: first, love; second, similar background, education, and environment; third, maintenance of a basic living standard.

As for divorce, I do not approve of it at the slightest provocation, but I do not approve of being patient and suffering for one's whole life. We must base the choice on innocent children. If both spouses try to succeed and can help the children toward happiness, then, of course, both parties should try to make it work, because a child is made up of their own flesh and bones. If, however, a divorce can help a child's wholesome development, then a divorce should take place. I always have felt that before marriage one must be careful and think three times. And after marriage we must forgive and understand. Only in this way can we diminish the chances of this type of tragic event happening.

In an agricultural society, today, this year, next year, several hundred years — society does not change much and people's thinking is always the same — conservative and less liberal. That is why early marriage did not affect the relationship between husband and wife. Wives also help in providing labor for production. But, now, in the process of speeding up modernization and industrialization, society has a trend of a new sun and a different moon every day. People's thought and way of life also change every year. That is why the result of an early marriage can be that, after a few years, the spouses feel that misunderstanding or differences are increasing with the passage of time. At the same time, a family always ties a person down somewhat and lessens his sense of adventure and opportunities to branch out. That is why a later marriage, after our own personalities are more stable and our work has a solid foundation — that type of family is perhaps more solid.

As for a profession, one can always work in any profession, if it is suitable. But a wife, once she has children, must stay home and take care of the children. For a woman, the most wonderful achievement is to educate good sons and daughters, to make a good and warm home, and to lessen the worries of her husband. But, she must never forget to absorb new knowledge. One day, when the children are grown up, she can still go out into society and use her capabilities for the benefit of everyone. The position of a woman in her family should be according to the laws of nature and the nature of man. I think that, no matter what the time period, we should not change the basic position of the family. The man faces toward the outside and the woman should stay inside.

*Comments.* Miss C's comments on various aspects of her life have a more general interest: first, the economic situation of her family was not uncommon among Mainlanders who stuck with the Nationalists and left their homes for Taiwan. While many Mainlanders because of their superior educational background recovered their former prestige and status, many other declined. Yet, as with Miss C, they instilled in their children a drive to improve through education, motivated, in part, by family traditions of education. I often met middle-aged Mainlanders whose fortunes had fallen below their former ones, but usually their children were well on the way to recovering the lost ground through education.

Second, the shift to Taiwan by the Mainlanders probably reenforced a tendency which often accompanies urbanization: a shift from dependance on the extended family. Miss C is an example of extreme individualization, necessitated, of course, by the death of her parents and the apparent dissolution of her family. Her extreme anxiety and insecurity in adolescence derived, in large part, from the absence of any paternal or maternal relatives to fulfill the role of parent or, at least, an adult authority figure. I have little doubt that on the Mainland either an uncle or brother would have tried to fill that role.

Third, Miss C's comment that no one worried about her emotional condition because she was achieving in school reflects a very strong trend among Chinese. The assumption is that achievement indicates stability; lack of achievement points to instability. This assumption, in turn, encourages moderation of any extremes of emotion which would interfere with scholastic effort, since approval results from achievement in school. Whatever one's inner feelings, outward composure is requisite.

I would guess that much personal unhappiness is channelled into renewed energy for academic achievement. There is a widespread assumption that, in the absence of illness or mental retardation, lack of achievement when schooling is available represents a flaw in one's character. There is no thought of immorality in such a judgement. Rather, a parent or friend would look upon a nonachieving person, particularly one who is from a "good" family, as an example of lack of recognition of the external necessities to which one must bend oneself without question.

The education period must be free from all other emotional concerns. The great fear of parents, reflected in the press, plays, and popular advice articles, is that their student-children will come under such bad influences as American teen-age behavior with its overt sexuality. Sexual interest in this period is regarded as damaging and is strongly discouraged. My students, who were in the upper middle and college age groups, for example, long after we had established a good rapport, honestly told me that questions of sex were irrelevant for them, because they were too young to think about such things. Their statements were made as a matter of fact, not as an indication of discomfort or embarrassment.

Fourth, Miss C's concept of an educated person as one who influences others by indirect example reflects a traditional view of the role of the educated man in society. It also shows the way that suggestions are normally made among the Chinese. Indirect confrontation is preferred; the famous middleman is utilized. In Confucian thought, the *raison d'être* for an intellectual was his harmonizing and uplifting influence on the masses.

Fifth, Miss C's comments on divorce represent a considerable shift, which seems to be increasingly widespread. Divorce in traditional China always resulted in severe criticism of the wife and often ostracism of her. Her moral or immoral conduct during marriage was usually irrelevant to the almost automatic condemnation of her in a divorce. She virtually had no rights to property, children, and so on.

Miss C's reason for approving of divorce in certain circumstances also reflects a very widespread attitude among young Chinese: marriage should serve the emotional needs of the married couple, not the interests or preferences of their parents. Surveys of young people's attitudes, such as my own, show that mutual love is regarded as a primary factor in marriage. This represents a fundamental shift in attitude from the traditional view that the primary function of marriage was continuation of the family line. The older generation therefore determined and supervised marriage, and the preferences of the young people were totally irrelevant. Thus divorce in the earlier system was more of an affront to a family than an individual matter. To return to Mr. A for a moment — when he described his marriage as "traditional," he was accurate in one respect: it was arranged by a third party. But, his views of marriage, like Miss C's, are anything but traditional in their explicit equalitarianism.

I have little doubt, however, that a divorced woman still faces considerable prejudice. But now, unlike traditional times, she can work, and that fact alone makes her life more bearable. The traditional divorcée had very few options except for prostitution or a dishonorable second marriage.

Sixth, while Miss C stresses the role of women as wives and mothers, she also recognizes that a woman in middle age may require some means of livelihood. An education can provide her with some alternatives in case the need arises. Many traditional devices for supporting older people may very well weaken with increasing urbanization, industrialization, and the splitting of family units into nuclear residential units. Older women, in particular, are facing increasingly independent daughters-in-law. With a rise in their education, economic, and employment levels, young women have less tolerance for an authoritarian figure in their homes. Formerly, a young woman had no home; she resided as a very unequal person in her mother-in-law's home.

### Miss D

Miss D, a young woman in her twenties, represents a similar situation to Miss B's. One significant difference, however, is that Miss D had begun to show academic promise when her famliy began to suffer from her father's habitual drinking. She had had a taste of praise, and it left her bitter and resentful over her lost opportunities.

> I was born in Taiwan on the eve of Chinese New Year. Everybody said that I was a lucky girl, but 'til now I have not felt particularly happy. No one can know about the future.
>
> My mother, an orphan, was raised by another family. When she was sixteen years old, at my grandmother's command and as the result of a go-between's work, she was married to my father. At first we lived in _____. In 1945, the Japanese made air raids on Taiwan. At that time, my eldest younger brother was born. During the war under such chaotic conditions, everybody went up into the mountains; but at that time I did not understand and was not afraid. Fortunately, not long after that, Taiwan was restored to Chinese rule.

My father opened a bicycle repair shop. Because my father likes to make friends and also likes to drink, he got drunk every day and did not look after his business. In less than two years, his whole economic situation began to fall apart. So, we had to sell our house and go live where we live now. It is small and it leaks. It's fortunate that there are houses on all four sides of our house; otherwise in the summer we would not have to open windows to get lots of air. When we moved, my father had no job; so the only thing to do was to help people repair bicycles.

Business was not very good. My father was still the same. He would be out all day drinking. My older sister, my younger brother, and I would take turns looking after the tools. We would wait and wait, sometimes for several hours. He still would not show up even after dark. We could not move the dirty and heavy tools. So, we had to ask other people to help us take those things home where we would feel that they were safe. In the winter, especially, when we were so hungry and cold, this was so hard to take.

My father is a very stubborn man and has a terrible temper. He would create so many incidents after he had become drunk. He would summon us children and, no matter what we had done, he would give us a lecture and then a beating. At that time, when I was small, I had such a feeling of horror every time he would come home drunk. No matter how hot the weather was, we would all go under our blankets. My mother was the most pitiful. Every day she was busy with the housework. Not only could she not enjoy life, but she was also often beaten black and blue by our father.

So, in this kind of environment, my brothers and sisters were born, one by one. In recent years, however, my father's temper has changed. He is not so irritable any more. But, he is still stubborn. Even when I was small, I, too, was stubborn. Every time I made a mistake, I would never, never confess it in front of other people, although I felt very bad deep down. When I had conflict with other people, I would never give in to them. Of course, sometimes my stubborness would go to extremes. For example, if someone had a misunderstanding with me, I would never explain it to him. I would much rather let him misunderstand to the end. Or, if I misunderstood other people, I would not let them have any grounds for explaining. This is my greatest lack, my greatest shortcoming.

I wanted to change my stubborn character and tried to do so, but I have not succeeded yet. But, now I have learned to be patient and try my best not to have any conflicts with other people. Sometimes, if I meet with something which is not happy, or, if I feel very depressed, I will take it to heart. But on the surface I will just pretend that nothing has happened. It is very difficult to be a person with such a strong sense of self-respect and competition and at the same time have a tremendous inferiority complex.

My younger brothers' and sisters' personalities are almost the same as mine. They are also very stubborn. At home, sometimes, because of a small matter, we will have a huge quarrel. I always have felt that, if a man is alive, he must have a meaningful life. If a man is to die, he must also die meaningfully. In my environment, I have often thought of committing suicide. But, I feel that I cannot be laughed at by others. They would call me a coward. This is only a test of life. I have my future and my profession. When I think about those things, I go on living bravely.

When I was in primary school, I did very well in my studies. I loved mathematics. I can say that mathematics was the best subject in all my courses. My teachers liked me very much because I was very bright. When I was small, I liked to do research. Every time I would meet a difficult problem, I would try to solve it. I would not stop. So, the teacher gave me a nickname, "the tyrant of mathematics." I took the joint examinations and was accepted into [an excellent school] upper middle school. At that time my father was working at _____. My sister was working as a bus conductor. My paternal grandmother lived with my aunt. In a family of ten, only two could support us. In this situation, we were not starving, but we also did not have enough to eat.

I had to stop school. I also became a bus conductor. I spent several years in the wind and rain and have had to take every type of insult in this type of life. Several years ago, when our family income became a little bit better, I entered English night school to learn English. I have worked half-time and studied half-time. Three years ago, I was selected for the information desk; so now my work is less taxing.

I am now staying with my paternal grandmother, four younger brothers, two younger sisters, my father and my mother. My father still works at _____. My eldest younger brother teaches _____. My second younger brother and my third younger brother are learning technical trades after their graduation from primary school. My fourth younger brother is still in primary school. My first and second younger sisters, after their graduation from primary school, are now working. Because my parents did not receive much education, their attitude and emphasis on education are not very high. So, the whole family, older and younger, except for my eldest younger brother, who finished upper middle school, did not finish anything except primary school.

As for marriage, Chinese old-style marriages were all arranged by parents and a go-between. Now we have progressed to free choice of mates. Old-style and modern marriages have basic differences. Old-style marriages depended on fate. They had their good and bad points. The modern-style marriage gives more opportunity for selection. But, even with free choice of mates, there are still fortunate and unfortunate cases. Some people, when they are in love, do not find out about the shortcomings of the opposite party. They do something which they should not do and when they discover it, it is too late to regret.

According to my belief, there are two kinds of ideal marriage. First, there is an introduction through good friends or relatives. After a long period of going together, say two or three years, if we feel that the other person is good in all aspects, then we talk about marriage. The second way is to select a person who is more suitable to yourself from among friends with whom one comes into contact in everyday life. And, after a period of going together, we will talk about marriage.

From ancient times until now, there have been two bad things, or disadvantages, or bad signs about Chinese marriages. One is the money spent by the male side, and the other is the dowry provided by the female side. Because of these two things, people who are poor cannot marry those whom they love. Even if they would be happy. Now, some modern parents no longer mind or put so much emphasis on these two items, but those who are still old-fashioned are quite stubborn about those two things.

I think that engagement and marriage ceremonies are very, very important; but when a country is in such a chaotic condition, things should be reduced to the simplest level.

I think that in an ideal family there should be two boys and two girls. Because both parents would probably work, if there were too many children, they would neglect them. Some who are poor cannot possibly maintain all the children's educational needs and daily living requirements. I think, though, that if one has few children or no children at all, then the house seems empty. The primary purpose of marriage is to build a lovely and wholesome family. Every girl hopes to have a nice, happy family life, and what she fears most is dissention at home or her husband's going for other women.

As for education — there are many bad elements in today's society. This probably results from parental neglect. In childhood, those people have had no one to look after them, and when they grow up, they become bandits and harmful elements in society. Whether a person is good or not, the environment surrounding him influences him a lot. To be a parent, one must take on a great responsibility.

There are two reasons why a person can go on the wrong track easily. Some parents only assume the material responsibilities of raising their children, and they neglect the educational and rearing duties of raising children. Second, some parents only put emphasis on their children's education and provide very little discipline at home.

Although I am not married, I do have views on this matter of educating children. First, the place where they live should not be very complicated, and there should be an environment which is good for the child. Second, when a child is very small, we must continually tell him that he must respect other people and how to say things with manners. Third, when a child is in school, being educated, the teaching at home is just as important and must not be neglected. Because a child joins in group activities, he can go on the wrong track quite easily. In the home, we should also buy good books with educational value for them to read. Fourth, the children's friends. As parents, we must be very careful about the friends that our children bring home. We should encourage them to hang around with good people and try to discourage them from hanging around with people who would be a bad influence. Teaching at home and education in school must go side-by-side. Only in this way can we train a child to be useful. I think that the Western and Oriental methods of teaching children are about the same. Every parent wants his child to go on a good road, on the road to becoming a good person.

As for the position of male and female at home, in former times men always walked in front of women. If one were a housewife, she could not go out to work. She had to stay home, do housework, look after the children, and serve her husband. In ancient times, this seemed to be the requirement and duty of women. One could describe them as good wives and mothers. One could also describe them as slaves. Sometimes they had to take a lot from their husbands.

Some husbands still think: "Well, I am providing for the family. I'm really something." But they never think about the fact that, if they did not have a good wife at home who provides them with such a happy and warm family, who would? The positions of the husband and wife in a family are equal. They must respect each other and they must cooperate.

In today's society, everybody is yelling about the equality of men and women. Although women's status is a lot higher than before, I do not think that there is complete equality yet. Although some housewives now go out to work, the minute they come home they have to work very hard around the house, and some husbands could not care less. They think: "Well, that's their job." I am not pointing this out about all men; some are very nice.

I think that in a lovely home there must be a stable husband and a very kind, wise, and understanding wife. Every man would like to find an ideal wife. Of course, every girl would like to find an ideal husband. A husband, in addition to his business toward which he must have a high sense of duty and competition, must look after his wife. He must praise her quite often in front of other people so that she understands that she occupies a very important position in his heart. At the same time, the wife must always encourage her husband to go ahead and give him spiritual comfort, help him in his business, and tell him that she is very satisfied with him and his family. This is an ideal wife in a husband's heart.

Modernization means being more up to the times than before. It also means science or industrialization. I think that the ways of people are getting wiser and wiser and brighter and brighter as time goes on. I think that the scientific and industrial revolutions, and the progress in all these areas, have lessened a lot of pain for most people, reduced the amount of wasted time, and also made a lot of people's lives more comfortable because of conveniences. In olden times, people's education level was very low. Maybe they would study their own language only; thus, they could not talk with other people. And there was no such thing as development of science or industry. In recent times, countries are getting to be very strong. Just taking China as an example, marriages are no longer as autocratic and dictatorial as before. There are fewer people without jobs. Most people have a normal way of living.

*Comment.* Miss D's situation is not uncommon. Chinese young women in Taiwan expect to work outside their homes, and education obviously determines the type of employment a young person can enter.

If the young woman's family does not provide support for her, even though she qualifies for schooling beyond the level provided free by the Government, she has no choice but to accept a job much lower than she knows her potential to be. The same may very well be true of her eventual marriage, especially in a place where female education level is rising and potential partners of equal education achievement are available to young men.

Other issues which Miss D raises are quite familiar to readers in the West. The problem of the working mother and her relationship to her children, husband, and home is the subject of considerable discussion among people concerned with the increasing tendency in industrialized areas for women to work outside the home. A complicating factor for Chinese women is that there are few quick ways of preparing meals. Time-saving partially-prepared foods have been a great help to American working wives and mothers. As young women in Taiwan establish homes separate from any older female relatives, these problems will increase.

## Summary

We have examined the lives of four young people who are using their night school training to produce major changes in their opportunities and life styles. These particular authobiographies were chosen because they represent many prominent trends in contemporary life in Taiwan.

Interestingly, all four persons have had to struggle against different degrees of parental discouragement, ranging from indifference (Miss B) to manifest alcoholic hostility (Miss D). Alcoholism has played a major and destructive role in the lives of both Miss C and Miss D. Only Mr. B's family has been relatively stable, and that has followed a period of drinking and carousing by his father. The stability of the Chinese family is proverbial, perhaps too proverbial. Perhaps even *that* solid social unit is yielding to the dysfunctional elements which our modern world offers in such plentitude.

## NOTES

1. Mobility for college graduates in Taiwan is available primarily through travel to the United States where income, opportunity, and advancement for Chinese have been most favorable. In the period 1964–67, for example, 500 medical doctors left Taiwan for the United States and fewer than 10 returned. This is a representative figure for professions.

# A Chinese Village:
# Taitou, Shantung Province

## MARTIN C. YANG

### VILLAGE ORGANIZATION

From a survey of the surrounding crop land one receives a strong impression of the unity of the village. The fields belonging to village families lie side by side in a circle around the cluster of houses. Although there are overlaps at many points, the boundary line is quite recognizable and there is never any doubt as to which village any piece of land belongs to.

Village solidarity can be seen in many things. Methods of cultivating crops, of threshing, storing, or preparing foodstuffs, of cooking or preparing feasts for the New Year celebration are exactly the same for every family within a single village. In a neighboring village, even though the

Reprinted from *A Chinese Village: Taitou, Shantung Province* by Martin C. Yang, by permission of the publisher, Columbia University Press, New York, New York. Pp. 143–148. Copyright © 1945 Columbia University Press.

activities are the same, there will be slight variations in technique. One often hears farm laborers who hire out to different villages tell each other that this village's food is superior (or inferior) to that village's.

Organizations in the village can be roughly divided into three categories: those which cover the whole village, those limited to a single neighborhood, and those based on family associations.

The first village-wide organization is the village defense program, in which every family is required to take part. The families are divided roughly into three or four classes according to the number of men in the family and to its economic status. Wealthy families are expected to equip themselves with rifles, pistols, old-fashioned tube-guns, and the necessary ammunition; other families need to have only a rifle and ammunition. Families that cannot afford to buy rifles are asked to contribute other materials useful in defense. The very poor are asked for nothing except that they behave themselves and obey the defense regulations. The able-bodied men of all the families are registered and organized into a number of teams. The recruiting system is based on the family unit, each family supplying one grown-up son for duty each night.

Two defense lines were built around the village, the outer one consisting of removable mines — iron tubes filled with powder and scrap iron and connected by wire. The villagers knew where they were and how to pass through the line safely, but a stranger could not enter the village without being trapped by the wires which exploded the mines. The defenses were removed in the daytime for the safety of the villagers. The second line, built within the limits of the village, consisted of a number of fortifications, lane gates, and gun placements on the backyard walls. At night, the young men were assigned, first to lay the explosive mines and wires for the outer line, and then to patrol the streets, lanes, and strategic points. Meanwhile, several other teams were on guard in two or three places in different parts of the village. When an alarm was sounded or a signal given by the leader or patrolman, the men on guard went immediately to the fortifications or gun placements with their guns ready. The teams alternated with each other nightly. It was estimated that at one time the villagers owned a total of fifty rifles, ten or more pistols, five or six big tube-guns, a great number of explosive mines and some ammunition. It was also reported that some of the young villagers could fire the modern weapons remarkably well. The village had not been attacked since the organization of the defense. It was rumored that bandits feared to come near it. Later, this organization was weakened, due to the bad conduct of several young men of the P'an families and also due to the gradual restoration of government control.

The village school, though it had been built by the P'an clan and was mainly supported by them, was attended by boys from the entire village. Until the establishment of the Christian school, this was the only general educational establishment in the village. Girls were not sent to school but trained in the domestic arts at home by their mothers. A few girls now go to the Christian school. At school, boys made contacts that were not dependent on the neighborhood or the clan. The school council was made up of the heads of families and this cooperation in managing and supporting the school brought families together; families too poor to send their children to school did not, of course, participate, but nonetheless the council was a village-wide organization.

The villagers regard education as a means by which a family can raise its position. Children are taught to read names, to understand the content of land deeds, and to recognize the different kinds of paper money orders so that they will not be cheated in business transactions. The sons not needed for farm work are trained for a career, for business or a trade. Calligraphy, account keeping, the use of the abacus, and the learning of the terms for farm products, farm implements, domestic utensils and manufactured commodities also held an important place in the curriculum, and there were some who regarded the school as the place where one learned good manners and observed the teachings of the ancient worthies.

In the past, most boys were not in the least interested in their schoolwork. The school itself was a one-room affair with a dirt floor. The walls were dark and the windows were pasted over with grimy old paper so that the lighting was very bad. The tables, benches, and stools were brought by the pupils from their homes. Boys ranging in age from six to twenty years were herded together in one room. The teachers' quarters were partitioned off from the schoolroom and here the teacher sat all day, except when he had calls to make, went to the market town, or was invited out to entertain a guest or to write documents for a village family. At school, his chief function was to maintain order.

The students were sent to school before the sun was up in the morning, about an hour before the teacher arrived. Each boy was expected to use this time in reading his assignment at the top of his voice and to memorize what he was reading. When the teacher appeared, another hour was spent in reviewing the textbooks. Then the boys were called upon to recite one by one. Each boy, as his turn came, placed his books on the teacher's desk, turned his back, and recited all or part of his assignment. All of this took place before breakfast. Both pupils and teachers went home to eat. When they returned from the morning meal, they practiced calligraphy and tried their skill at filling in couplets and composing poems. Occasionally there were lectures on good manners and on the ethical doctrines of Confucius. The teacher gave out the new assignments to each pupil individually, as there was no class system.

At noon the school closed again for luncheon. After luncheon the teacher took a nap and the boys were ordered to sleep at their tables. The teacher usually woke about three o'clock and gave a cough or some other signal to rouse the boys, who were pretending to be asleep. The teacher then heard the lessons of those who had not been reached in the morning session, and corrected the calligraphy with a pen brush dipped in red ink. Calligraphy was very important under the old system and the teacher devoted a great deal of time to it. Then there followed another period of recitation and until the close of the day the school resounded with chanting.

In summer the school day ended around eight o'clock, when supper was served. In the winter, however, when supper was served much earlier, it was followed by another two-hour period of school. These evening sessions were usually spent in reading advanced textbooks or in writing short essays and poems. The local people regarded these winter evening classes as the most important part of the school term. Those parents who wanted their boys to prepare for the Imperial Examinations made sure that their sons did their best in the evenings. There was a common saying that any degree won from the Examination was the result of a great deal of oil and fire.

There was no systematic curriculum in the old-fashioned village school; each student advanced at his own speed. In his first year, a boy would usually be taught to read the *San Tze Ching,* a reader containing the rudiments of national history, politics, economy, literature, philosophy, geography, and ethical principles. It was written in short and rhythmic sentences, each sentence composed of three characters; hence the title. The other reader was the *Pei Chia Hsing* which contained one hundred family names. The first-year boy was required to read these two books, but he did not have to understand the contents. It is doubtful that the teacher understood them.

The second-year textbooks were the first and second parts of Confucius' Dialogues. Supplementing these were the *Jih Yung Za Tze,* a dictionary of everyday words and terms, and the *Sze Yen Za Tze,* a collection of rudimentary biology, chemistry, geology, and physics, which was some-what Taoistic. To the teacher, the two parts of the Dialogues were most important, because they contained the essence of Confucian doctrine and were the main source from which the standards of morality were derived. Practice in calligraphy was continued throughout the second year.

In the third year the boy read the first and second parts of Mencius' Dialogues, the Great Learning and the Principles of Mean (Chung Yung). If the teacher was capable, he might begin to interpret some parts of the Confucian Dialogues to the boy at this time. In the third year the pupil also started to learn how to use the abacus.

In the fourth year the regular textbooks were the *Tso Chuan,* Annals of the Chou dynasty, the Book of Poetry, the Book of Rites, and the *Shu Ching,* China's earliest history. These were never interpreted; the boys simply read them without knowing what they meant. Ordinarily, a fourth-year student was a senior in the school. He was supposed to learn how to make couplets and to compose poems and short essays. But in the country school this was neglected, since very few of the boys were expected to take part in the Imperial Examination. Therefore, most of the boys in the fourth year learned more of the abacus and calligraphy instead. Intelligent students sometimes finished in three years. If their parents were not ambitious for them, they left school and either returned to the farm or learned a trade. The few boys who excelled and who were able to continue at school prepared for the Imperial Examination as soon as they finished the regular courses. They studied the poems and essays written by the early scholars and also wrote some of their own.

We have said before that most of the boys did not like the school. They learned their lessons by rote without understanding the meaning of what they were required to read. Except for the *Jih Yung Za Tze*, all the textbooks were completely incomprehensible to them, but they were compelled to read and to remember what they had read. It was painful work. Unfortunately, neither the teacher nor the boy's parents had any interest in remedying the situation, and the boys were forced into endless memorizing and were punished severely if they failed in this dull task. Fear of punishment also made school hateful. Once a six-year-old boy, who was reading his *San Tze Ching*, fell asleep at his table. The teacher woke him with a thunderous call, scolded him harshly, and then asked him to recite his lesson. The boy was too frightened to do it well, and for this failure he was beaten. This sort of thing used to occur very frequently.

The old-fashioned school offered no recreation. As a rule, a schoolboy had to sit on his seat and keep quiet all the time. When he heard the noise, the laughter, and the wild running of the boys out on the street, he and all the other pupils felt a great longing to join them but did not dare. The only chance for fun was when the teacher was not in school. On these rare occasions the boys' energy, imagination, and joy broke forth immediately and simultaneously. They overturned tables and piled up benches as a stage for an impromptu "show." They threw paper balls and water holders in a game of "war." They stole into the vegetable garden near the schoolhouse to pick fruits, cucumbers, or radishes. The shouting, swearing, and laughing could be heard even by distant neighbors. One or two small boys stood guard at a far corner to watch for the teacher's coming. As soon as he was sighted and the signal was given, all the boys ran wildly back into the schoolhouse and put everything in order. Occasionally they were discovered and punished.

Thirty years ago, the first modern school was established in Hsinanchen by the county government. Following this, several semimodern schools were opened in different villages. The school in Taitou was also modernized to a certain extent. In these new schools life was interesting to the pupils and, as a result, the attitude toward going to school changed. The textbooks were fascinating; they were written in the contemporary idioms familiar to the pupils and were beautifully illustrated. Above all, they contained interesting stories about children's daily life, which were entirely comprehensible and opened new vistas to the young minds. The arithmetic was new and interesting. Learning the symbols of numbers and new methods of counting was most fascinating. The chalk, the blackboard, the clay stick, and the clay plate were all delightful things which had never been seen before. In the old school, singing had been absolutely forbidden, but now the young teachers cheerfully taught the boys to sing as part of the curriculum. They sang the songs of the coming and going of the swallows, the joy of study, of patriots, and of the flowers, and the stars. The boys also learned the symbols of music. Few had any musical talent, but they liked to sing and imitated the teacher with great gusto. Physical education was a regular part of the school day. This was most exciting. In the old days they were punished for making noise or for having fun, now they were taught and led by the teachers in exercises and games. They also had some military instruction. The teacher sometimes made a short address before the lesson was over. "Do you know that our nation is in danger? Do you know that we have been attacked and disgraced many times by foreign countries? The Japanese devils looted our grain and animals. They attacked our sisters and beat our brothers. We hate them, we want to fight them to death. It is well for you to remember these things. We will some day avenge our national disgrace, but now we must know what has made it possible. It is because we are weak. Our people are weak, so our nation is weak. Our body is weak and our knowledge is weak too. Our people do not know how to work together, therefore, the foreigners can attack us one by one. We have no good soldiers, so we cannot defend our nation. Therefore, the first thing we must do is to make ourselves strong — strong in body and strong in knowledge. Our young people must become good soldiers because only good soldiers can defend our nation and protect our people. Do you all understand? Physical education is to train our body and to teach us how to march together. The other lessons are to give you knowledge so that you will know our nation and other nations. Do you all agree with me?"

# Report From a Chinese Village

JAN MYRDAL

### HAN YING-LIN, HEADMASTER, AGED 28

I am the head of Liu Ling Basic School. I was born in 1934 in Lochuan. My mother is dead and my father is a farmer. He can neither read nor write. I went to school in Lochuan. By the time I was ten, I had been through the first section of the basic school, and I then went to Lochuan Normal School. In 1949, I joined the League of Youth. In 1953, I joined the party. That same year I began as a teacher. In 1958, I began as assistant to the head in Yenan Middle School. In 1960, I studied at Yenan University. In 1961, I was appointed headmaster of Liu Ling Basic School.

I was fourteen when Hu Tsung-nan's troops withdrew from the area. All my conscious life has been spent in the new society. I am a rural intellectual of the new type.

The school has ten teachers, one of whom is an assistant teacher who works in the whole of our district, helping schoolteachers with their own education. Most of the teachers are new. Our experience is short. The most experienced of us has ten years' service. Three of the teachers are women. We all belong to the trade union. The school is, of course, mixed; 109 of our pupils are boys and 68 girls. We have six classes. The first four classes constitute the lower basic school and the two highest the higher basic school. The school was started in 1940 with 24 pupils. It closed down during the occupation, but reopened in 1949 with 8 pupils. The higher basic school was opened in 1956. Our pupils come from this and surrounding labour brigades, and also from Seven-mile Village.

Our school fulfils the task the party has given us. Teaching has to serve the policy of the proletariat, and teaching has to be combined with productive work. We are to inculcate the fundamentals of knowledge and basic techniques. The pupils study, but after lessons they have to contribute, as well as they can, in productive work in the school's vegetable garden. They have to know the honour of working, so that they don't look down on work. There are many good little workers among our pupils. I myself can remember that in my schooldays the pupils never cleaned out the latrines. If we met a farmworker carrying a couple of buckets of human excrement, we felt unclean and hid. But now, in our school, the pupils have such a feeling for the honour of work that they will crawl into the latrines with enthusiasm and bring up the shit. This teaches them cleanliness and respect for work.

At the parents' meetings, people often say that, before, their children had not helped in the house, but that now they sweep the yard, carry the rubbish away and collect grass for the pig. But it is not just a question of production. It is also a matter of proletarian policy. Of knowing how. The teachers are young and enthusiastic and they work hard and prepare their lessons well. Before the teachers never bothered about anything. Now they all study so much that I have to go round at night and myself see that they put their lights out and go to sleep.

The pupils have two kinds of preparatory work: that which they do in school during private study hours, and proper homework. We have rather a problem with this latter. It is often difficult for the pupils to study undisturbed at home in their caves. We have discussed this with the parents at the parents' meetings. The teachers are, besides, in touch with parents over various questions. If any problems arise with pupils, if their work is not satisfactory, or if there are difficulties at home, we discuss this at the parents' meetings and in the school management. Teachers will also go to a home and have a talk with a pupil's parents. They discuss how the pupil concerned is studying, how he lives, how he works at home. They assess his good and his bad sides. We try to foster his good side and correct his bad side. It may also happen that parents do not consider that their children should go to school. Perhaps the family is badly off for labour and want to have the child at home in order to put it to work. We then have a talk with the parents about the necessity for education.

We try to get them to understand this and to agree. We had one of these problems some time ago. Tuan Fu-yin, whose son, Tuan Shao-tang, is one of the best pupils in the school, forbade him to go to school. This was during the spring term 1962. Tuan Fu-yin wanted to have his son at home, so that he could work and earn money. It took three visits before we could get this father to agree to his son's staying on at school.

All forms of physical punishment are forbidden. For a teacher to raise his hand against a pupil is a crime, no matter what the circumstances under which it is done. We discuss problems with the pupils, we discuss them with the parents. In extreme cases we can expel a pupil. But that is only on paper. We have never had to expel anyone. We have never come up against a case as grave as that. We also have different kinds of activities outside school hours. We organize the children's play, because children ought to learn as they play. Then we have the work in the vegetable garden I mentioned.

The methods we use are different from those of the old days. We have no learning off by heart. We try to stimulate the pupils' own interest in what is being studied. They must want to learn the thing. School education must be such that they of their own accord long to go to school and love their studies and understand why education is necessary. The new school must be attractive. Especially now, when education is still not compulsory, and it will certainly be some time before that can be introduced.

Before, school used to train bookworms who had no understanding of real life. One of my classmates had a father who was a farmer, too. When this father came to visit his son at his school in Lochuan, the boy used to run away and hide, because he was ashamed before the others of having a father who worked with his hands. Now, pupils are brought up to do work with their own hands and to love their parents and have respect for all who are elderly. Children no longer learn mere theory, but practice as well. In mathematics, for example, we teach them to work with an abacus. One of our pupils from Seven-mile Village is already doing all the family's bookkeeping.

Because we explain to the children that the purpose of their studying is to make them fit to build up their country, our pupils now work with great enthusiasm. That was not the case in the old days. Then, one just learned things by heart. In general, the children do obey us. Their grades are not particularly good, but they themselves are good. We attach great weight to their moral education. We hold up various models and heroes as moral examples for them. We tell them what they should do, and what they should not do. We make it clear to them where the line runs between right and wrong. If something seems not clear or doubtful to them, we announce a class discussion, and, when this has been held, the teacher draws the conclusions from it for them, emphasizing right and wrong.

We instruct the children in hygiene and cleanliness. They do not know much about this when they first come to school. This is, of course, a backward, dirty part of the country. People here do not have good habits in hygiene. After our training, the children become better. We help their families to change their habits. We teach the children gradually to persuade their parents to change their habits, where hygiene is concerned. We certainly do not encourage them to argue stubbornly with their parents. On the contrary, we attach great importance to their respecting their elders. Our task is to collaborate with their parents. School and home must stand united. Our aim is to turn the children into healthy bearers of culture, willing to work with others and loving their socialist country.

We do not want any smooth, slippery personalities. But it is very necessary that they should have the feeling of being ready to work and be collective-minded. Children ought to be group-conscious. We teach the children to help each other. Not to compete with each other, but to help each other. Take, for example, the river-crossing down here. After rain it is not easy, and so the older children have to help the younger, and the boys the girls. The older ones carry the young ones across. We also train them to be honest. If they find anything on the road, they are to bring it to school. . . . The school year begins on 1 August and ends on 20 June. The school works six days a week. Together, the year's holidays amount to seventy-five days. The time of the winter holiday depends on the weather. There are eight individual holidays: two at the National Day in October, one on 1 May, one at the New Year, one on International Children's Day and three at the spring festival, if this does not coincide with the winter holiday.

The teachers are quite free during the holidays. They can go home if they wish, they can go away somewhere, they can do further study or anything else they like.

If a pupil fails in two basic subjects, like mathematics and Chinese language, he cannot move up to the next class. If a pupil fails in one basic subject, he has to be reexamined before the autumn term and can move up if he passes. If a pupil fails in three other subjects, he cannot move up. If he fails in two other subjects, he can move up. Last year, we had seven who had not moved up. A pupil who has failed to move up twice and then again gets such grades that he cannot be moved up has to leave the school. Pupils can be absent owing to sickness or with the special permission of the head.

The numbers in our classes are high, of course. Last year the numbers in the different classes were:

| First Class | 42 | Fourth Class | 24 |
|---|---|---|---|
| Second Class | 31 | Fifth Class | 37 |
| Third Class | 28 | Sixth Class | 21 |

Certain children transfer to other schools or leave school altogether. There are also children of school age who do not attend school. We speak with their parents and often succeed in persuading them to send their children to school. Though not always. Sometimes the children themselves don't want to go to school. They manage to get their grandmother to feel sorry for them, and some parents are unable to stand up to their elders. Then, of course, there are also parents who want to exploit their children's labour.

We did, however, succeed in getting Hu Yen-ching back to school. Last year, when she was eight, she ran away and refused to live with her parents. She went to her grandmother, Ching Chung-ying's wife. Granny thought the poor child was made to work far too hard at school, and she even accused the teachers of having a grudge against her. She loved her granddaughter and let her stay with her. But now we have managed to persuade Hu Yen-ching to go back to her parents and come to school again.

We have no real difficulties over discipline. The only difficulty is that certain children are late for school. Of course, we have this period both in the morning and afternoon with reading aloud to give them time to get to school, and we try to get the children to help each other keep to the hours. But some of the children have a long way to come, and it is difficult for them to keep to the hours. The farthest any of our children has to come is eight li. Seven of the children have so far to come that they do not go home for the midday rest. They bring food with them, and the cook heats it up in the staff kitchen, then they have their rest in the school. We have one room for the boys to sleep in and another for the girls.

Another difficulty is that certain children find it difficult to sit still and be quiet. Thus, in the first class there is not much discipline. There everything's more of a game. The children must think all the time that school is fun. Then gradually, as they become older, they see the necessity of work discipline, and then we require more of them.

There is a certain amount of fighting and quarrelling. We try to quell this and sort it all out with discussion and persuasion. As I've said, no teacher must ever try to settle anything by striking a child. We have to check disorder by other means. And it always succeeds. Before, in the old days, schoolmasters used to beat their pupils, but then the children had no real respect for their teachers. They were just afraid of them. That was why the teachers found it difficult to keep order. Now teachers and pupils love one another, and all goes well.

We take certain fees from the parents. There is an instruction fee of 1 Y per pupil per term. Then there are certain school costs which the pupils have to pay themselves: gymnastic apparatus, water for the children's tea and heating during the winter. The gymnastic costs are 0.50 Y per pupil per term; the boiled drinking water costs 1.50 Y per pupil per term;

the cost of fuel for the winter works out at 1.50 Y per pupil for each autumn term. Parents also pay the cost of school material. In the first class this amounts to 0.30—0.40 Y per term for each pupil, and in the higher classes it rises to 0.50—0.70 Y.

The teachers' salaries are paid by the hsien authorities. This school in Liu Ling is, of course, wholly state-supported. With us the highest salary is 49.50 Y a month and the lowest 35 Y. Salaries are calculated according to education and length of service. On questions of salary, the teachers make suggestions, and the amount is fixed by the hsien authorities. Free dwelling quarters and a cook paid by the state are supplied in addition to the salary. We receive full pay during the school holidays. We are not expected to take other work. Teaching is an exacting task, and for a teacher to be able to give of his best, it is preferred that he both rest and continue his own studies. Then there is the staff garden. This is not the same as the school garden. We look after the staff garden ourselves. In it we grow vegetables and corn and keep chickens and pigs. This does not mean that we are anything like self-supporting as far as food is concerned. We eat communally, and we usually reckon on having to contribute five yuan a head each month to the catering fund for outside purchases.

Teachers are duty-bound to spend nine hours a week on private study over and above their teaching duties. The teachers' timetable is three hours for teaching subjects, four hours for pedagogy, and two hours for private study. Lu Huan-ping is in charge of this instruction and supervises it.

The school's budget is quite simple. In the spring term 1962 it was as follows, apart from wages to staff, headmaster, teachers and cook:

*Income* | Y
---|---

| | Y |
|---|---|
| From Education Office in Yenan hsien | 1,375.33 |
| Fees from pupils | 177.00 |
| Total | 1,552.33 |

*Expenditure*

| | Y |
|---|---|
| Installation of electric light | 1,100.00 |
| Two-wheeled hand-cart with rubber tyres | 125.60 |
| Indian ink, paper, chalk, sickles, mattocks | 236.24 |
| Total | 1,461.84 |
| Balance at the end of spring term, transferred to following year | 90.49 |

Expenditure on gymnastic apparatus, water and heating have its own budget, since it is paid direct by the pupils:

*Income, Spring Term 1962*                                           Y

| | |
|---|---:|
| Gymnastics fees | 88.50 |
| Water fees | 305.50 |
| Fuel fee (not applicable in spring term) | |
| Fuel in hand, carried over from autumn 1961 | 69.72 |
| Total | 463.72 |

*Expenditure, Spring Term 1962*

| | |
|---|---:|
| Gymnastic apparatus | 84.96 |
| Boiled water | 216.28 |
| Fuel in hand consumed | 69.72 |
| | 370.96 |
| Balance at end of spring term, carried over to next school year | 92.76 |

The staff garden comprises four mu. There we grow food for our own account. Any surplus we sell. In 1961, my share of the year's crops sold amounted to twenty yuan.

The children's garden, the school garden proper, in 1961 produced goods to a total value of 740 Y. Of this we sold produce to the value of 147.19 Y in the market and bought prizes for the pupils.

Each pupil got some sort of prize. Its size depended on his or her grading. These prizes consisted of such things as pens, books, notebooks, and similar things. When we had put aside what was needed to increase the following year's production, we were left with produce to a value of roughly 300 Y. This the pupils ate.

The school garden, you see, is not run for income, but to teach the pupils to love agricultural work. That, too, is why we do not distribute the produce in accordance with the amount of work put into it by the pupils. We sell or exchange part of the produce in order to buy foodstuffs, and with these the school cook makes one or two 'feasts' every year. All the pupils come to these feasts, even those who have not done any garden work. We do this to induce a right attitude to work. It is part of the pupils' moral upbringing to grow their own food and eat it, sharing it and their labour with others.

The school is run by a headmaster's council. This consists of five people: the headmaster, convener and representative of the party; Li Juei-chen, deputy head; Chang Chang-li, in charge of administration; Chang Chung-fang, representative of the staff; and Lu Huan-ping. This headmaster's council is there to discuss the school's educational work and its internal administrative problems. Questions raised at the headmaster's council are taken up at the staff meeting, attended by every member of the staff in the school: the head, the nine teachers and the cook. There, they are discussed, decisions are reached and recommendations may be sent to the education office in Yenan hsien.

Another group which is of great significance is the school council. I am the chairman of this. On it are representatives from all the labour brigades from which we have pupils. The school council studies relations between the labour brigades and the council, between the pupils' homes and the school; it investigates any problems that may arise. Last year there was, for example, electrification: that was a question that had to be solved in collaboration with the labour brigades. The school council can, on the one hand, only recommend measures to the education office in Yenan hsien; but, on the other hand, it has the power of decision in certain questions, namely those concerning cooperation with the different labour brigades.

There is yet another school group, the parents' representation. In each village, the parents of our pupils choose one to represent them. There are seven of these representatives, and they come under the headmaster's council. I am their chairman by virtue of being head. Their duties are undefined; but one can say that the school council concerns itself with the practical problems, whereas the parents' representatives deal with the more personal problems. One can discuss the children's work with them and any faults there may be in the liaison between school and home. The parents' representatives have only advisory powers.

If, for example, you could imagine one of the children behaving so badly that it really became necessary to consider expulsion — but I must once again emphasize that this has never happened here — the matter would be discussed first at a meeting of the parents' representatives. If no solution to the problem was found, then the headmaster's council would have to discuss it and finally propose expulsion. After the school council had discussed this decision, it would have to be referred to the education office in Yenan hsien and approved by it before it could be put into effect.

All the teachers are members of the trade union. The trade union's duty is to help the teachers in their studies and to see to their social welfare. One percent of the teacher's salary goes to the trade union's funds. The union receives an equal amount from its central office, and this is used to ensure the teachers' material welfare, to buy study material for them and for other similar purposes. I am the head of the trade union here in Liu Ling Basic School.

It is essential for the school to have good contacts with the people in the village. The pupils are expected to help teach at the reading classes in the winter; that is, of course, only the older pupils in the highest classes. The school has its own library, but here, too, we have established close co-operation with Liu Ling's Labour Brigade. We have over 300 volumes, and we have borrowed a further 300 from the labour brigade's library. These are mainly works of fiction suitable for children and pure children's books. The older children borrow them. In addition, each class has a class library. That of the sixth class comprises almost forty volumes.

The children elect a leader for each class. The leader's job is to help the teacher maintain order; and he also has to help organize the pupils when on excursions and that sort of thing. He also presides over the committee of three that the pupils of each class elect to manage the various jobs the class does jointly. The committee of three consists of the class leader, a study leader and one who is responsible for practical matters, such as keeping the classroom clean, work in the garden, etc.

# Education and Modern
# National Development

JOHN WHITNEY HALL

### JAPAN'S EDUCATIONAL HERITAGE: CONFUCIANISM, *BUSHIDO,* AND APPRENTICESHIP

Education in Tokugawa Japan is only now receiving the attention it deserves from Western scholars. In the works of Ronald P. Dore and Herbert Passin we now have the bases for understanding what Japan's educational heritage was in terms of its availability to the several social classes, its content and consequent effect upon the culture, and its influence in preparing the various segments of the population for the reforms of the early Meiji period. The common tendency until now has been to dismiss Tokugawa education as "feudal" and "Confucian" and, except for the *terakoya* (the small parish schools), which admittedly provided the basis of the Meiji elementary school system, to assume that Japan

From *Twelve Doors to Japan* by J. W. Hall and R. K. Beardsley. Copyright © 1965 by McGraw-Hill, Inc. Used with permission of McGraw-Hill Book Company.

literally had to start from scratch after 1868 to build its modern educational system. The truth is that Tokugawa education did much more than lay the foundation for primary schooling; above all, it instilled a favorable attitude toward education throughout a wide segment of the population. Nor should Confucianism, that supposed philosophy of social and political conservatism, be so lightly discounted, for whatever its political limitations, it provided a sound base upon which a modern educational system could rest. Confucianism firmly believed in the importance of education, and it was under Confucian tutelage that the Japanese after the sixteenth century erected a system of schooling with extensive textual and pedagogical support. Confucianism taught attention to the affairs of government and social order. As in the case of the scholasticism of Europe, its knowledge of the psychological and physical worlds may have been faulty, but its categories of thought were useful and at least orderly.

To say that education in Tokugawa Japan was Confucian is only to acknowledge the fact that the Japanese had based themselves on the only fully developed system of knowledge common to East Asia, namely, that of China. Given the country's historic dependence upon China, this was to be expected. And while certain types of schooling were available in Buddhist monasteries and like institutions, almost inevitably the Confucian literature that came into Japan from the fifth century onward made up the bulk of the textual material which formed the basis of instruction. Traditional Japanese "book learning" was fundamentally Confucian. So also were the basic attitudes toward education, especially regarding the importance of moral instruction and the cultivation of proper attitudes toward the state and the family. During the Tokugawa period this reliance on Confucian or Chinese practices reached its height, but it also began its decline, as Japanese thinkers began to take up the study of their own "classical heritage" of works written in Japanese or to experiment with the fragments of Western science which managed to seep through the wall of seclusion. But it is also true that even the decidedly un-Chinese tendencies in Tokugawa thought seldom broke out of the enveloping framework of Confucian rationalism.

Whether entirely Confucian-inspired or not, there was a great expansion in education and in the pursuit of learning during the Tokugawa period. The achievement of peace and comparative prosperity under the Tokugawa shoguns gave the Japanese the leisure and the means to stress the arts and letters. There were changes in the structure of society as well, particularly as greater and greater numbers of persons turned to urban living, which stimulated the desire for education. For some education was a means of self-cultivation, but for most it had become the practical requisite for better performance of the role of soldier, bureaucrat, merchant, or village headman. By the end of the seventeenth century Japan was beginning to achieve literacy on a wide scale. This meant that the ability to read and write, indeed, the capacity to enjoy literature or to be amused by short stories, had passed out of the hands of a small minority composed of priests or aristocrats. For one thing the samurai class (by definition expected to be literate) constituted a sizable 5 to 7 percent of the population. Added to this were a growing class of urban commercial families and a wealthy stratum of villagers who not only found the ability to read and write necessary for their business or administrative duties but also had the leisure to indulge in the reading of the classics or the composition of poetry. Historians have in fact talked about an intellectual renaissance during the seventeenth century, and while the analogy with Europe may be somewhat farfetched, it is true that some of the most creative products of the Tokugawa period were in the field of letters and philosophy. Not many of these products have continued to attract the attention of presentday scholars. (It is the popular literature which we now admire.) But we should remember that Tokugawa scholars produced literally hundreds of national and local histories and thousands of treatises on political economics and social morality. While these works are no longer informative to us today, they reveal a remarkable degree of intellectual sophistication, given the limitations within which they were written.

Learning in Tokugawa Japan was first of all a requirement for the samurai class. Education was both a badge of social distinction and a practical necessity for a class which had turned from military to bureaucratic pursuits. It was thought sufficiently important, in fact, so that by the eighteenth century enough government-supported schools and colleges had been established to assure at least a minimum education for the entire class. Chief among the schools patronized by the Tokugawa shoguns was the one begun in the Hayashi residence in 1630 and dedicated to the teaching of Confucian ethics and philosophy. In 1690 it was enlarged and renamed the Shōheikō. It served as the main Tokugawa college and, with its excellent library, became the seat of official scholarship and of the orthodox Chu Hsi branch of neo-Confucian doctrine (*shushi-gaku*) favored by the shogunate. The Hayashi family continued throughout the Tokugawa period to serve as hereditary rectors of the college. The Shōheikō became the model for a large number of schools established by the several *daimyō* — perhaps three hundred of them by the end of the Tokugawa period — for children of the samurai in each domain. Members of the samurai class, at least by the beginning of the nineteenth century, had a course of study available which began with the local domain school, then continued for some at the Shōheikō or other private academies for more advanced training, and might even include special study in Edo or Nagasaki.

Education for the samurai, though it may have had its literary overtones, was essentially the schooling of a ruling class. As such it was expected to instill both technical competence in reading and writing and a knowledge of principles of the social and political order and a strength of character and personal discipline becoming a military officer. The basic code of the samurai stated in its very first clause that the gentleman must cultivate both letters (*bun*) and military training (*bu*). And whatever the authorities may have meant by the term *bun*, in actual practice the content of education was left to Confucian-trained teachers who were as much concerned with the ethical message of the text they expounded as with the linguistic skills it instilled in the students.

Confucianism provided the philosophical rationale for both public and personal morality. The leading educational theorist at the outset of the Tokugawa era, Hayashi Razan (1583–1657), drew from the Confucian classics the ethical principles for statecraft and a loyal officialdom, justifying the shogun's authority and the special status of the samurai. To a later Confucianist such as Kaibara Ekken (1630–1714), the aim of education was to promote filial piety and benevolence, the supreme Confucian virtues of personal conduct. For him the end of personal cultivation was to bring the individual into harmony with the social order by practicing the five classic virtues of benevolence, justice, courtesy, learning, and integrity of character. Women were to cultivate chastity and submissiveness. Despite the abstractness and overly didactic quality of so much of the Confucian borrowing from China, in the early years of the Tokugawa period at least, the message was remarkably revelant to the political needs of Japan. The texts and theories with which samurai education was nourished helped immeasurably in easing the transformation of the samurai from the rough military man he was at the outset of the period to the officer and "gentleman" he had become within two or three generations.

But the exhortations of shogun and *daimyō* would have had little influence in raising the standard of literacy among the samurai or in encouraging erudite studies in general had not the age also required men of scholarly training. The increasingly bureaucratic nature of government, the premium placed upon the ability to read and write, in fact, the competition for preferment on the basis of some sort of administrative competence created a constant demand for education. The requirements of the age also put their stamp upon the kind of "military training" which the samurai received. For with the elimination of all possibility of further civil war, the samurai put his muskets upon the wall and turned his sword and bow into less warlike instruments. His zeal for military preparedness was converted into a passion for social and moral discipline. Swordsmanship and archery were gentled into pastimes calculated to deepen the concentration of the mind, while military training itself stressed the achievement of qualities of decisiveness and vigorous leadership. *Bushidō* (the code of the samurai) became a way of life as much for civil administrators as for the officer in the field.

Education for the common people, though not formally provided for by the authorities, was not by any means neglected. The Tokugawa government encouraged, though it did not subsidize, common schools (*terakoya*). These were rudimentary affairs, conducted in local temples or the homes of priests or laymen, and provided elementary schooling, watered down from the samurai version, for a few of the common people. The parish schools relied on the simplest of Confucian texts and emphasized certain practical subjects, such as calligraphy, oral reading, arithmetic on the *soroban* (abacus), and etiquette. The teachers were priests, both Buddhist and Shinto, unattached samurai, Confucian scholars, or educated merchants or villagers. In all there may have been some fifteen thousand *terakoya* in existence at the time of the Meiji Restoration. It is these schools which literally formed the basis of Japan's modern elementary school system.

At an educational level above the *terakoya* there came into being a variety of semiofficial schools known as *gōgaku*, or country schools. More numerous than the domain academies and colleges, these schools provided a more advanced level of instruction in both Confucian studies and practical subjects. They were usually open to both samurai and commoners, but their main purpose in most localities was to improve the quality of the men who headed the organs of local government, the village headmen or the town ward heads.

Most diverse in size and subject matter were the large number of private boarding schools, called *juku* or *shijuku*. Most of these were quite small, depending upon a single master who surrounded himself with a few disciples and gave instruction in his particular scholarly specialty or in some particular accomplishment. Such private schools met a variety of educational needs and operated at a variety of levels. They became particularly popular toward the end of the Tokugawa period, as samurai and commoner alike sought special skills or gained the leisure to indulge in further education. An estimated fifteen hundred *juku* were in existence in Japan in 1870. And many of the outstanding leaders of the Restoration received their inspiration for political action at the feet of such *juku* teachers as Yoshida Shōin (1830–1859), the fiery Chōsū activist, or Fujita Tōko (1806–1855), the Mito loyalist.

It is sometimes asked why, if Tokugawa education was essentially Confucian, it should have produced such different results from what it did in China. The answer, in part, is that Japanese education was not simply Confucian. Perhaps what most differentiated the educational and intellectual climate of Tokugawa Japan from that of China at the same time was that, though Confucian principles were admired by the Japanese, they were never considered the only basis of pedagogy or the only source of educational philosophy. The Tokugawa commitment to Confucianism was strong, but it was never absolute, and it was actually on the decline after the beginning of the nineteenth century. As a doctrine providing religious certainty and comfort, Buddhism was by no means dead, and Shinto was in the course of a strong resurgence. To those inclined to secular learning, studies of Japanese literature or Western sciences competed more and more strongly with the Confucian classics. Perhaps the eclecticism of the early nineteenth-century Japanese intellectual stemmed from the fact that all intellectual systems (except Shinto) were to some extent alien. Finding his psychological security increasingly in the rediscovery of "Japanese" values (pride in country and Emperor or dedication to military discipline), he could take a more relaxed view of Confucianism and its practical consequences. Securely dedicated to particularistic national values which had their source in the incarnate symbols of the Emperor or the warrior's code, he was relatively free to accept or discard the metaphysical systems upon which his "schooling" rested. Toward the end of the Tokugawa period, the parallel spread of Western learning (Dutch language and science) and "imperial learning" (chiefly Japanese history and literature) gave witness to a growing intellectual ferment.

Aside from its strong Confucian element, there were other aspects of education that affected the quality and style of learning which the Tokugawa Japanese received. It has been said that education in Japan was conducted in a *feudal* atmosphere. The term is not particularly appropriate, but it does serve to identify certain features of the pedagogical system which contrast strongly with the principle of universal education to which the Japanese eventually turned. Tokugawa education was first of all class-based. There was a frank adherence to the view that education was more necessary to the highborn than to the low, and classroom procedures were organized to give privileges to samurai over commoner and high samurai over low. That this attitude toward education was not at all unique to the Japanese needs no elaboration. (We need only to compare Japan with England of the same time.) And that such class restrictions in education were breaking down in nineteenth-century Japan, particularly in the *shijuku* and in the non-Confucian branches of study, is also important to bear in mind.

There is another side to this complex of attitudes toward education which remained more strongly characteristic of the Japanese instructional system even after 1868, namely, the assumption that knowledge was something acquired by apprenticeship from a master. Thus, even in the larger schools, the transmission of knowledge was accomplished through a system of personal or highly intimate associations between student and teacher. The student was often bound over to the teacher by his parents, or at least he was obliged to acknowledge his absolute authority over his mind and body. Of course, the apprentice system, in the strict sense of the term, was most commonly used as the means of imparting a trade or manual skill. But the same basic approach to learning, whereby the master disclosed increments of his special knowledge in carefully controlled lessons which the student then took on faith and learned by rote and in which the student once graduated became the lifetime disciple of the master, pervaded all branches of education. It is this approach to learning which tended to drive all skills, whether artistic or intellectual, into restricted channels transmitted generation after generation within certain families or "schools." It made for rigidity and imitativeness. And although this practice is no longer common in the academic world in Japan, certain arts, such as the nō drama, the tea ceremony, flower arrangement, and most of the traditional crafts, are still transmitted in this fashion. It is still true that one of the persistent comments about differences between the American and Japanese attitudes toward learning is that there is a heavier reliance in Japan on rote learning and on the acquisition of a professor's "system." Emphasis on originality was not part of Japan's educational heritage.

Still another feature of the educational process which was accentuated both by the master-disciple system and by the heavily religious orientation of learning in Tokugawa Japan was the assumption that education should "train character" as well as impart useful information. Training in certain arts was considered useful as a way of developing self-discipline or inculcating proper social attitudes. We have already noted that the substance of learning (Buddhist or Confucian) was largely ethical; one of its foremost aims was to make the student virtuous by teaching him the wisdom of the past and so to shape his character as to meet the needs of his society. Calligraphy, the basis of literacy, was taught for its character-forming (mental-disciplinary) effect as well as for its practical value. Teachers were supposed to be models of virtue; they were honored as much for their character as for their erudition. Such attitudes of reverence toward teachers, unthinking devotion and willingness to take directions, were to have both their admirable and less desirable results. For if Japan in the early years of its modernization was fortunate that its people were filled with a zeal to follow leaders of a remarkably enlightened quality, the zeal to follow led to disaster during the 1930's, when those leaders had been replaced by men of more xenophobic aims.

In final assessment, then, we see that Tokugawa education showed a great diversity and complexity of institutional and ideological facets. The volume of education was remarkably large, as indicated both by the number of persons estimated to be in school (perhaps 1,300,000 in the late 1860's) and the quantities of publications consumed by the Tokugawa reader. While most schooling was highly moralistic and didactic, it was also practical, and furthermore there had already come into existence by

the end of the period several levels of instruction which recognized varying social and occupational needs. Moreover, there was diversity in subject matter which made it possible to choose unorthodox fields of study
without great stigma. And, finally, things were changing. This above all
seems to characterize the late Tokugawa scene, for in all aspects of
education, in school attendance, in the number of schools, in variety of
courses, in heterodox subjects being pursued, it was in the years beginning
with the 1840's that the greatest changes appear to have taken place. As
Japan came increasingly into contact with the West, the counteractions
(both defensive and acquisitive) were rapid and decisive. The vigor
with which the Japanese samurai drew his sword upon the foreigner as
well as the inquisitiveness with which he sought to penetrate the secrets
of Western power were remarkable testimony to his intellectual alertness.

## THE MEIJI RESTORATION AND EDUCATIONAL POLICY

Education was very much in the forefront of the thinking of the leaders
of the Meiji Restoration, who once they came to power worked quickly
toward the formation of an educational policy consistent with the aims of
the new government. Some of the earliest decisions made by the restoration government were concerned with state ideology, education, and popular instruction. But the educational aims of the new government and the
nature of the policy which should guide the training of the new subjects of
the Emperor were by no means agreed upon. The Japanese of 1868 faced
critical decisions regarding education and the role of the state in the
setting of public attitudes. What was to be the philosophical basis of a
formal educational system? Should it be Western in content and conception, or should it attempt to retain traditional elements? What should be
done about the religious content in education? What of the competing
claims between Confucian- and Shinto-based morals? Or should Japan
adopt an entirely new ethical system from the West? Was some sort of
compromise possible in which the Japanese could become modern and
yet retain their traditional social values? What, indeed, was the relationship between Western morality (and more specifically Christianity) and
Western success in modernization? In the early years after the restoration
there was no clear consensus of how to deal with these questions, except
that all leaders were agreed that education should further national development and patriotic unity around the symbol of the Emperor. The
years between 1868 and 1890 saw a struggle over matters of ideology and
educational theory while the practical steps of creating a new school system and eliminating the remnants of illiteracy were steadily carried
forward.

# 10 ................

# Suye Mura
# A Japanese Village

JOHN F. EMBREE

## THE LIFE HISTORY OF THE INDIVIDUAL

### Education and School

During the first year a child is the favored one in the family. At any time he may drink milk from his mother's breast, and whatever he cries for will be given to him. He is cuddled and fondled and rocked to sleep. He learns by imitation as his mother repeats unendingly baby talk for this and that.

But almost inevitably his mother bears another baby, and the child faces his first hard knocks. While the mother devotes her attention to the newcomer, the child is turned over to an older sibling or nursemaid who carries him about on her back or sits him down somewhere to play. When he cries, he may not be listened to, for his mother no longer gives him first attention. This rapid weaning from milk and maternal attention results in several weeks of temper tantrums. Occasionally, the tantrums are effective, especially if they last long enough, but eventually the child readjusts himself; he gets acquainted with other children also put out to play, and he is soon a member of a new age group of the two- and three-year-olds of the neighborhood. He learns to get along with his contemporaries.

Even in these early years a boy receives a few special educational influences different from those of his sister. On a walk to some shrine festival the mother may tell the sister to walk behind because she is the lady and he the gentleman. And, if a first son, the boy will always have preferred treatment over his younger brothers.

He learns about sex early because older children frequently engage in sex play, his mother often draws attention to his genitals when playing with him, and he sleeps in the same room as his parents.

In general, children are very much spoiled. They can and do strike their mothers in a rage and call them the favorite Japanese epithet of *baka!* (fool). Anything a child asks for or cries for long enough he gets. He learns the ways of society not through discipline but through example and instruction patiently and endlessly repeated by his mother. The father, softhearted to the younger children, becomes more strict as they grow older. As a child grows older and finds other people not so inclined to do his bidding, he develops a strong sentimental love for his mother.

At full six years the child goes with all the other little six-year-olds and their fathers or mothers in April to the village shrine of Suwa-san. Here, with teachers and other older school children, a short Shinto ritual is performed. The priest gives the young a little talk on the virtues and greatness of Japan, the Emperor, and the gods and then hands to each of the neophytes a copy of the first-year book of ethics[1] published by the department of education. This is a child's first introduction to a world beyond his *buraku* and *mura*. After the shrine service he attends schools for the first time as a student, dressed up in a new black uniform and cap. (He has been here often before with his mother when she came to some meeting or party held in the school auditorium, or with his nurse to play in the schoolyard.) The trip to the shrine did not mean much to him, but it was significant of the close association of official Shinto and the public school system.

At school he meets for the first time children from all over the village. His constant association with them for the next six years is an important one both for him and for the unity of the village. The ties of men who were classmates in school are very close.

The school building, a long one- or two-storied wooden structure, is

partly paid for by village taxes, partly by prefectural and central government funds. As there are no heating facilities, children shiver and sniffle
their way through the winter months. There is a confirmed belief that
cold and discomfort are good for learning and mental discipline. If any
child complains of the cold, the teacher tells him to think of the brave
soldiers in Manchukuo, where it is *really* cold. Every day after school
hours pupils clean up the yard with straw brooms, while girls get on their
hands and knees to wipe up the floors. A school servant exists but chiefly
for the purpose of running errands and making tea for the teachers to
drink between classes.

Every morning now the child gets up about five and washes; he need
not dress as he probably slept in his school uniform. After bowing to the
household gods, he has a breakfast of bean soup and rice and runs out of
the house and off to school. If he lives far from school, this trip by foot
may be as long as two or three miles; if close by, it may be only a few
yards. On the way he plays games, chiefly a kind of cops and robbers.
These games are played with boys and girls alike amid shouts and shrieks
as someone is captured. On entering the school grounds, he bows toward
the closet in the main auditorium where the Emperor's portrait is housed.
(More well-to-do schools have a special concrete house costing a thousand
yen or more to house the sacred photograph.)

At school shortly before eight all the children from first grade to sixth
line up in the schoolyard for radio exercises. From 7:50 to 8:00 the entire
youth of the nation under the leadership of hundreds of teachers goes
through the same daily dozen to the shrill directions of the same government radio announcer.

After this, the school children break ranks and file into their various
classrooms. Here the boys or girls find their places, small fixed cramped
wooden benches and desks, each sex on a different side of the room. The
teacher in black uniform comes in — all children rise and bow to him,
receiving a slight bow in return — and class begins, with singing perhaps.
Many of the songs are simple little nursery rhymes about birds and insects,
but the first one the children learn describes the "beautiful national flag
with the red sun on it" and the next one is called "The Soldier" ("With
the gun over his shoulder the soldier marches, to the sound of the bugle
he marches; the beautiful soldier, I love the soldier"). Then they learn to
read and write. In their first-year reader they again read of the soldier
and the flag.

The older children are expected to help the newcomers find their way
around school. From now on for six years the child goes to school from
April to July and from August to April again. School is from nine to twelve
noon for first-year children, eight-thirty to three-thirty after that. Most of

the time is taken up with singing, reading, and athletics — all three with a leaven of nationalism. No attempt is made to teach children to think critically either in primary school or in high school. The schoolmaster of the primary school sets as his aim the rules for primary school education of the department of education in Tokyo, the schoolmaster of the middle school sets as his aim the rules of middle school education of the department of education, and so also for the agricultural school, girls' high school, etc. The schoolmasters vary from the sacred word of the department only on the side of greater nationalism. In the agricultural school in Menda, for instance, boys are given many lectures on Japanese spirit, and second sons are encouraged to emigrate to Manchukuo.

The great difficulty of learning two or three thousand characters in the first six years, in addition to two sets of fifty-syllable characters, gives but little chance for a student to do much original composition. Geography arithmetic, and drawing are taught. The drawing is European style, but in arithmetic emphasis is on the use of the *soroban* (abacus) — so much so that many a man can scarcely add two and three without the aid of this device. In Suye boys and girls are also given some practical lessons in farming on a few *chō* of paddy and upland fields belonging to the school.

In higher grades some geography, history, and general science find their way into the curriculum, but the major part of the child's time is still taken up with readng and writing, singing, and ethics. The reading lessons are performed by the deafening method of the whole class reading aloud at once.

In rural schools practically all children are promoted every year, the emphasis in teaching being more moral than intellectual. Teachers feel that, if they left some child behind his class, he would feel very badly about it and that the resulting psychological effect and family chagrin would not be compensated for by any good the child might receive mentally by repeating a school grade. Similarly, at school athletic contests all entrants, not only first, second, and third, receive prizes. By giving prizes thus generously, no one feels unduly slighted. While occasionally people are shown the virtues of initiative and leadership, they are more often shown the virtues of cooperation, and the good but mediocre child is held out to be superior to the bad but brilliant one.

Unquestioning acceptance of everything the teacher says at school is the rule. Occasionally, this causes trouble at home when the father says something to the boy, and he replies that the teacher did not say so. The more a child is educated, the wider becomes the gap between the old people's folkways and the young people's ideas. By the time they reach university the gap is too wide to bridge, hence college graduates from villages almost never return to their homes.

To solve this and other behavior problems that arise, there is an annual parents' day on which old people, many of whom went to no school at all or to only a four-year elementary course, come to the school, see classes in action, and later have discussions with the teachers. With a touching faith in the rightness of their children's teachers, the parents discuss their parental troubles.

At frequent intervals during the school year there are other special days. Some are national holidays, such as the Emperor Meiji's death day, when there is a general assembly with a solemn reading of the Imperial rescript on education while all present bow their heads, followed by an uplifting lecture by the schoolmaster and by the singing of the national anthem. On other occasions the students have more fun; for instance, at the annual athletic meet, for which they train for weeks ahead. This is attended by practically everyone in the village, the families coming with lunch baskets to stay all day. People of a *buraku* sit together. Another big day is the old students' day, when the graduates come to watch the present students perform skits and dances.

After six years a boy or girl has learned enough to read simple things. He has also imbibed a good deal of nationalism and martial Japanese spirit by means of games of war and the watching of young men drilling in the schoolyard four times a month. If he leaves school at this point, he will probably forget much of his reading ability and his nationalism will be dormant in a life whose primary object is to raise good rice and get along amicably with his neighbors.

At school the children, especially boys, form close friendships with their own classmates, children mostly of the same age. Classmates are called *dōkyosei;* people of the same age, *dōnen.* It is the *dōnen* tie which is more important. All through life male *dōnen* remain close. When two men meet for the first time, if they turn out to be of the same age, they are well on the way toward being friends. The ties of *dōnen* increase with age. As a man grows old and the sexual desires die down, parties of *dōnen* are the only true pleasures left in life, and the farmers of Suye say that a *dōnen* then becomes closer than a wife.

The primary school came to Suye about sixty years ago. It was then a four-year course. Most of the older generation have attended this. Thirty years later a six-year course was begun, and more recently have come the continuation classes called *seinen gakkō* and *kōtō shōgakkō.* The *seinen gakkō* is a young people's school that meets at night and on *mura* rest days. The *kōtō shōgakkō* is full-time regular school for two or three years after the sixth grade. The *seinen gakkō* instructs girls in sewing and cooking and boys in fencing, wrestling, some general knowledge, and a lot of military drill.

All young men in the *mura,* including young servants from outside, are expected to attend *seinen gakkō.* The women's participation is much more limited; some do not go at all, and those who do go, go only on *mura* holidays, there being no night school for them.

Before leaving the classroom all pupils stand and bow to the teacher, and before leaving the schoolyard at the end of the school day all classes line up for dismissal by the schoolmaster, and every child bows in the direction of the Emperor's portrait. If not going home right away, a boy may while away the afternoon with other little boys playing war games. The girls will play at juggling beanbags or bouncing a ball, as often as not with a baby sibling bouncing in rhythm on their backs. Parents like to have their children come home first, say, "I have returned," and then go off to play.

There are many songs to go with ball-bouncing and other games, also many lullabies sung by older children to soothe a baby carried on the back. An example of each is given below.

### HAND-CLAPPING GAME SONG

| | |
|---|---|
| Arutoki Hanako no | At one time Hanako's |
| Namida ga hori hori | Tears poured down |
| Hori hori | Poured down. |
| Ammari deta no de | Too many tears |
| Tamoto de nugūimasho | With the sleeve let us wipe |
| Nugūimasho | Let us wipe |
| Nugūta kimono wa | The wet *kimono* |
| Araimasho | Let us wash |
| Araimasho | Let us wash. |
| Aratta kimono wa | The washed *kimono* |
| Shiburimasho | Let us wring |
| Shiburimasho | Let us wring. |
| Shibutta kimono wa | The wrung *kimono* |
| Hoshimasho | Let us hang out |
| Hoshimasho | Let us hang out. |
| Hosh'ta kimono wa | The hung *kimono* |
| Tatamimasho | Let us fold |
| Tatamimasho | Let us fold. |
| Tatanda kimono wa | The folded *kimono* |
| Naoshimasho | Let us put away |
| Naoshimasho | Let us put away. |
| Naoshita kimono wa | The put-away *kimono* |
| Nezumi ga poki poki | The mice (ate), *poki poki* |
| Poki poki | *Poki poki* |
| On puku pon—na—pon | *On puku pon na pon.* |

## LULLABY (*KOMORI-UTA*)

Nenne ko Torahachi baba no mago
Baba oraren jī no mago
Jī wa doke ikaita
Jī wa machi fune kai ni
Fune wa naka tokya uma kōte
Uma wa doke tsunagaita
Uma wa sendan no ki tsunagaita
Nan kwasete tsunagaita
Hami kwasete tsunagaita

Go to sleep Torahachi, granma's grandchild.
Granma is not here, granpa's grandchild.
Granpa, where did he go?
Granpa went to town to buy a boat;
There was no boat, he bought a horse.
The horse, where did he tie (it)?
The horse he tied to a *sendan* tree.
What did he feed (it) tethered?
The bit he fed (it), tethered.

If a child's family is rich, he will probably be sent to high school. A girl will go to the girls' high school (*jogakkō*) in Taragi or, more exceptionally, in Hitoyoshi. A boy will be sent to the agricultural school (*nōgakkō*) in Menda or, more exceptionally, to the middle school in Hitoyoshi. A high school education helps a girl's family to make a good marriage for her.[2]

More boys than girls receive education outside Suye. In the last ten years nine boys and no girls went from Suye families to some college or university. Of these, one became a government official in Tokyo; two, doctors in Hitoyoshi; one, an army doctor; one, a newspaper man in Tokyo; three are still in college. Only one has come back to Suye. He came back because of illness while working at an office job in Kumamoto and because his father died, forcing him to come home and take care of his household consisting of his mother and three unmarried younger sisters. He has made a virtue of his necessity by deploring the fact that educated citizens of Suye leave the place and saying he must now stay here as a duty to his native village.

At fourteen or fifteen a young person begins taking his full share of farm work. At twenty about one boy in four goes off to the barracks; girls continue helping their mothers or perhaps work as maids for some richer families. Young men of poor families also work out as menservants.

## *NOTES*

1. As generally translated. Actually these books, one for each grade, are more concerned with national civics, the virtue of being a soldier, of revering the Emperor, etc.

2. Today all social classes except the nobility are said to be equal, but on every boy's file is recorded whether or not he is descended from a *samurai,* and whether or not he is from the *eta* class.

# 11 .................

# City Life in Japan
# A Study of a Tokyo Ward

RONALD PHILIP DORE

## EDUCATION

The educational system was singled out for special attention by the reformers in Occupational Headquarters. It was believed that those features of the Japanese state — authoritarianism and militaristic nationalism — which were considered morally the most objectionable, and expediently the most dangerous in a Pacific neighbour, had their roots in the training given, and in the values and beliefs implanted by, the prewar schools. In 1946 a large committee of American educators was invited to make a lightning tour and report on the modifications necessary to turn the educational system into one more befitting a democratic state. It was largely on the basis of its recommendations that the Fundamental Edu-

Reprinted from *City Life in Japan* by Ronald Philip Dore. Berkeley and Los Angeles: University of California Press. Reprinted by permission of The Regents of the University of California. Copyright: © R. P. Dore 1958.

cation Law of 1947 (a statement of general principles) and the School Education Law of 1948 were enacted. Meanwhile, by administrative regulations, thorough-going changes had been made in school organization and curriculum, the most noteworthy being the replacement of the former ethics, history, and geography courses by a combined "Social Studies" course.

The changes enforced in the system of higher education were generally deplored by the Japanese, but the new primary and secondary system less so. They set about making the new system work with perhaps more enthusiasm than was shown for any other of the postwar changes. Large numbers of new secondary schools were built, in villages often at the cost of a direct levy on the villagers and sometimes with the help of voluntary labour. There was a great vogue in American educational theory; Dewey became almost a best seller and words like "homeroom," "recreation," and "core curriculum" were used with great fluency and determination, if not always with full comprehension, by teachers in the far corners of the land.[1] Possibly the bewilderment of the ordinary primary schoolmaster, but certainly his anxious desire for enlightenment, are reflected in the vast number of books on educational practice and theory, averaging thirteen a week in 1950, or 5 percent of the total number of titles produced in that year.[2]

A few visits to schools near Shitayama-cho and some conversations with teachers and parents hardly provide sufficient material on which to base a detailed and systematic analysis of the education Shitayama-cho children were receiving. They were, however, enough to gain some impression of the problems, the bewilderment, the enthusiasms and hesitations which go to make up the atmosphere of the modern Tokyo school.

The Ikegami primary school (catering for Shitayama-cho and four other wards) has just short of a thousand children (aged 6–11) divided into twenty classes (three or four for each age group). The average size of class (forty-nine) is about the average for the borough, though some schools have classes of seventy. Of the twenty-seven teachers (sixteen men, eleven women), three have largely administrative and secretarial duties — the headmaster, the senior master and one other teacher. There are three specialists, an art teacher, a music teacher, and a "nurse teacher" who is chiefly concerned with the pupils' health.

Before the war it was one of the model schools for showing to foreign visitors, and as such was well provided with equipment, but it was burnt out in the bombing. With gradual rebuilding it progressed from three-shift to two-shift, and now finally to one-shift working. It is still bedraggled in appearance, and one wing remains a mass of scarred walls and twisted window frames, but the drab classrooms with their resounding wooden boarding, are made gay with maps and drawings, flowers, models and insect cages. There is the inevitable loudspeaker system[3] (provided by the Parent-Teacher Association) and the school still has a good reputation, which prompts some parents from neighbouring districts to send their children here by getting them officially registered as "lodgers" with relatives or friends within the Ikegami school district. The source of the school's comparative superiority, says the headmaster modestly, lies in the type of homes the children come from. The parents are all more or less of the same lower-middle-class level and they are all keen supporters of school activities.

Discussions of education in Shitayama-cho nearly always led round to a comparison of the present with the prewar state of affairs. In our first conversation the headmaster, a very forceful and articulate man in his fifties, seemed very anxious to stress how far the spirit of the modern education was removed from the old inculcation of formal knowledge and abstract principles of loyalty and filial piety. Nowadays, he said, he is concerned to impress on the children their rights as citizens — the parks they go to on school outings belong to them, not to the Government — he believes not in rigid authoritarian discipline nor in the encouragement of moralistic precocity, but in awaiting the natural burgeoning of the child's moral sense. There are stages of development, . . . tender plants . . . fertilization . . . hot-house blossoms . . . .

Certainly there was nothing rigidly disciplinarian about the assembly with which each day began. The pupils lined up in class formation and raggedly and haphazardly measured distance from the front on the orders of the senior master. As the headmaster came on to the platform, the head boy (President of the Pupils' Self-Governing Council) stepped forward to say "Good morning, Headmaster" and all the pupils bowed. After the headmaster's few remarks on the fact that it was the day the Japanese plenipotentiaries were due back from the San Francisco Peace Conference, that the next day was old people's day, and that parents had complimented him on the efficiency of the Traffic Section of the School's Self-Government Association, they filed off in ragged line talking and laughing the while.

Until the end of the war strict military discipline prevailed on these occasions. After the war they stopped lining up altogether and just gathered in higgledy-piggledy groups. Then someone discovered that the children were lined up at one of the American schools in the Occupation housing estates. So they started lining up again, but they keep such discipline to the "minimum necessary to maintain group life." The headmaster, having elicited from me the information that children did not bow to the head teacher in English schools, supposed that "there is still a lot of unnecessary formalism we could do away with."

Nor was formal discipline very marked in the class teaching. One class of fifty seven-year-olds presented a scene of good-natured chaos as the teacher attempts to tell a story about a sparrow, but eventually gave way to the persistent interruptions of one boy who had a story of his own that he wanted to tell. In the art room ten-year-olds were making a sort of propeller toy which rises up into the air as it is twisted. They were scraping away absorbedly at pieces of bamboo with penknives, kitchen knives, table knives, anything they had been able to persuade their mothers to let them have. Their 23-year-old teacher was wandering round the room giving advice, and occasionally shooting his own propeller into the air with boyish whoops of delight.

Another class, of ten-year-olds, was doing arithmetic. Problems were written on the board. When they had done them or wanted advice the pupils came individually to the teacher. But there was no question of working in silence; the problems were obviously being worked on, but to the accompaniment of conversation, consultation, shouts across the room and tussles over rubbers. There seemed to be a good many children walking about the room, not all in the direction of the teacher. One boy, convinced that he had been misinformed protested "Teacher, that's wrong!" The teacher ignored him, having turned by that time to one of the other pupils crowding round him and shouting "Teacher! Teacher!" like a press of autograph-hunters. One certainly did not get the impression that these children were being brought up in the fear of authority.

The quietest room in the school, in fact, contained the boys of a class of eleven-year-olds left alone to work out some arithmetic problems while the girls were away for a domestic class. (Boys and girls take domestic classes together until the age of ten. The fact that boys are now taught to sew was often commented on by male parents as one of the least comprehensible whimsies of the new education. It is generally justified, and approved by many mothers, on the grounds that it should help to induce in men an understanding of the woman's lot.) These were working with quiet concentration which my entry and interrogation of one of them did little to interrupt. One boy, obviously recognized as an authority, would occasionally be asked if such and such was the right answer for number so-and-so. Once he adopted a very elder-brother tone, did not give the answer, but said instead, "Look, you see that . . . Well, multiply that number by that number . . . See?"

This much would seem to provide some confirmation of Ruth Benedict's theories concerning the discontinuity of child training in Japan — the undisciplined freedom of early childhood suddenly replaced at about the age of ten by rigid repression which breaks the spirit and prepares for the strict formalism and obedience to convention of adult Japanese life. The period may mark a change, but it is doubtful, however, if sudden repression plays much part. If this were the case, then this could not be other than conscious parental and pedagogic policy, based on commonly held views concerning the nature and responsibilities of the child. But there was little trace of this in parents' answers to interview questions, questions concerning the teaching of respect language, bowing to guests, silence at meals or the age at which they thought the child's *monogokoro ga tsuku* (not quite the same as "develop a sense of right and wrong"; it means something more like "develop the ability to behave with discretion and responsibility"). The answers (from 100 parents) show a great variety in which it would defy any statistician's ingenuity to discern a predominant pattern. Girls certainly seem to be taught manners more strictly than boys and from an earlier age, but there was no suggestion that the age of ten or eleven had any particular significance in parents' eyes. Nor, one gathers from teachers, in their eyes either.

It seems though, that boys at least develop a certain sense of responsibility and self-importance at about this age — perhaps the Pupils' Self-Government Association helps in this. They also develop a sense of sex-separateness. An eleven-year-old-boy once answered my question asking when they stopped playing with girls in unhesitatingly precise terms — in the third term of the third year (i.e., at about the age of nine), and he affirmed that this was "fixed," a convention of the School Teachers also remarked that by the fourth year girls almost without exception used more respectful women's language, not the rougher language of boys.

Corporal punishment is not used in the school, the only punishments being scolding or making children stand in a corner or outside the room. They are invoked, said a group of teachers, chiefly as a means of dealing with quarrels or uncooperative behaviour in group activities — when children "make a nuisance of themselves to others." It is, indeed, surprising how often, in modern Japan, one hears *hito ni meiwaku wo kakete wa ikenai* — "one must not make a nuisance of oneself to other people" quoted as the cardinal principle of morality. Of all the traditional moral precepts, this, in itself somewhat negative and unsatisfying, seems to be the only one which has come unscathed through the fire of "democracy."

Each class has a Self-Government Association. (*Jichikai* sounds somewhat less pompous in Japanese.) A president and three vice-presidents are elected every term, the elections being preceded by speeches by each of the candidates declaring his policy and what he will do if elected. These act as monitors when the teacher is absent, and (except for the two lowest years) sit on the School Self-Government Council. Teachers are careful to confine the Self-Government Council to the making of the rules — no running in corridors, no leaving of litter, etc. — and to organize the performance of duties such as school cleaning or traffic control. (Every morning in the main road outside the school a ten- or eleven-year-old boy or girl would appear with a large red flag inscribed *Ikegami Primary School, Pupils' Self-Government Association, Traffic Section* to hold up the traffic while the children crossed.) They do not give these councils any judiciary powers. In some schools after the war there were class courts in which children judged rule-breaking fellows. They were far too reminiscent of Communist self-criticism meetings — the "stringing-up" of unpopular children against whom the whole weight of outraged group sentiment was brought to bear, an experience of traumatic proportions for the emotionally insecure child. They also have to be on their guard against the class president developing too great a sense of his own importance and becoming a gang leader of the worst sort.

The children are not allowed, moreover, to write penal provisions into the rules, though they have often asked to be allowed to do so. One teacher said that if he asks the class "What shall we do with him?" of some offender, they are usually in favour of punishment. There is very little sense of pupil solidarity *vis-à-vis* the teacher, except among girls in the top classes.

This, teachers insisted, used not to be so. The elder brother attitude was not considered consonant with the teacher's dignity. There was a smouldering state of war between pupils and teachers. Children used to hate having to go to the staff room. Now they thought nothing of it. Parents have remarked how impressed they were at seeing the headmaster walking away from the school hand-in-hand with one of his charges.

In the School Self-Government Council, the ten- and eleven-year-olds obviously take the lead, but teachers do their best to correct for their predominance and bring the younger ones forward. No powers over lower forms are given to upper forms: — so much for the "traditional emphasis on seniority" of Japanese society.

No teacher bothered very much about respect language. It used to be part of the ethics course to teach it and they used to insist on it in the classroom. Now there is a certain amount of teaching of respect language in the Japanese language periods, but they do not go out of their way to insist on it in the classroom. Children learn it at home, and there is a considerable difference in this respect between the "well-spoken" boy from the professional class home and the children from, say, the Public Assistance Hostel.

There is no streaming by ability. It is, said teachers, a bad system. Effective from the intellectual point of view, but man does not live by intellect alone. Feelings have also to be considered. The sense of inferiority of the downgraded and the arrogance of the élite are to be avoided at all costs. Marks are not given in positional order. In reports a child's performance is compared not with that of other children but with his previous term's record. (Teachers fill in the most ludicrously complicated reports sheets for parents, each child being assessed in each subject on three or four criteria, e.g. for the Japanese language, on "Ability for verbal expression," "Ability for written expression," "Ability for comprehension," "Attitude to study," etc.) The head stressed as a cardinal principle the importance of not letting any child feel inferior or unappreciated. Even if a child was good at nothing but sweeping floors, he would be praised for that. (The really subnormal are supposed to go to a special school, but the number of places at such schools is insufficient.) At a recent summer Handicrafts Exhibition about a third of the children got prizes — awarded more for effort than for skill.

The complaints of parents suggest that the teachers are not exaggerating in saying that there has been a big change in the disciplinary atmosphere of the schools. The majority of parents are, on the whole, favourable to the new education. The innovations are generally summed up in the phrase that whereas education used to be guided on "packing-in" principles — the mere cramming of a lot of information down children's throats — now teachers made children study by themselves and gave them guidance. One mother described with unmistakable delight how her ten-year-old son had set off alone to interview the stationmaster at Tokyo station to get material for a social studies period. Another group of mothers agreed that intellectual training probably suffered — whereas the old was narrow and thorough the new education is broad and shallow — but they marvelled at their children's sense of independence and were pleased to see them enjoying their schooling far more than they themselves did in their youth. On the other hand, when asked whether the prewar ethics course should be reinstated in the curriculum, more than eighty parents out of a hundred said that it should, and the most frequently expressed reason was that the children are "badly behaved," "don't know how to be polite," and "have no respect for their elders."[4] The other most common theme in justifying the need for an ethics course was that the children are no longer told the stories of famous men to inspire them — the old stories of Ninomiya Sontoku, Benjamin Franklin, Jenner or Noguchi. (Of these the most frequently mentioned was the first, the "peasant sage of Japan," an agricultural productivity expert and moralist of the early nineteenth century, himself a shining example of upward mobility overleaping all the feudal barriers of estate distinctions, whose statue — always showing him reading a Confucian classic as he walks down from the mountains, back bent under a load of firewood — stood before the war outside nearly every primary school. At Ikegami it was destroyed in the bombing and has not been replaced.) The necessity of teaching children to be filial to their parents is the next most common theme. Two people thought that children ought to be taught to respect the Emperor and another thought it shameful that children nowadays did not even know the national anthem.

The postwar Parent-Teacher Associations have, at least, brought parents into frequent direct contact with the schools. At the Ikegami school the most common form of meeting was by class, the "home-room" teacher meeting the parents (almost exclusively mothers) of his pupils at regular intervals. There were also three parent representatives for each class who, in addition to arranging outings and social activities of their particular class, also sit on one of eight committees concerned with "general affairs," "education," "culture," "welfare," "equipment," "school meals," "out-of-school activities" and "finance." It was apparent from the remarks of some mothers that they derived a good deal of both pleasure and information from these class meetings, but answers to a few interview questions about the P.T.A. suggested that the organization as a whole was not altogether popular.

Very few parents have nothing to do with it at all. On the other hand most go out of a sense of duty, i.e., it is on the same level as the Ward Association — a meeting at which it is necessary that *one* representative from each household should "show his face" as a matter of obligation to the local community. Thus, of fifty-five parents with children at school, only six said that nobody from their house ever went to the P.T.A. meetings. In thirty-six houses only the wife went, in seven only the husband, and in five either the husband or the wife according to circumstances. But in only one case did husband and wife go together. (This may also to some extent be due to lingering ideas of the impropriety of married couples being seen out together, and to the necessity for someone to stay home to look after the children.) One woman said at the interview that "everybody grumbles about *having* to go to the P.T.A. Nobody likes going."

There were, too, a fair number of specific criticisms of the running of the P.T.A. Only about a dozen of the fifty-five proclaimed themselves fully or even mildly satisfied with the way the Association was being run. The criticisms were very much on the lines familiar from newspaper comment. Chiefly, first of all, that it was primarily a means for wringing money out of parents. This had been especially the case at the Ikegami school where parents bore a large share of the cost of the first stage of rebuilding. With the gradual rehabilitation of its finances, the borough had taken over the whole burden of the later stages of rebuilding, as, of course, it was its responsibility to do from the beginning. (A Ministry of Education survey of educational expenditure for 1949 showed that the money derived from P.T.A. and other contributions amounted to 72 percent of the amount provided from public funds for primary schools, 66 percent for secondary schools, and even 15 percent for high schools.[5])

The contributions were more or less proportionate to means, but since this involved a public self-evaluation of one's standing in the community, it was naturally unpopular. There were complaints that the rebuilding fund targets and the general level of contributions had been decided by the small clique of relatively wealthy members who run the affair and on whom the eventual publication of the subscription list would be most likely to reflect honour and prestige. Such criticisms applied especially to the *per capita* contributions for class activities the collection of which was the class representatives' chief function. Each parent of eleven-year-olds, for instance, was asked to contribute 500 *yen* (About 10*s.*) towards the cost of a graduation photograph album, a graduation outing, and a memorial present which each class of school-leavers presented to the school.

The very widespread complaint, which recurs in newspaper comment, that the P.T.A. is "boss-ridden" and run for individual ends, also came up in these interview replies. One or two said that the accounting was distinctly loose and the annual statement left scope for quite sizable speculation. How justified such suspicions were it was impossible to tell, but it would seem more likely that the leaders of the P.T.A. (the President was also President of the Shitayama Ward Association) were attracted more by the opportunities for the minor exercise of power and for "improving their connections" than by possibilities of financial profit. The former P.T.A. President had already reaped the fruits of his presidency in election to the borough council. There were possibly other advantages, too. The headmaster's room at the school was liberally provided with ashtrays, each of which bore an advertisement for the former President's glassware and kitchen equipment.

Another criticism of the leadership was that too much was spent on unnecessary and expensive conviviality for the exclusive enjoyment of the officials. That "the women seem to have very little say in what goes on" was the complaint of another man whose wife always represented his household at the meetings. And, indeed, there did seem to be a strong tendency for the meetings to be composed of a small oligarchy of managing men, and a large number of docile women. This is, perhaps, one reason why women rather than men go. It would be somewhat humiliating for the man to have to join the docile herd of those not in the inner circle and it is not easy to lead an opposition in local community organizations of this sort in Japan.

Nevertheless, in spite of these criticisms — most of them justified — the P.T.A. does succeed in bringing parents and teachers together. Of forty-eight parents of primary school children, only ten (eight of them men) had never talked to their children's teacher in the past year.

Coeducation, one of the chief postwar innovations, seems to be generally accepted and approved by parents, to judge from replies to interview questions. Women, in particular, approve on the grounds that their daughters are now able to enjoy an education equal in quality to that given to boys. It is most anxiously watched at the high school level, where, if anywhere, the new conventions governing adolescent friendships appropriate to a society which marries 'for love' rather than 'by arrangement' will have to be created. Some local authorities went over to coeducation with a single thoroughgoing reorganization. In Osaka half the pupils and staff were transferred all at once from one school to another. Tokyo, however, believes in gradualism, with the result that a former boys' school (referred to hereafter as the Ueno School) takes two-thirds boys and one-third girls, and a former girls' school (the Mita School) takes two-thirds girls and one-third boys. Moreover, since the former boys' schools still have the reputation of being the best for boys, and the former girls' schools the best for girls, owing to the nature of the entrance examination, the Ueno school tends to consist of two-thirds bright boys and one-third dull girls, and the Mita school of two-thirds fairly bright girls and one-third boys who could not make the grade for one of the better former boys schools. Although this was denied by teachers, there seem some grounds for suspicion that the Municipal authorities were not keen to have the system work successfully. There are, at least, some headmasters who are strongly opposed to the change. At Hibiya, for instance, which formerly had the reputation of being the best boys' middle school — the sure route for entry into the First High School and thence into Tokyo Imperial University — the headmaster has publicly said that he has no intention of starting domestic studies or providing other special facilities for girls. Only one woman teacher has been appointed and a firm line is taken with girls who do not reach the standards required, fifteen of whom were expelled in 1950.

The boys at the Mita school were a very depressed group. The girls despised them, which suited the teachers since there was little probability of "problems" arising. In the early days there were rumours that a third-year girl had written love-letters to a first-year boy, but since then there had been no difficulties. All classes except those in physical education and domestic studies were taken together and seating was determined by height with the sexes mixed. There were also joint class excursions, but the school definitely frowned on "pairing off." The school rules had the following section on "friendship."

(1.) With respect to friendships, always consult with your parents or your class teacher and respect their advice.
(2.) If you have specially intimate friends, always introduce them to your family.
(3.) In relations with members of the opposite sex, always observe proper decorum.

(4.) Relations with members of the opposite sex should be open and healthy. Always observe strict decorum and etiquette.

(5.) Strive to build a happy school atmosphere, each helping the other and supplementing the other's shortcomings.

(6.) It is not proper etiquette to be alone in a room with a member of the opposite sex. If it is unavoidable, see that the door is left open.

Girls did have boy friends outside the school — mostly boys older than themselves and most frequently students of nearby Keioo University. It was considered bad form to have a boy friend who is working. Prohibition of make-up and permanent waves was written into the school rules, but was not very effective. Girls could be observed tying up their hair at the school gates and letting it down as they leave.

The *essu* ("s") or *shisutaa* ("sister") — the "very special" adolescent girl friendships which were so much a part of the prewar Girls' High School culture, seemed to have disappeared. The all-female Takarazuka troupe still performed its insipid musicals, but it no longer aroused the passionate interest of the High School girls, and "pin-ups" of its leading stars — always Eton-cropped and dressed in dinner jacket and black tie — were no longer in favour. "Crushes" can now, presumably, take a more adult heterosexual course without too great an accompanying sense of sin.

At the former boys' school at Ueno (where the intellectual inferiority of the girls fits more neatly into established cultural patterns) the atmosphere was somewhat different. In the second year of coeducation there were the beginnings of particular friendships between boys and girls. Sometimes they would go to the cinema together, but more commonly (for economic reasons) call at a tea shop for a cup of tea and a cake on the way home from school. Often it was the girls who paid and frequently the dominant feature of the relationship was a protective solicitude of the girl for the boy. The girl would often bring cakes for two to eat together during the break. (Perhaps freedom of adolescent courting in a society where male superiority is well-established necessarily tends to make the girl the "admirer.") The attitudes taken by teachers vary; some made clear their disapproval of paired visits to cinemas. But the general policy of the school was tolerance provided there was no attempt at secrecy and the parents approved. On one occasion, when the relations between one third-year boy and a first-year girl appeared to be developing excessive intensity, they were both given a talking-to, but there was no question of repressive measures.

Club activities and class outings were all mixed. One teacher who had recently taken a class on a trip to the mountains said that there was no tendency to split up into separate sex groups; boys and girls came down the mountain hand-in-hand. On the other hand mixed groups for school study was not a success, the girls were boycotted by the boys, who refused to take them seriously or allow them to do anything. Class seating was segregated. The four double rows of desks were alternately boy rows and girl rows, and during a break of five minutes in one class when there was much talking and joking going on, no boy appeared to speak to any girl.

At both schools, particularly the Ueno one, the children are very much examination-oppressed. At Mita before the war, according to the headmaster's estimate, about 10 percent of the girls went on to a women's university, 3–4 percent took jobs, about 15 percent stayed on for the Supplementary Course — in which they learnt flower arrangement and the tea ceremony and other polite accomplishments — the rest stayed at home to be trained for an early marriage by their mothers. In 1951 about a third went on to university and a third took jobs — not for family economic reasons so much as to "see the world." Every afternoon from 3 to 4.30 there were special examination classes for those who want to take university entrance examinations. There was still a supplementary "bride's school" course, but the girls showed little eagerness to enter it.

At Ueno 95 percent of the boys aimed to get to a university. Many had private teachers and there were again special examination classes every afternoon. The whole school curriculum tends to be organized around the needs of the university entrance examinations. The teachers deplored this, but saw no way out. The parents want it, the children want it, and the school, to maintain its reputation, must keep up a good record for getting its pupils into Tokyo University. It was even difficult to get boys to take on the jobs of officials in the Self-Government Association so reluctant were they to spare time from their studies.

Competitive personal rivalry becomes keener with the approach of the highly competitive university entrance examinations. There was a curious system of allocating positions only to the upper strata in examination results. In the trial run for the university entrance, held in the third year, the first fifty were numbered, the also-rans were simply classified as "upper," "middle," and "lower."

The most worried men in these schools were the teachers of social studies. It is not an easy subject at this level, where they can no longer stick to the safe primary school topics of the transport system and the fire brigade. "What is the ultimate object? That's what bothers us," said one. "What is the 'good citizen' we are supposed to produce? The person who is obedient to his leaders? Someone who has enough powers of independent criticism not to be fooled by his leaders? Or someone who is capable of rubbing along with his fellows and merging cooperatively in his group?" The Ministry of Education produces its Outline Course of

Study but it only lists the scope to be covered with little guidance as to the object in view. As one of them said, "It used to be easy enough in the old days when everything centered on inculcating 'loyalty' (he used the English word — the same psychological mechanism as produces a new polite word for "lavatory" every generation), but now it's impossible to bring everything coherently together." Another showed the circumspection of a Vicar of Bray. "Who knows how Japan is going to change in the future? [This was in the last year of the Occupation.] It is impossible to visualize what sort of society it will be like, or what will be the type of good citizen which that society will demand." Too much is left to the teacher, and at the same time prudence demands care in the expression of his political opinions. (Most schools are still fairly liberal, but in others left-wing opinions have been the end of a promising career.) But the real trouble is that most of them have not got any firm opinions. As one of them said, their *nayami* — their worried confusion — transmits itself to their pupils.

Sometimes, indeed, it seemed in 1951 that only the Communists and the American-worshippers had succeeded in really finding something to believe *in* since the defeat. For them it was easier since it was not so much abstract principles or values as a source of authority to which they were required to pin their faith. But those who tried to get some clear idea of the moral implications for the individual and the political implications for contemporary Japanese society of the "democratic" outlook were often as much at sea, and as insecure, as the conscious trimmers — than whom, was one's impression, they were rather more numerous.

The result, at any rate, was that the Social Studies periods tended to concentrate on the retailing of nearly packaged factual detail. The mere description of the established order was thought to be "safe" and "non-political." It may be safe, but it is certainly not nonpolitical. A general conservative bias is inevitable, which, however, the *nayami,* the worried confusion of the teacher may do something to subvert.

One first-year class, for instance, was being taken through the taxation system. (General Social Studies continue through the Secondary School to the first year of High School. For the last two years of High School it is split into Japanese History, World History, and Human Geography.) The explanation was based on pamphlets provided by the Tokyo Municipality and the Ministry of Finance, copies of which every child had. They explain the mechanisms of taxation. The teacher did promise to touch on the "social policy aspects" in a later lesson, but today there was no approach to normative questions except in discussion of the system of graduated income tax, when the teacher said that the alternative system of equal *per capita* taxation might cut some people's income below the minimum, and so the progressive system was designed to meet this objection. His only comment on indirect taxation was that it was originally the most common form and was easier to apply since people were taxed without noticing it.

There was no mistaking the feelings, in any of these schools, that things had changed. Nor did one feel prompted to doubt the genuineness of frequent statements that the change was for the better. Many really felt that a dead weight of oppressive formalism had been lifted. In the former Japan the sacred had expanded its sphere of competence too far at the expense of the profane. The most frequent adjective used to describe the old days was *kyuukutsu* — "stiff," "crampingly formal." So much of life was sacrosanct; — the transcendental supremacy of the Emperor and his scriptural utterances, the glory of the army and the nobility of Japan's destiny, the principles of the established order and the ideals of the educational systems, even the authority of the teacher. To treat these sacred symbols lightly and objectively, verbally to criticize or in behaviour to fail to conform, was unthinkable outside a small stratum of intellectuals. To do so was not only prudentially dangerous in a local community in which sententious solemnity held absolute sway and reacted with hostility against nonconformity, it was also to cut oneself off from the emotional security of identification with the aims and values of a thoroughly integrated society carving its way to success against a hostile world. The teacher, on whom devolved a special responsibility for upholding the values of the society, was more especially circumscribed by the solemn formality which the sacred elements of life demanded.

Now the frontiers of the sacred have been rolled back; the dreadful consequences of sacrilege no longer follow a joke about authority or a confession of honest fumbling doubt. A lapse from dignity is no longer a betrayal of the ideal role of the teacher which society formerly imposed. Many undoubtedly feel freer and happier. But there must also be some, both among the conscious trimmers and among those who honestly confess themselves uncertain in their basic value beliefs, who find this new freedom painful and distressing. Implicit acceptance of the sacred symbols undoubtedly gave many an assurance and a security for which the new age provides no substitute. How many are now in the grip of Erich Fromm's "fear of freedom?"

And how many such individuals will the new generation now being educated contain? What was to be seen in these schools certainly did not suggest the educational system which one associates with an authoritarian society. The freedom and the gaiety of the primary school child does not foreshadow the adult personality which fears authority but stills its fears by appeasement, by subservience to and identification with authority, directing the hate which accompanies its fear towards external objects. But perhaps this is not the whole story. It may be that the new methods were the more easily assimilated in the primary school in that they fitted into already established patterns of tender indulgence for the young child. But there was something a little ominous in the deadly earnestness of the High School boy whose life, with the whole weight of parental ambition behind him, centres on approaching competitive examinations. It was an earnestness which left little time for questioning, little time for anything but the amassing of knowledge primarily related to its instrumental value for "getting on." It was necessary for them to prepare themselves to answer the question: "The present system of income tax is a (regressive, progressive, indirect) system of taxation. (Put a ring round the most suitable)" rather than to concern themselves with the question whether the present system of taxation was just or unjust. And what if the society whose workings are thus being taught in much the same way as the laws of physics are taught — a society whose prospects of economic expansion are rigorously limited by poverty of natural resources and by defeat — fails to offer some satisfactory fulfilment of their strivings to a large number of those now caught up in the greatly expanded higher-education system? Will there be sufficient fluidity in the economic system to enable such individuals to go on hoping for something to turn up, or at least to secure a working-out of their own thwarted ambitions by projecting them onto their children? Will the training in school self-government associations be sufficient to enable the frustrated to express themselves in the organization of democratic political parties and economic pressure groups? Or will their understanding of the forces which control society be so imperfect, will they feel so strongly the need for an immediate inspiring hope, the need, as the traditional proverb has it, "to wrap up in something long" — to find some reassuring symbol of inviolate authority as an escape from the powerless isolation of the individual — that a new regime of authority and conformity develops? It need not necessarily be on the pre-war Japanese pattern — for the resuscitation of the old symbols would require an act of salesmanship of which the present political leaders are probably incapable — but the recent history of Europe and of Russia provides no lack of suitable alternative models.

## NOTES

1. "Anyone who has ever peeped into a primary school staff meeting will certainly have an entirely new slant on the Japanese language. You will find even the venerable headmaster contorting his vocal organs to discuss what is to be done about the *koka-koramu*, the importance of *skoppu* or of *shiiken*. You may be tempted to ask what language it is he is talking.

"*Koa-karikyuramu* (core curriculum), *Sukoopu* (scope) and *Shiikuensu* (sequence) and the rest are now such thoroughly acclimatized Japanese words and have so lost touch with their originals, that perhaps the venerable headmaster is to be forgiven for getting mixed up with Coca-Cola." (Takata Tamotsu, *Daini Burari-Hyootan*, 1952, p. 96). Another writer, deploring the tendency to use foreign words without much appreciation of their meaning, claims to have overheard the remark, "That's a very good school. They say they have a *karikyuramu* (curriculum) there" (Gotoo Iwao *et al.*, *Zooho Atarashii Kyooikuhoo*, 1949, p. 129).

2. Shuppan Nyuusu, *Shuppan Nenkan* 1951, pp. 840–1. This does not include textbooks which account for another 15 percent of the total book production.

3. One of my most vivid impressions of the mixture of new techniques and traditional attitudes resulted from a visit to the headmaster of a village school in the mountains of central Japan. Soon after our arrival he walked to the microphone in the corner of his room and relayed a message throughout the school asking Teacher Suzuki to come to the headmaster's room. Teacher Suzuki, the only woman member of the staff, arrived from her class, not to be introduced to the visitors, but to pour water from the always simmering kettle into the teapot and to serve us tea.

4. A newspaper opinion survey reported that 63 percent believe that children are worse behaved than before the war. The most common reason given by the 14 percent minority who thought that they were better behaved was that they have "learnt to speak up for themselves frankly and clearly" and that they are "more open and active." (*Yomiuri Shimbun*, 4 May 1951. A large sample of Tokyo dwellers.)

5. *Yomiuri*, 31 March 1951.

## SUGGESTED READINGS FOR PART TWO

### China

BAUM, RICHARD AND FREDERICK C. TEIWES
    1968    Ssu-ch'ing: The socialist education movement of 1962–1966. Berkeley: University of California Center for Chinese Studies. 128 pp., appendixes, bibliographical footnotes, glossary.

        Discussion of Chinese attempts to bring ideology and education into harmony

FRASER, STEWART (ED.)
    1965    Chinese communist education: Records of the first decade. Nashville: Vanderbilt University Press. xvi+542 pp., bibliography.

        Presentation of documents illustrating the currents of debate about education in Mainland China

## *India*

DAKIN, JULIAN, BRIAN TIFFEN, AND H. G. WIDDOWSON
   1968    Language in education: The problem in Commonwealth Africa and
        the Indo-Pakistan sub-continent. London: Oxford University Press.
        xi+177 pp., glossary.

        Discussion of one of the most pressing issues in India — the prob-
        lems of separatism based on language

LASKA, JOHN A.
   1968    Planning and educational development in India. New York:
        Teachers College Press, Columbia University. xi+129 pp., bibli-
        ography, tables.

        The problems of planning in an overpopulated and poor nation are
        put into perspective.

USEEM, JOHN AND RUTH HILL USEEM
   1955    The western educated man in India. New York: Dryden Press.

        A view of the problems of people educated in one culture and liv-
        ing in another

## *Japan*

DORE, RONALD
   1965    Education in Tokugawa Japan. Berkeley: University of California
        Press. xi+346 pp., illustrated, map.

        Analysis of education in the crucial period in Japan before Western
        influences modified education there

PASSIN, HERBERT
   1965    Society and education in Japan. New York: Bureau of Publications,
        Columbia University. xvii+347 pp., illus.

        Relationships between Japanese social structure and Japanese edu-
        cational networks are examined in detail.

In terms of education, Europe is often divided into two major units: Communist and non-Communist. Such a division is inordinately simplistic, however, and observes only a rough political criterion. Actually, the diversity of educational systems and the complexity of their problems go far beyond even the national divisions reflected in a map of contemporary Europe. Educational problems often reflect linguistic-cultural divergences which, in turn, are usually aspects (or causes) of economic and social inequalities within nations. Examples range from the conflicts between the Flemish (Dutch-speaking) and Walloon (French-speaking) groups in Belgium to resentment of the residents of Brittany against the central government of France; from the struggles of the Basques for greater autonomy (including educational) in Spain to the small but insistent group of Welsh nationalists who insist on, among other demands, use of Welsh (with English) in a bilingual educational system; from the great ecological differences between Sicily and northern Italy to the efforts of the Russian Tartars to gain recognition in the ethnic conglomerate of the U.S.S.R.

## PART THREE

# EUROPE

While language is often the popular issue, there is an increasing tendency for some of the struggle to center on efforts toward truly mass education as opposed to traditions of elitism. Scandinavian nations, especially Sweden, have gone far in democratizing their educational systems. The United Kingdom, France, and Germany are also involved in varying degrees in debates over whether the role of education should be the creation of an intellectual elite or, following the American model, the educational standard should be the preparation of masses of skilled and fairly literate citizens.

Both Laurence Wylie and Leila Berg draw relationships between educational experiences and the reenforcement of the types of "social personalities" which are anticipated in the groups they are describing. By "social personality" is meant a pattern of overt behavior and decision-making which is deemed "appropriate" to the rank, status, and prestige of the group to which the individual belongs. Both France and England have an elitist tradition in the educational systems which quite early makes clear, irreversible distinctions between the small minority intended for higher education and the great majority destined to terminate education in their early or midteens. In addition, both nations have common problems of industrialization: marked rural-urban differences in school systems, slum-nonslum distinctions within urban areas, and class and occupational limits on aspirations. England, the oldest industrialized nation, also has an increasing racial problem in the presence of nonwhite Commonwealth residents and the prejudice against them which is being increasingly expressed by white citizens.

The two readings on Europe offer very different situations. In Laurence Wylie's article the people in Peyrane would be seen by most other Frenchmen as good, reliable, hardworking citizens. The same judgement would not hold for the students at Risinghill described in Leila Berg's article. The students in Peyrane come from well-integrated families and feel relatively secure in their lifestyles. In both respects, the students at Risinghill are different. While the prevailing standards in the school in Peyrane reenforce generally accepted values and norms, it is obvious that the standards which Mr. Duane was trying to change at Risinghill and the ones he was trying to introduce differed, on the one hand, from what society expected in the education of economically deprived, urban young people, and, on the other hand, from what most Risinghill students absorbed in their family lives.

A major point in the selection of these two readings is that a student of education and anthropology must be aware of the very high level of generality and abstraction represented in terms such as "English" education or "French" education. Very old educational systems, new technological and social conditions, and internal, local differences require a much lower and more specific level of analysis for significant anthropological study.

# 12 .................

# Village in the Vaucluse

## LAURENCE WYLIE

### SCHOOL

Madame Biron, the butcher's wife, lived in Apt before she moved to Peyrane. She likes living in Peyrane, but she says that life in a city has one great advantage for a woman with a three-year-old boy like her Jeannot, for in the cities three-year-old children can be sent to school. In small schools like the one in Peyrane the teachers refuse to take children before their fourth birthday. Madame Biron talked to Madame Girard, the teacher of the *classes enfantines,* and tried to persuade her to take Jeannot a few months before his fourth birthday, but Madame Girard refused to make an exception, even though Jeannot was big for his age.

If Madame Girard had made an exception in this case she soon would have had all the three-year-old children in Peyrane. All the mothers are eager to send their children to school as soon as possible. A child in

Reprinted by permission of the publishers from Laurence Wylie *Village in the Vaucluse.* Cambridge, Mass.: Harvard University Press, Copyright, 1957, 1964, by the President and Fellows of Harvard College.

school is one less responsibility at home — at least for six hours of the day — and mothers welcome the opportunity to share their responsibilities with the teacher.

The fourth birthday is important in the life of a child, for he starts school that very day. The event does not come as a surprise to him, since there has been much talk about it in the family. He has new shoes, sturdy boots big enough so that heavy woolen socks may be worn with them. If the family purse is large enough he has a new cap or beret, new smocks, and a heavy muffler which his mother has knitted. He also has to have a briefcase to carry his pencils and crayons and papers. The town furnishes school materials, but children usually prefer to have a set of their own, and Madame Girard will not allow them to be left at the school. If private materials disappeared she would be blamed for the loss, and she is unwilling to assume this needless responsibility. So even though children are given no homework until they are six or seven years old, they often begin to carry a briefcase to and from school at the age of four.

The only children to undergo a special ceremony before starting to school are boys with pretty hair like Jeannot Biron and Bébert Favre. They have their long curls cut off and get a boy's regular haircut with a part on the side and a long lock held back with a bobby pin. Bébert's father cut his hair the day before he started to school, but Madame Biron, who was more accustomed to city ways and whose husband's business was prosperous, took Jeannot to Madame Avenas's beauty parlor because she said she wanted his first haircut to "look just right." One boy in the *classe enfantine* still had long curls, and his mother felt it necessary to explain that she had a special reason for postponing his haircut. His aunt was to be married in a few months, and she wanted Loulou to look his best for the wedding.

On the day that the child is to start to school his mother accompanies him if she can arrange it. Otherwise an older sister or brother or a neighbor's child will take the responsibility of introducing him to the teacher and showing the required papers: birth certificate, diphtheria inoculation certificate, and vaccination certificate. Madame Girard greets a new child with a show of affection and interest. She shakes hands with him, hugs and kisses him, and tells him how happy he is going to be now that he is grown up and can go to school with the big children. When the child's mother leaves or when the older sister goes off to her class the child may cry, and Madame Girard does her best to console him. She may hold him on her lap and mother him without interrupting her work with the older children in her room. If he is too demanding, she will call in Odette Peretti or one of the other big girls from the *classe des grands* to care for him until he adjusts to the new situation.

As soon as the child accepts the situation, and it rarely takes more than an hour or so, no more nonsense is expected of him. He must submit to the same rules and routine followed by all the other children. He must sit quietly at his desk for three hours in the morning and three hours in the afternoon. He must not fidget or talk to other children. He can move around freely only during the fifteen minute recess periods, one in the morning and one in the afternoon.

Officially, the *classes enfantines* are considered only a sort of *garderie,* a nursery where little children are kept for a few hours every day to free their mothers. Now and then Madame Girard may take the time to work with them formally, teaching them the alphabet, showing them how to copy letters and numbers, helping them learn songs or poems by heart, but most of the time she is kept busy with the older children on the other side of the room who have regular lessons to learn. The younger ones must learn to amuse themselves without making any disturbance. Paper, crayons, a few blocks, a few books are provided for them. A four-year-old may play with them or he may just sit still and listen to the older children recite. Now and then he may put his head on his desk and take a nap. Madame Girard lets the little ones sleep when they wish, for she knows that they may have been up until very late at a family dinner or at the movies the night before. And then she says, "There is nothing serious that they have to learn for a year or so."

The four-year-old and five-year-old children, however, *do* learn important lessons. They learn to sit still for long periods. They learn to accept the discipline of the school. They even learn about learning — that is, they are impressed with the fact that to learn means to copy or to repeat whatever the teacher tells them. They are not encouraged to "express their personality." On the contrary, they learn that their personality must be kept constantly under control. These attitudes are so thoroughly inculcated in the four- and five-year-old children that by the time they are six years old they are considered mature enough to begin their formal education.

When we moved to Peyrane our older son was almost five years old, and naturally he was expected to go to school. Madame Girard said we might do as we liked about sending him but she would be glad to have him. To us it seemed cruel to ask a five-year-old child to sit at a desk for six long hours a day listening to a language he did not understand, so we sent him at first only in the morning. After a few weeks, however, he asked if he might attend both the morning and afternoon sessions. He said he liked the Peyrane school much more than the kindergarten he had attended at home. "At home we always had to keep playing all the time. Here we can learn real letters and numbers and things."

One reason we hesitated to ask our son to spend six hours a day in the schoolroom was that the school and the room seemed unhealthy to us. Like most of the buildings in Peyrane the school seems ageless, but it is only about two hundred and fifty years old. Built originally as a Charitable Home for the Poor and Aged, it has served as a school since 1833 when public primary education was introduced in Peyrane.

It is a picturesque building, but everyone agrees that as a school it is a disgrace to the community. The roof threatens to cave in at several points. There are cracks in the walls that run from the roof to the ground. The masons do their best to patch up the building so that it will hold together, but they say that fundamentally it is beyond repair. They have warned the Municipality, and the Municipality has warned the Department of Education that the children in the upstairs classroom are constantly exposed to the danger of a cave-in.

The teachers complain that, apart from the question of danger, the classrooms are inadequate. They may have seemed satisfactory fifty years ago, but by modern standards they are too small, too dark, poorly ventilated, and poorly equipped.

Each room is about twelve feet wide and twenty feet long, just large enough to accommodate the ten double desks for the children assigned to the room. In the center is a small wood stove surrounded by an iron guard rail. Hanging from the center of the ceiling is a sixty-watt electric bulb without a shade, the only artificial light in the room. Even on sunny days there is not much light because there is only one window, and the dark yellow walls reflect little light. In warm weather when the window and door are open the air is sufficiently fresh, but in the winter the room grows stuffy. Each teacher keeps a pan of water with strongly scented herbs simmering on the stove.

There are few questions on which all the people of Peyrane agree, but there is unanimous agreement that Peyrane should have a new school building, a beautiful, modern *groupe scolaire* like the one in the neighboring town of Goult. Just why Peyrane does not have a new *groupe scolaire*, in spite of this extraordinary unanimity, is a complicated question which cannot be discussed at this point because it would take us too far away from the actual problem of education. In 1950–51 it looked as though a new *groupe scolaire* might soon be built, but the old school itself was a fact, the only fact that mattered to the child who went to school and the only fact that concerns us here.

The teachers point to the old school building as evidence that the parents are indifferent to the education of their children. "If they really cared," said Madame Girard, "they'd work together in the *Conseil de Parents d'élèves* and force through this business of a new school. But they won't even come to meetings of the *Conseil.*"

Madame Girard was undoubtedly right in assuming that concerted action on the part of the parents would bring about the construction of a new school, but it was unreasonable of her to expect concerted action and unfair of her to blame the lack of action on the indifference of the parents. The adults of Peyrane do not unite to work together for any cause, as we shall see. They also avoid as the plague any involvement with the Government which they are not forced to accept. To expect them to organize spontaneously for the purpose of forcing the hand of the Government, even for a just and important cause like the erection of a new school building, is unreasonable.

Far from being indifferent to the education of their children, parents have a profound belief in it. This belief goes beyond the practical aspect of the question. It is obvious to them that all children should learn to read and write and do practical problems in arithmetic, that they should learn some history and some science and some geography. Such knowledge is recognized as essential for practical reasons. But quite apart from practical considerations they believe that education is a good thing in itself. "One can never know too much," was an aphorism that many parents used in talking to me about the school.

They are incapable of acting in an organized, official manner to support the school, but in the sphere of action where they feel secure and where their authority is supreme, that is within the family unit itself, they cooperate wholeheartedly with the teachers. In the first place, they see to it that their children attend school regularly. If a child is absent from school there is almost always a good excuse. There are legal sanctions to which the authorities can resort to enforce school attendance. The town can even cut off the government family allowances of a family which disobeys the school law, but it is never necessary to invoke these sanctions. People send their children to school voluntarily because they are eager for their children to be educated.

Naturally, there are exceptions. One of the least responsible inhabitants of the village, a Spanish ochre worker named Mariano, sent his older son off to work in the cherry harvest in another part of the department without securing the temporary work permit that can be obtained for children twelve years old. He told Madame Vernet, the boy's teacher, that he had gone to the city to visit a sick relative, but indirectly she learned the real cause of his absence from class. Even in the case of Mariano, however, it was not necessary to send the *garde-champêtre* (the constable) to remind him that he was disobeying the law. Madame Vernet simply told him that she knew the real reason for his son's absence. Two days later the boy was back in Peyrane, attending school regularly.

Most parents not only insist that their children attend school regularly, but they demand of their children the best possible performance in school. If the teacher tells a family that their child is not doing as well as he might in school, that he is not working hard enough, the child's life at home becomes uncomfortable. He is constantly reminded of his deficiency. He is told that he is disgracing the family. He is deprived of play opportunities and given extra work. Every possible pressure is brought to bear on him so that he may be forced to live up to the teacher's and the parents' expectations. The parents cooperate so wholeheartedly in this matter that the teacher sometimes has to intervene to prevent the child from being overworked at home. One of the problems of the teacher is to moderate the desires of parents who insist that their children be given supplementary lessons. Parents want their children to work hard, and they complain if they think the teacher is not sufficiently demanding.

The parents also cooperate with the teachers in enforcing the rules of social conduct. If a child is punished for misbehavior at school he can expect no sympathy from his parents when he gets home. In fact, he will try to hide from his parents the fact that he has been punished in school, for he knows that if they find out about it they will inflict another punishment on him. They will not even listen to his excuse, for they say there is no excuse for misbehavior. "One does what is expected! That's the way it is!" Only if the child can convince his parents that he has been discriminated against or punished unfairly can he turn their anger against the teacher.

A successful teacher must be very careful in all matters relating to the family. She must be scrupulously impartial in meting out punishments. She must never criticize parents in front of their children or in any other way weaken the parental authority. She must never take part in family arguments or clan feuds. In a general way she must never interfere with or imply criticism of a family as an institution.

The teachers are keenly aware of the importance of these unwritten rules, and far from wounding the pride of the families, they make a constant effort to flatter it. Two months of the school year are almost completely devoted to the preparation of programs in which the children perform as brilliantly as they can before their parents and the assembled community. Most of the month of December is devoted to rehearsing songs and skits for the Christmas party. Every child is given a role in which he may appear to the best advantage. Even Loulou Favre, who has a speech difficulty, is given a part, a silent part in which his difficulty will not be noticed. At the party every child is given a Christmas present chosen for him by the teacher.

From the middle of June until the middle of July the school building is almost deserted. The teachers and the children spend most of their time in the bleak *Salle des Fêtes,* practicing for the program of the Distribution des Prix, the Prize Awarding Ceremony which closes the school year. When the ceremony takes place every child in the school takes part in the program, and every child is awarded a prize for his work during the year. Obviously not every child deserves a prize, but it is important for every child to receive some recognition so that his family will feel that its dignity is respected.

If a teacher in a village school acquires the reputation of being a conscientious person capable of making the children work hard, if the parents think that the children both fear him and love him, if he is mindful of the honor of each family, if he has the tact to avoid becoming embroiled in village quarrels without being considered *fier* (aloof), if he is punctilious in making clear how every franc in the school budget is spent, if he gives gossips no cause to talk, then he will enjoy a favored position in the community. Obviously these conditions are not easily met; it would take a saint to fulfill them.

In spite of these conditions the life of a teacher is appealing. Socially the teacher is second to only the Notaire (the lawyer, broker, banker, and recorder of deeds). Culturally he is the incarnation of knowledge and civilization, which are highly respected in the community. Economically he is respected because he earns more money than any other salaried person in the village. He enjoys the prestige of being a representative of the government. People also respect him because of the security of his position and because of the pension he will receive when he retires. In some villages the teacher is more than a leading citizen; if he has the energy and tact he may become Town Clerk, and the Town Clerk is frequently the real manager of the community, even though the Mayor remains the titular authority.

Economically and socially, then, a career as a village school teacher has an appeal. It is especially attractive to children of farm or lower middle class families who demonstrate unusual intellectual aptitude in school but whose ambition is modest. To qualify as a teacher in the primary school system is not easy, however. Before a candidate gets his permanent certificate he must have the equivalent of the baccalaureate degree; he must have studied in Normal School; he must have had two years' experience as a practice teacher; he must have passed a series of difficult oral and written examinations and practical demonstrations. There are few teaching positions open, and there are many candidates, so the competition is severe. There are no local school boards to exert pressure or to relax standards in behalf of a favored local candidate. The whole system is a part of the Department of National Education, which sees that standards are kept high.

Consequently, the three teachers in the school at Peyrane are professionally competent. Unfortunately they have no interest in the community of Peyrane itself. They were assigned by the Inspecteur d'Académie to their present positions and were forced to accept them because their seniority was insufficient for them to secure the positions they wanted in larger towns. All three have applied for positions elsewhere and will leave Peyrane as soon as more attractive positions open up. As a result, Peyrane is deprived of needed leadership, the kind of leadership teachers give communities in which they are interested.

Madame Girard, the teacher of the youngest children, spends most of her free time in the city of Apt where her little daughter lives with an elderly aunt and uncle. She is an attractive, rather stylish woman about twenty-eight years old. She became a teacher when she divorced her husband only a few months after their marriage in 1945, and she has been teaching in Peyrane ever since she completed her teaching certificate requirements. She has applied for a transfer to the schools in Apt so that she can be with her daughter.

Madame Druetta, who has charge of the intermediate grades, is the youngest of the three teachers and is still teaching on a practice teacher's license. She has been at Peyrane only one year and will not return next year if she can secure an appointment near the city of Pertuis, where her husband is an employee in a bank. She spends Saturday and Sunday nights at home. Monday morning her husband brings her to Peyrane on his motorcycle. Monday and Tuesday nights she sleeps in the lodgings supplied for her by the town of Peyrane. Wednesday evening her husband comes for her again and brings her back early Friday morning. On Saturday afternoon he comes to take her home for the weekend. When he is unable to make the trip she rides her bicycle seven miles to Apt and takes the bus to Pertuis. Madame Druetta obviously has little interest in remaining in Peyrane.

The head of the school and the teacher of the classes of oldest children is Madame Vernet. She is thirty years old, but she looks younger because her physical frailty gives her an air of immaturity. She came to teach in Peyrane during the war, and when she married Philippe Vernet, the son of the *garde-champêtre*, it looked as though she might spend her life in the village. However, Philippe was one of the most attractive, intelligent, and ambitious young men in the village, and he had no intention of spending the rest of his life driving a truck at the ochre mines. For the six years he has been married he has been taking correspondence courses, and with the help of his wife he has become a master mechanic. He hopes eventually to become a teacher in a technical school. Meanwhile Madame Vernet has applied for a transfer to a city school so that Philippe can work in a garage where he can get a better job than driving a truck.

Even though the teachers have little interest in the village as a whole, they are genuinely interested in the school and in the children in their classes. It is obvious that teaching is a true vocation for them. They are devoted to the children of Peyrane as they would be devoted to the children in any school, and they fulfill their duties conscientiously. Their superiors, their pupils, and the parents of the pupils all agree that Madame Girard, Madame Druetta, and Madame Vernet are good teachers.

It does not follow, of course, that they are not criticized by the villagers. No one can live in Peyrane and escape criticism. In spite of the respect in which they are held, the teachers are especially vulnerable to criticism. Their social prestige and privileges arouse resentment among the villagers who say that the teachers "have it easy," that they are well paid but do not have to work hard, that they have a long summer vacation and many shorter holidays throughout the year, that they have to work in the classrooms only thirty hours a week! Of course, those who make these criticisms freely admit that they would be unwilling to trade places with the teachers and spend six hours a day, nine months a year cooped up in the same room with twenty children. People also know that the teachers spend many hours correcting papers and working with pupils outside of class. Nevertheless, the basic resentment against teachers exists and is often expressed.

Probably the best testimony of the community's real approval of the teachers lies in the fact that the sixty-nine children enrolled in the school represent a large proportion of the children of school age of the commune of Peyrane. Thirty-nine of the children live outside of the village, and some of them living on the edge of the commune would find it more convenient to go to other schools located nearer their homes. The Marchal family, for instance, lives only two hundred yards from the school in the hamlet of Les Pins; still the Marchal children go to school in Peyrane despite the four-mile walk in the daily round trip. Madame Marchal told me she disliked imposing this hardship on her children, but the teachers in Peyrane were so much better than the teacher in Les Pins that the sacrifice was worthwhile. The teacher at Les Pins had been given his teacher's license during the war when the scarcity of good teachers forced the Vichy régime to relax standards.

The schoolyard starts to fill up at eight o'clock in the morning. The children who live the farthest away from school arrive first. Villagers sleep later than country people. The village children drift down to school only a few minutes before the eight-thirty deadline. Even five or ten minutes after school has started one may hear a door bang up the street, then the thumping of a child's heavy boots as Yves Biron or Colette Favre runs down the street, late as usual but hoping to avoid in some way the usual scolding.

At eight-thirty Madame Vernet blows her whistle, and lines form in front of the three entries to the classrooms. There is some jostling in the ranks of the four-, five-, and six-year-olds among those who want to be first in line, but Madame Girard with a sharp word and clap of her hands stops the confusion at once. The children seven to nine years old in front of Madame Druetta's door, and those ten to fourteen in front of Madame Vernet's door stand in a dignified manner and look at the scuffling younger children with an air of amusement and superiority. When order has been completely established the teachers open the doors and the children file in, hang their wraps on the proper pegs, sit down at their desks and start arranging materials from their brief cases.

The school day begins with a fifteen-minute *leçon de morale*. The teacher reads a short story or tells an incident from which she draws a moral lesson which may be summed up in a sentence, repeated in chorus and learned by heart by the children. Officially, the purpose of the *leçon de morale* is to teach the children to practice "the principal individual and social virtues (temperance, sincerity, modesty, kindness, courage, tolerance), to inspire in them the love for work, the taste for cooperation, the spirit of teamwork, the respect for one's word of honor, the understanding of other people, the love of one's native soil, the obligations toward one's family and toward France" (Le Livre des Instituteurs, 1948:161).

Most of the teacher's moral tales are taken from ready-made texts like Souché's *New Moral Lessons* or *On the Straight Road* by Leterrier and Bonnet, and when she can she tries to relate them directly to the life of the children. This is an easy matter if, for instance, it concerns family obligations. It is harder if the moral lessons concern cooperation and teamwork, which are not characteristic virtues of the people of Peyrane. A few lessons are so completely in conflict with the customs of Peyrane that it seems futile to teach them.

One morning Mrs. Wylie was at school when Madame Girard was giving a moral lesson designed to increase the children's love and respect for Nature. The anecdote, from Souché's *New Moral Lessons*, concerned "Two Poor Little Birds," and the sentence which the children repeated and learned by heart was, "Let us be the friends and protectors of the little birds." In a region where a favorite dish is roasted little birds, where a husky man boasts of consuming fifty or sixty warblers at a sitting, there is little likelihood that this lesson will have much effect.

When the *leçon de morale* is finished, work is begun in earnest on the subjects in the curriculum. At ten o'clock the children file out to the school yard for a recess of fifteen minutes. Sometimes, especially at the beginning of the year, the teachers organize singing games for the girls and younger children, but usually the children are left to their own devices. They may run and yell and play at will so long as they do not attack each other physically, get wet or dirty or expose themselves to danger. The children break up into groups spontaneously, the younger children playing with friends of either sex and the older children playing only with friends of their own sex. The boys play tag or may organize a game of soccer if one of them has brought a ball to school. There is no play equipment of any kind in the school yard except for a climbing rope which children must learn to climb in order to get their *brevet sportif scolaire* (athletic certificate). The older girls sit in a sunny corner of the yard gossiping and petting one or two of the youngest children who turn instinctively to them when they need affection. The younger boys and girls run about madly in groups of two or three or four, often chasing and verbally tormenting a current scapegoat. The three teachers stroll about the yard, chatting and vaguely keeping an eye on the whole situation. Play is stopped only in case a child gets hurt or is punished. Then all the children crowd about the victim. If the child is hurt, faces of the other children are filled with sympathy, and there are murmurs that "he shouldn't have been doing that; he was sure to get hurt." If he is being punished, there is a mocking expression on their faces. Usually, of course, the play continues uneventfully until Madame Vernet blows her whistle and the children line up to march back into the school.

At a few minutes past eleven-thirty Madame Vernet sends a child out in the school yard to look at the town clock. When he runs back to report that the time is up, there is a scuffle to put away books. The two older classes are excused, and the children leave the classroom at will. The little ones in Madame Girard's class must line up outside the classroom and wait until all are ready to leave. They line up by twos, with boys and girls paired up and holding hands. When all is ready they march to the break in the wall between the school yard and the street where they stand poised for a moment. Madame Girard has them wait until they are all calm and until she makes sure no cars are coming down the street. Then she calls: "Avancez!" The children answer in one voice, "'voir, Madame," and they start down the street, running and yelling, temporarily freed from the restrictive weight of discipline.

Most of the village children hurry straight home, for they have errands to do before lunch. Jacques Leporatti must carry a bucket and a pitcher of water home from the public fountain, for there is no running water in the Leporatti house. Georges Vincent has to bring bread from the bakery for his father's restaurant. Tatave Pouget has to run to the store to get a bottle of wine. Colette Favre has to take care of her little brother while her mother is finishing preparations for lunch, and when lunch is ready she has to go call her father at the café.

Back at school, lunch is being served to the children who live too far away from school to return home and to a few village children whose mothers are working and cannot prepare a proper lunch for them. Now and then children who could return home persuade their parents to let them eat at the cantine, for the children all enjoy eating there. They like eating together, and they say that the food which old Madame Bardin prepares is very good. It consists of three courses — two substantial dishes (stew, thick soup, spaghetti, or something of the kind) and dessert (usually jam or stewed fruit). Each child brings his own big piece of bread to school with him. This meal costs twenty-five francs, about eight cents.

Discipline at the cantine is strict. The children must sit up straight, keep their wrists on the edge of the table, and finish everything on their plates. There is a double purpose in requiring the children to clean up their plates. It teaches them not to waste food, and it also reduces the number of dishes which have to be washed. At the cantine as in most homes, when the main course is finished and each child's dish is wiped clean with a piece of bread, the dish is turned over so that dessert may be served on the back of it. The spoon is also inverted so that jam may be eaten from the handle.

During the meal absolute silence is maintained. A child may speak only if he receives permission from the teacher in charge. The teachers justify this rule of silence by saying that the acoustics in the cantine are such that the place would be a bedlam if the children were allowed to talk. They also say that lunch would last forever if the children were allowed to distract each other. As it is, lunch is so disciplined that it lasts no longer than fifteen or twenty minutes. Then the children are turned loose on the playground and play as they do during recess until class begins at one o'clock.

The afternoon session differs little from the morning session. It lasts three hours with a recess of fifteen minutes in the middle of the period. The children are dismissed at four o'clock in the same way as at eleven-thirty, with this difference, that at the end of the morning all the children leave the school. At four o'clock, five or six children are required to remain in their seats for any time from a few minutes to an hour in order to make up work that they have done improperly or as a punishment for misbehavior.

By five o'clock the school is cleared, and the cleaning woman comes to scrub and sweep. After she leaves, the school is ready for the next day, and the shutters and doors are locked until morning.

When the village children leave school they run directly home for their *goûter*, or midafternoon snack. Since supper will not be served for three or four hours the *goûter* is important, and if a child does not return home directly after school his mother will send someone out to look for him. Some children sit down at the table for a fairly substantial meal, but most of them are impatient to get outdoors. They are given their large hunk of bread and a piece of chocolate or cheese and go out in the street to eat it in the company of other children.

After the *goûter* the younger children may play, but the older ones have work to do. Water must be carried from the public fountain. Armloads of wood must be carried from the basement room down the street where wood is stored. Trips must be made to the edge of the village to gather fresh grass for the chickens and rabbits or to pick mulberry leaves for the silkworms. When these chores are finished there is homework to be done. Finally at six or six-thirty the older children may go out in the streets to play, but even then the older girls have the responsibility of keeping an eye on their little sisters and brothers.

When the country children leave school they start their long walk toward home. Some of them live as far as two miles from the village. In winter when it gets dark early and the mistral is blowing, this walk is accomplished as fast as possible. In nice weather, however, groups of five or six children dawdle all the way home. This is the only time of the day when they are free from adult surveillance. They learn how to get along with other children without the pressure of adult authority but with the severe social pressure that can be exercised by other children of their group.

The groups grow smaller and smaller as children reach home and drop out. In the last few hundred meters there is usually a sudden rush to get home, for the children remember that they will be scolded if they have lingered too long. They may be late for the *goûter,* which is always a more formal, more substantial meal in the country than in the village. The men come in from the fields and the whole family sits down to a heavy snack of bread, cheese, sausage, jam, and wine.

After the *goûter,* all but the smallest children have their chores, more numerous and more important than the chores of the village children. They have the problem of carrying wood and water and getting grass for the rabbits and chickens, and when this work is finished they have to help work in the field or in the garden. They have to take their turn watching the sheep or goats, bringing them into the fold when it starts to get dark, and milking the ewes and nannies that are fresh. If there is time to spare between chores and supper it must be devoted to schoolwork. There is no time for homework after supper, for supper is not served until the men have stopped working, usually well after dark. By the time supper is finished it is time to go to bed. The next morning they must get up early to get to school on time, and in the cold early morning one has neither time nor inclination to dawdle or play. The walk home from school in the afternoon gives the country children their only playtime.

The four-year-old child who has just started to school soon falls into this routine. He has no homework. He has no chores. The routine is hard, however, and he must accept without complaining. He knows that complaining would not relieve him of the pressure, for no one would listen to him. He has already learned that there are unpleasant aspects of life that must be faced. He is told that he is old enough to face the school routine, and he does so stoically. He is partially rewarded by his feeling of pride in being considered old enough, reasonable enough to accept the inevitable with resignation.

For ten years, until the child is fourteen, the school routine is the most important part of his life. His parents, his teachers, his friends constantly remind him of its importance. Confronted by this unbroken social pressure, he accepts the school routine as a serious responsibility to which he must measure up.

The educational program of the school of Peyrane is the same as that of every other public primary school in France. It is formulated by the Department of National Education which sends out precise and detailed instructions concerning educational goals, subjects to be taught, methods to be followed, distribution of class time, and all other aspects of the functioning of the school. As one reads page after page of these instructions, one gets the impression that the officials of the Department of National Education do not recognize the special needs of different communities and leave nothing to the imagination of the teachers. Even the games to be played in the nursery school are "determined by the decree of July 15, 1921."

In practice, of course, the program is far from being as rigid and impersonal as it seems. The teachers know that these official instructions are intended as a guide and should not be taken too literally. After all, the teachers are French and consequently recognize the gap that usually separates laws and regulations on the one hand from actual practice on the other. They know that they need not follow the daily program blindly so long as over a period of time they observe the relative proportions for the important subjects indicated in the program. They know that for everyone in Peyrane it is more important for a child to be able to read well than to take part effectively in choral singing. If they take the time allocated for singing and devote it to drill in reading no one will object.

Monsieur Valentini, the Primary Inspector from Avignon, who supervises the primary schools of the district, shares this flexible, reasonable attitude. The teachers speak as though they were in constant fear of his annual inspection visit and of the unexpected visits he pays now and then, but confidentially they admit that this anxiety is superficial, for Monsieur Valentini is a genial, tolerant person who expects teachers to carry out the spirit of the official program as best they can in their own specific, local situation. He calls the teachers of the district together for a meeting once or twice a year to discuss with them the program and their problems and to go over the new regulations sent out by the Department of Education. At one of the meetings I attended he explained at length a new ruling which some of the teachers had not understood. He concluded his remarks by saying, "That's what the regulation says, and I hope you all understand it now. Unofficially, of course, I might add that no one is going to object if you follow your own judgement in this matter."

Although the official curriculum prescribed by the Department of National Education is long and complicated (*Le Livre des Instituteurs,* 1948:150 ff), it may be described in simple terms as it is put in practice in the school in Peyrane. The children of the school are divided into five classes: *Classes enfantines* (Nursery Group) with children from four to six, *Section préparatoire* (Preparatory Section) with children from six to seven, *Cours élémentaire* (Elementary Course) with children from seven to nine, *Cours moyen* (Intermediate Course) with children from nine to eleven, and the *Classe de Fin d'Etudes* (Concluding Course) with children from twelve to fourteen. Of course, the age division is by no means rigorous. A bright five-year-old may be placed with the six-year-old group, and a dull twelve-year-old may be kept with the seven-year-old group. Paul Jouvaud, who is mentally defective, remained in the room with the smallest children until he was thirteen years old and the biggest, strongest child in school. He was "graduated" from the Nursery Group and dropped from school, according to Madame Girard, when the stirrings of puberty made him too difficult for her to handle.

Madame Girard has charge of both the Nursery Group and the Preparatory Section. We have already seen how the Nursery Group spends its time. The Preparatory Section, to which Madame Girard devotes the major portion of her energy, concentrates on learning to read, write, and do simple problems in arithmetic. In an average six-hour school day about two hours are devoted to reading, a half-hour to writing, a half-hour to grammar, and an hour to arithmetic. The use of the remaining two hours depends on the mood of the teacher and of the children and on a variety of other human factors. Usually the time is split up into brief periods which are given over to singing, drawing, paper and scissor work, the *leçon morale,* short talks on such subjects as divisions of the year, points of the compass, parts of the body, hygiene, and so on. Recess, of course, takes up a half-hour.

There is no radical difference between this program and that of the children in the Elementary Course, which is Madame Druetta's sole concern. The same time is spent on reading and writing, but the emphasis is slightly shifted. Less time is devoted to reading and more to the formal study of grammar. Two new subjects are introduced, but in moderate amounts: history and geography take up about fifteen minutes of the school day.

In Madame Vernet's room are both the Intermediate Course and the Concluding Course, and it takes a teacher as skillful as Madame Vernet to handle these two quite different sections in the same schoolroom. The Intermediate Course is a continuation of the Elementary Course, and one sees in its program the same tendencies. Half the school time is still devoted to reading and writing, but the emphasis is shifted somewhat further: the study of formal grammar replaces reading as the primary concern of the class. No new subjects are introduced at this level, but the time devoted to arithmetic, geography, and history is doubled. Together these three subjects take up a third of the class time. Arithmetic alone takes up an hour a day. We noted that in the Preparatory Section, Madame Girard now and then gave brief talks on practical subjects such as divisions of time. By the time the children have reached the Intermediate Section these talks have become a formal subject to which a half-hour a day is devoted and which is called *leçons de choses*. This might be translated "lessons in things" or "exercises in observation," but it may be best understood as a kind of practical approach to the study of science.

The program of the Concluding Course is rather different from the programs of the other Courses. The study of French is still the primary consideration of the class, but the time devoted to it is reduced to an hour or so a day, the same time that is now given over to the study of arithmetic and science. History and geography take up about a half-hour, and what used to be called the *leçon morale* has now become civics, which the class studies for a half-hour daily. This makes for a more balanced program than that of the other courses, but of course the balance may not be evident from day to day. If the class is especially weak in one subject, most of the time may be spent on drill in that subject until the students perform adequately. This is especially true with the study of French, which is recognized by everyone as the most important subject taught in the school. Any other subject may be slighted or sacrificed in order to increase the time for drill in reading (silent or aloud) and writing (penmanship, spelling, grammar, composition).

The program is frequently interrupted. The visit of the Inspector or some other official, the illness of a teacher, preparations for the Primary Certificate Examination, a teachers' meeting which the teachers must attend in Apt, a visit to the ochre mine, the annual excursion to Marseille, and many other events frequently interrupt the routine. And then there is always the preparation for the two public performances — the Christmas Party and the Prize Awarding Ceremony — to which a substantial part of two months of the school year is devoted, as we have seen.

In spite of these interruptions and in spite of the rigidity, more illusory than real, of the official curriculum, when a child leaves school at the age of fourteen he has learned approximately what his parents expected him to learn in school. He can read with ease. He can write without making too many grammatical errors. He can solve most of the practical problems in arithmetic with which he is confronted in daily life. He knows enough of history, government, geography, and science to make him aware of his relationship to his environment; he is aware of the moral and ethical values professed by society.

To an observer who studies school life in Peyrane over a period of time it is apparent that the children learn much that is not explicitly stated in the curriculum. From the attitude of the teachers, from the way in which the school work is presented, from the textbooks, the children learn to make basic assumptions concerning the nature of reality and their relationship to it. These assumptions are not mentioned in the directives of the Department of Education. They are not prescribed by the Primary Inspector. If the teachers are conscious of them they never discuss them directly in class. Yet these assumptions are so important that they will determine to a large extent the frame of mind and the manner in which a child will approach the problems with which he is confronted throughout his life.

In teaching morals, grammar, arithmetic, and science the teacher always follows the same method. She first introduces a principle or rule that each pupil is supposed to memorize so thoroughly that it can be repeated on any occasion without the slightest faltering. Then a concrete illustration or problem is presented and studied or solved in the light of the principle. More problems or examples are given until the children can recognize the abstract principle implicit in the concrete circumstances and the set of circumstances implicit in the principle. When this relationship is sufficiently established in the minds of the children, the teacher moves on to another principle and set of related facts.

The principle itself is not questioned and is hardly discussed. Children are not encouraged to formulate principles independently on the basis of an examination of concrete cases. They are given the impression that principles exist autonomously. They are always there: immutable and constant. One can only learn to recognize them, and accept them. The same is true of concrete facts and circumstances. They exist, real and inalterable. Nothing can be done to change them. One has only to recognize them and accept them. The solution of any problem lies in one's ability to recognize abstract principles and concrete facts and to establish the relationship between them.

Another basic assumption is most clearly seen in the way history, civics, geography, and literature are studied, but it is important in all subjects. In learning history the children are first presented with a general framework which they are asked to memorize. Studying history consists partially in filling in this framework, that is, in learning how the facts of history fit into the framework. An isolated fact is unimportant in itself. It assumes importance only when one recognizes its relationship to other facts and above all its relationship to the whole framework. In learning geography a child first studies his own countryside, then the surrounding region, then France, then the world. Heavy stress is placed on the relationship of each geographical unit to a larger whole. In the study of morals and civics the children learn the proper relationship and reciprocal obligations of the individual to the family, to the community, to France, and to humanity.

This emphasis on the relationship of the part to the whole is also seen in the rather rudimentary study of literature that is carried out in the higher grades. No attempt is made to understand or to appreciate the text which is presented to the class until it has been thoroughly dissected and analyzed. It is broken down into its logical divisions, and the author's purpose in each division is explained. Difficult or obscure words and expressions are explained. Only when each of the component parts of a passage is understood and when the relationship of each part to the whole is made clear is the passage put back together and appraised as a unit.

Thus a child comes to believe that every fact, every phenomenon, every individual is an integral part of a larger unit. As in a jigsaw puzzle each part has its own clearly defined and proper position. They make sense only if their proper relationship is recognized.

Finally, it is assumed that knowledge is important only as it is related to human beings. There is no stress on learning simply for the sake of learning, no stress on the accumulation of facts without regard for their usefulness. This is most evident in the study of arithmetic and geometry. The principles studied and the problems solved are chosen exclusively on the basis of their usefulness in teaching the students to solve the problems which they will be confronted with after they leave school.

The purpose of the rudimentary instruction they receive in science is equally related to the children as human beings. No effort is made to have the children collect butterflies, learn to recognize different kinds of birds, study rocks simply for the purpose of being able to classify them. A bird offers no interest in itself. It is interesting because it is good to eat, or because it is harmful to the crops or eats harmful insects, or because it has beautiful plumage or a beautiful song. In the same way the study of geography does not consist in memorizing the capitals of all the departments of France; its purpose is rather to show the relationship of the people of Peyrane to their surroundings.

The learning of grammatical rules is so emphasized that at times it appears that the rules are considered important in themselves. This impression is false, however. The rules are considered important because it is believed that a person cannot express himself properly unless he knows them thoroughly. It is difficult for an Anglo-Saxon to comprehend how essential this language study is to the French. The French judge a person to a far greater degree than we do on the basis of his ability to speak and write correctly. Even in a rural community like Peyrane the way a person speaks and writes is considered an important indication of his social status. The study of grammar is thus strongly emphasized in school, not because of its intrinsic value but because it will be important to the children throughout their life.

The history course shows the same orientation. The framework of dates and facts must be memorized, it is true, but is important because it lends perspective to the two aspects of historical study which are emphasized in the course: the life of the French people at different periods of history and the study of the lives of great men.

In 1938, Monsieur Jean Zay, then Minister of Education, sent out a circular which Madame Vernet and Madame Girard told me they consider the most authoritative statement of purpose and method in primary education. Concerning the study of history the statement says:

> In teaching history the teachers should emphasize the role played by those men who have helped bring about progress. Today we no longer believe that history can provide a means to foretell the future; we no longer believe that the study of history can provide us with solutions for present-day problems. It does teach us, however, to meet events in their unfolding with a more impassive attitude, and that is a valuable contribution. It teaches us the value of honest labor, the value of great example, the comfort to be derived from healthy admiration. Children should be told of the effective role played by those men and women whom we consider the benefactors of humanity. If they retain only a genuine feeling for such people we shall have accomplished much. For they will have learned that this material progress of which we are so proud was accomplished at the cost of great effort, that it is the ever-threatened result of an immense collaboration, that in enjoying it we are responsible to the great men who created it.[1]

Not dates or facts alone then, but human beings in relationship to dates and facts, should constitute the study of history.

So in their study of arithmetic, science, geography, grammar, and history, children learn that man is the measure of all things. Facts are important and must be recognized, accepted and learned, but they are important only as they may be related to human beings, and especially to the human beings living in the commune of Peyrane.

The most successful child in the school of Peyrane is the child who goes beyond the subject matter to grasp these basic assumptions. Without consciously realizing that he does so, he learns to recognize the relationship between abstract principle and concrete fact, the relationship between the part and the whole, and the relationship of knowledge and experience to himself as a human being.

Even the average child, who certainly has only a partial grasp of these relationships, is sufficiently imbued with their importance that they will help determine the manner in which he seeks a solution to any problem — in human relations, in politics, in mechanics. He will approach the problem as he was taught to approach all problems in school. In every problem he knows there is a principle involved, and it is important for him to recognize the principle. In every problem lurk practical, concrete difficulties which make the application of the principle difficult. There is no isolated problem; every problem is related to a larger problem. The only problems worth worrying about are those which affect people. To approach problems with these assumptions is to approach them sensibly, reasonably, logically, and therefore, it is assumed, correctly.

Of course, these assumptions are not new to the schoolchild, for they are also implicit in most of the home training he has received.

### NOTES

1. Jean Zay, "Enseignement du Premier Degré. Instructions relatives à l'application des arrêtés du 23 mars 1938 et du 11 juillet 1938," *Journal officiel, Annexe,* 24 septembre 1938.

# 13 ..................

# The Teachers

## LEILA BERG

*Both boys and girls will be faced with evolving a new concept of a partnership in their personal relations.*

Risinghill, like every school, has a Punishment Book. Risinghill's has one entry only:

| Date | Name of child | Age | Form | Offence | Details of Punishment | Signature of master or mistress who inflicted the punishment | Initials of headmaster or mistress |
|---|---|---|---|---|---|---|---|
| 18.5.60 | John Roderick | 13 | D2 | Theft | 2 on seat | Andrew Thorpe | M.D. |

This incident took place within a short time of the school opening, and was discussed at a staff meeting. Johnny Roderick came from Gifford School; the school faces Pentonville Prison, and while Johnny was in

Reprinted from Leila Berg, *Risinghill: Death of a Comprehensive School* (1968), by permission of the publisher, Penguin Books, Ltd., London.

school, his father was frequently opposite — in prison for theft. He was there, in fact, when Mr. Thorpe caned Johnny for theft.

The staff meeting decided it was wrong to cane a boy who was imitating his father; and that not only was corporal punishment wrong in this specific case — it was unnecessary, always. Mr. Duane was not present at this meeting, and he knew nothing about it; but when the decision was passed to him, he was pleased. The next day, he announced to the assembled children that there would be no more caning.

Educated people today tend to see words as a shield against action. Many of the teachers had probably never thought of translating what they said into fact; they had merely been entertaining themselves with indulgent philosophy. When Michael Duane made his announcement, these teachers were angry, because they were frightened and because their ordeal had been decreed by themselves. They said nothing at the time, but much later they said "We didn't mean you to tell the children," and Michael Duane said, simply, "But you are not doing away with corporal punishment unless you tell the children."

The children were incredulous. To them the point of being big was that you could hit littler ones; adults at home and at school had always taught them that; it was the whole basis for growing up.

Michael Duane himself had no illusions about what would happen. He did not imagine that these children would instantly become grateful and angelic. If he had ever thought so in theory, he had all the experience of Howe Dell to teach him otherwise. But he believed that if we were to set human beings free we would have to put up for a while with all the scars of their slavery.

But not only the children, the adults too had to cope with freedom. How many of them could stand it? Most of the teachers had gone from school straight into training college, from training college straight back into school. Nothing in the imposed pattern of life had ever changed for them; they had only taken a step up the authoritarian ladder, so that when decisions were handed down they would not now be the lowest rank to receive them.

When Risinghill opened, a third of the staff vacancies were still not filled; this third had to be filled up with constantly changing supply teachers, and this situation continued pretty well throughout the life of the school. Getting a good staff was the central problem, and remained the central problem. Cyril Ray, the writer, who was one of the governors and took a very affectionate interest in the school, told me, "We had to accept people we knew were second-raters on to the staff — second-raters academically as well as personally," and, on another occasion, Mr. Duane said, "All our problems of discipline and organization stemmed from this. They did not know how to deal with children who are uninhibited and therefore a threat to the authoritarian standard . . . and they were not trained for a big school where the head is not present as a perpetual father figure and continually within reach to sort everything out for them."

When I went to the school, it was very evident that many of the teachers resented very much that he was a father figure to the children but not to them. Such a remark may come as a shock to people who do not accept that teachers are as neurotic as the rest of us today. On that occasion the staff of Risinghill seemed to me to divide into three; and I suspect they always did.

Some were very good, generous and imaginative. But they were in the minority, and were being fought by other staff as well as by the environment (though the environment was not the deliberate enemy that some of the staff were, but rather a material that they had to learn to work creatively with). Because of this, and because they were creative people, they were frequently exhausted. They brought to the school their own individual ideas, and their own appreciation of, and pleasure in, the children. They were mature human beings. They would have been an asset anywhere. At Risinghill they were gold, because they gave equal friendship to children who had known very little of it and only knew adults as enemies. They could walk alongside the children; they knew, as so many teachers do not know, that children do not have to be battered and badgered and hectored and moulded, but that they simply have to be helped to grow by people who have faith and delight in their growing. I have called them child-centered teachers.

Some teachers did not want freedom at all. Some of these were old and some were not; but they had long ago surrendered their personality, the wishes and beliefs of their own personal life. If anyone were to question the validity of this sacrifice they could not have borne it, for it would have meant their whole life had been wasted; and who can bear to think of the waste of what will never come again? So they could not stand seeing children saying and doing things that they were never allowed to say or do, or watch them beginning to frame possibilities that for them were crushed in childhood, and not always (eventually) by other people; and there was not only resentment and jealousy in this, but a hopeless sense of waste which they could never face. So they told themselves that children should be quiet, that they should be so afraid of you that you should be able to hear a pin drop when you crossed the playground, that children were naturally bad and needed the badness beaten out of them, that individuality must be crushed down by will-power, and that there was satisfaction in this, and that God would reward people who kept their desks tidy, their lines straight, and never splashed outside the lavatory bowl. Such teachers do not make schools into joyous places bubbling over with vitality, and do not intend to; and in fact if you hint at such possibilities they will say contemptuously, "Well, of course, if you think that a school is a place where you *enjoy* yourself . . . !"

Everything and everyone had its one proper place for people like this. They said things like "I've never taken work home before and I'm not going to start now." They were astounded at the mild suggestion that they might be friendly with the children's parents.

In fact, informality altogether was to them a very suspect quality indeed. So you would later get Inspector Macgowan condemning Mr. Duane's familiarity to the children, and his familiarity to his staff. So you would get Mr. Carr accusing Mr. Blaize of "immoral purposes" because he was taking some boys on a camping weekend. Such teachers had never seen their pupils as fellow human beings before, as Martin Buber's "I" and "Thou," and the very suggestion of it unnerved them as much as if they were Southern whites and the children were Negroes; and in the same way many of them translated it sexually.

They were used to a system where you were *told* by the person above you, and then you *told* the person below you. (A teacher told me that he went to a weekend conference where teachers, Institute of Education lecturers, and training college lecturers led discussions; but that the training college lecturers took it as a personal insult when students in the body of the hall questioned what they had said, so that discussion was impossible.)

Such teachers went their own way. Since Michael Duane had, in their sort of language, "demoted" himself by being friendly to them, and friendly to the children, and friendly to the parents, they ignored him. At least one of them (several of them, according to the children) went on caning; and at least one of them "shut the classroom door firmly" every day on all that rubbish. (Mr. Carr used to say to his class, "Don't worry, I'll cane you before Mr. Duane gets to you.") But though they tried to ignore him, the fact that their new head did not approve of the outlook that had hitherto brought them full marks, was emotionally exhausting. I have called them the traditionalists, disciplinarians, authoritarians.

But a third section had first been bewildered, and then, under the influence of Michael Duane's personality, decided of their own accord to try to do what *he* wanted — to help him to accomplish *his* aim. These teachers took Michael Duane's warm spontaneity personally, so that they felt their work was a symbol of a special relationship between them; and when he merely took their work with a quick "Thanks," or "Right you are," they felt rejected. Simply because he did so much, they assumed he meant them to lean on him; and when he showed that on the contrary he expected them to stand on their own feet and make their own de-

cisions, again they felt humiliated. So then they began to say things like
"He takes us for granted," and "He cares more for the children than for
us," and — astoundingly — "We have the right to be led" (each of which
statements has been made to me, the first two by several teachers).

In their immaturity and their sudden freedom from the chains — and
the certainties — of authoritarianism, these teachers found it very difficult
to accept that he expected more strength from them than from the children. They were in a continual state of conflict. You would find such a
teacher flaring off in an appalling outburst against coloured children, and,
reprimanded for hitting a coloured child, saying, "Well it doesn't hurt
them like it does white children!" . . . and then taking some children
away on a trip entirely in his own time and at his own suggestion. Children would tell you of another, "He has no control over his class. They
just walk out of his class and he spends all his time trying to find them.
We just laugh at him" — and you would find that sometimes this man
would speak with sentimental philosophy of the needs of the children,
that at other times he would attack the children in front of the press. . . .
You would find another treating the children with contempt, cutting
destructively through their intimate, troubled conversations — then in-
viting a group of them home to tea. Such teachers thought of themselves
as quite different people from the people they really were. They would
describe their philosophic ideas glowingly, so that when you saw what
they really did you were shocked; yet occasionally they actually *did* what
they thought they were doing all the time, like a clumsy child who for a
second manages to fit his tracing over the first colourful picture; these
moments must have been very satisfying for them, for the children loved
them at such times and, generously, forgave and understood a great deal.

But they would do destructive things and constructive things quite
unpredictably. And since their conduct was based on the unconscious
treasuring of Michael Duane as an adult's father figure, and since he
refused, with some amusement, to be an adult's father figure, they too
were exhausted, filled from day to day with frustrations, resentments,
and anxieties, which they took out on the other teachers, on the children,
and at critical times on Michael Duane. Personally, in the particular
context of Risinghill, this group alarmed me. For such people, being
anxious, often lean a great deal on authority, and can therefore be easily
made use of and manipulated by an authority which despises them. Such
people can do a great deal of damage without ever intending to, or even
being aware that they are doing it; and when it is done they are appalled.

One of the Risinghill staff said later to me:

In such a building, and with such a background, the children would
only behave well if they *supported* the staff; the staff who believed they

could rely on force were relying on a fallacy. But it was so difficult for Michael Duane to convince them, because this was so new; there was no research to support him.

And also, at the beginning of Risinghill, the staff knew nothing of the difficulties other comprehensive schools had had. After the Kidbrooke affair, the L.C.C. invited reporters to go into selected comprehensive schools; and it was only then that one heard of difficulties that had had to be met elsewhere in the first year, and knew that Risinghill was not unique. We should have had this explained beforehand, by the inspectors — or else, as they knew this, the inspectors shouldn't have given us such a bad start.

I knew they were children who would not normally be interested in reading. But I had the idea, as so many do, that if you are simply pleasant, the children will instantly respond. But in that first year, the children didn't; they were very hostile to anyone in authority. And teachers from grammar schools — and people like me — were very hurt that their desire to help should be rebuffed in this way. We didn't realize then that their previous schools had been broken up in the same way; now we know ourselves how they must have felt twice over. I suppose the hostility extends to their homes as well as their schools. It seems to me fantastic that the authorities should not have realized the resentments and difficulties when they first uprooted these four schools and put them together.

The teachers felt inadequate, and looked for someone to cope with their problems for them, and when this wasn't done looked for a scapegoat. Some of the *most experienced* teachers told me they expected things to be sorted out for them. I even sometimes felt this myself though I didn't say so.

I don't think we were able, most of us, to identify with the children's future, and to know what their adult life was going to be like. We were terribly in the dark. We had to keep going back in our minds and trying to think what life should be like, and how different the life we were thinking of was from the life the children were thinking of.

The teachers who wanted only to teach specific subjects were very hurt because what they felt they had to give semed often so inappropriate. What the children needed one often did not know. What one had to give did not fit — it was often what one had wanted oneself, but one's life had been so very different from these children's.

Why should teachers expect every child immediately to respond to them and be attentive? When the child doesn't, the teacher becomes so hostile that caning follows.

Some teachers knew they couldn't play the "family" part demanded of them. Others tried, and went to the extreme and became too emotionally involved. It would have been much easier with children from good homes. But do we then intend to give good education only to children from good homes?

In fact, the children from good homes responded well, and became very cooperative, and wonderfully tolerant of the difficult children — it amazed me. I felt that many children had *benefited* by the responsibility they had taken for other children. Ben Andrews, for instance — during his holidays he worked with a playgroup, and was appointed over the heads of grammar school children because his attitude to younger children was so good. An inspector coming to a school wouldn't see this, and wouldn't talk to the children; I think he might think it unethical.

I think perhaps Mr. Duane felt his duty was more to his pupils than to his staff. Sometimes a teacher became upset, and wanted to be put first; then the teacher didn't want impartial fairness, but comfort. I know this is irrational, but in a place with such emotional pressure it tended to happen.

It would be unreasonable to expect teachers to be less neurotic, less unstable, less psychotic than the rest of the population of London today, and I do not do so. We are all suffering from the strain of contemporary society. But it may possibly be that teaching attracts more than its fair share or having attracted just a fair share gives power and approval to their neuroses. . . . And besides one needs to be well balanced to keep one's optimism in an area like Islington (though one must remember that areas like Islington are where most of London's citizens live).

Yet if we looked for teachers among those who loved their fellow men as well as pensions, and among those who were adventurous as well as afraid, the quality would improve. But we would then have to face the fact that unneurotic teachers might want to carry out unneurotic education, and that would make a deep upheaval.

I asked several of the child-centered teachers what proportion of the staff they thought any use at Risinghill. Estimates varied from a generous "less than fifty percent," through "twenty percent," down to "six out of seventy."

Apart from keeping his day as clear of paperwork as possible, so that he always had time to discuss difficulties and successes with his teachers, Mr. Duane organized very frequent staff discussion meetings — two a week to start with — so that everyone would be free to come at some time. At first sixty teachers used to turn up to each discussion. One teacher said she went over to the lavatories and found some girls there smoking, and when she told them off they said . . . something . . . well, she couldn't repeat it. "But what was it?" he asked. She said, "No, I couldn't possibly tell you." He sensed it was really something *she* wanted to say through their mouth, and he said, "Was it something about me? If it was, say it — I'm used to hearing rude comments." So she said, "They said 'That silly old bugger won't mind!'" He laughed; he was genuinely pleased because he was getting some truth, and because the teacher had found a way to release some hostility undangerously.

But one of the senior members of staff became very distressed and anxious, and would not stay at meetings where junior members of the staff were permitted to say whatever they liked, and this teacher gave very emotional reports on such meetings to County Hall, who didn't like it either.

County Hall did not have to worry. The discussions were broken up by the teachers themselves. A group of men teachers from one of the four original schools pushed corporal punishment as the solution to every problem, at every meeting; and after weeks of this incessant drumming, the rest of the staff was bored and angry, and refused to come any more. The discussions had been broken up by imposed force, of which corporal punishment is, after all, merely another facet. From then on, the only discussions that could ever be held were casual, spontaneous ones in the head's study, and in these, naturally, only already sympathetic teachers were participating: the others were so embarrassed and disturbed by informality in surroundings that they felt should be august (people actually drank wine as they talked!) that they kept as far away as possible.

Later, I was very puzzled to hear his staff complain Mr. Duane did not give them leadership. I had never come across a school where the head initiated, or tried to initiate, both spontaneously and with specially duplicated papers (of a standard incidentally so thoughtful that I fancy this too rather narked some important people), so much discussion about policy and methods. Afterwards I realized that many of the staff did not want discussion — they wanted to be "told"; and secondly that they wanted to be led in a completely different direction from the way Mr. Duane was going. This is what "no power of leadership" meant, a phrase which later on the L.C.C., pulling determinedly in the opposite way to him, was to use too.

Furthermore, Mr. Duane himself, like all or almost all the adults around him, had also been brought up by authoritarians. But unlike most of them he had not succumbed, and had preserved his honesty. He was resolved that no child should experience the humiliations, the violence, the undermining of integrity that he had experienced, but should instead be allowed and encouraged to grow from his own inner source. All this made him a person of tremendous value to growing children, and to education in practice. But from his own fight with authoritarianism, he still retained, at this stage, a weakness. He was overconcerned that all adults should understand what he was doing and concede that it was good. And this made him try over and over again to win over those teachers who were against him, rather than face up to the fact that they were incompatible, and he must make them go. It was this quality that was to vaguely irritate Inspector Macgowan, so that he complained in his 1962 report that Mr. Duane "esteems cordiality among the major virtues." But the inspector thought that if Mr. Duane could demolish this "cordiality" in himself he would treat the children differently; in fact, he would have treated the staff differently, those who opposed his creative approach, and *just possibly* this might have saved Risinghill.

This was a wild time. The children found it difficult to believe that Mr. Duane had meant what he said. They tested him, they tested the other teachers. Some of the teachers felt they had been cheated anyway, tripped up by their own willingness to give an opinion which their training and service had taught them was a dangerous thing to do. Several went on caning, and the L.C.C. Inspector, apprised of this by Mr. Duane who asked for disciplinary action, would do nothing about it. Every time a teacher did cane, the testing time was made a little longer.

The teachers who were frightened of children either caned them or fawned on them. The children used the word "soft" for both these types of teacher; they were unerring in this summing up. But Michael Duane (at any rate in my experience, though one good child-centered teacher who warmly supported Mr. Duane queried this) they did not consider "soft." One boy said to me, "Some of them come from schools where they used the cane, and they reckon you can't manage without it. Trouble is they don't get trained for this kind of school. They're too soft. If they were all like Mr. Duane, this would be a terrific school." And another told me "Mr. Duane has proved that if you don't use the cane, people respect you. The pupils respect him. It's the *teachers* who think he's soft not to use the cane — not the pupils. Things are much better here now — people behave better."

Cyril Ray said to me, "Mr. Duane told me how a boy waiting outside his room to see him was beaten up to teach him not to crawl to the head; and a man who, in the circumstances, decided to face violence with deliberate nonviolence, since to face it with violence merely demonstrated that violence pays, was in my view absolutely magnificent."

Boys were indeed often beaten up, at the beginning, for telling Mr. Duane things, and he was much aware of this danger, and concerned for them. Children would come to him, obviously under a great emotional strain, saying they wanted to tell him something, "but please *please* don't let anyone know it was me that told." He always assured them that he wouldn't, and would go to great trouble to find an alternative source for the same information, so that if it was necessary to back it up he could do so without bringing the child in. As for the children who did the beating up, he would talk to them, talk and talk: "What else can you do? What is the sense of you beating *them* up? Then there is no end to it. You must simply talk and talk and talk without ever getting tired."

One day a boy came to school feeling murderous. It had begun the previous day, after school. The events of these children's lives were the events that have made blues and folk-songs and ballads, and at this safe move from reality middle-class adults will view them with equanimity, nostalgia, and a sense of beauty. So I jotted down a somewhat altered version of this incident to be sung to the tune of "If I had the wings of an angel."

> My friend, oh my friend he is Joey,
> And my girl she is Mary Malone,
> Oh it's women who cause all the trouble
> Because they won't let you alone.

> We walked after school through the market,
> And we lingered and lingered outside,
> With the barrows piled up in the middle
> And the homes falling down at the side.

> We climbed in a big empty barrow,
> And the cider was golden and cool,
> And drinking three bottles of cider
> Is something to do after school.

> Oh my mother she works as a cleaner,
> My dad is a betting man,
> My sister's a slag¹ in the market,
> And I do the best that I can.

> My mother's a couple of husbands,
> My sister has any lad,
> The baby belongs to my sister,
> But I know my own true dad.

> It was cold, so I lay down on Mary,
> It was cold in the barrow that day,
> So I started to love up my Mary,
> And Joey he pulled me away.

> He shouldn't have treated me roughly,
> He shouldn't have handed me blame,
> He shouldn't have pulled me off Mary
> And called me a dirty old name.

> The church struck ten when we parted,
> And Mary she cut round the stall,
> And Joe walked the stinking alley,
> And I climbed the gap in the wall.

> The chopper I took in the morning,
> It was one of my father's own tools,
> I took it from under my jacket
> And I followed my Joe round the school.

Poor Joes he was scared of the chopper,
He ran like a whippet, and cried.
He ran through the door of the classroom
And the blade split the door outside.

Oh Joey, oh Joey, why did you?
Why were you so unkind?
You knew I was drunk on the cider,
You shouldn't hit a friend when he's blind.

Oh Joey my friend, how could you?
You made my blood run cold,
I was only loving up someone
Who scarcely is twelve years old.

It's women who cause all the trouble,
It's them get you caned at school,
And when you get sent off to borstal
They've a new boy to make look a fool.

And when you're grown up and you're married,
They take the whole of your pay,
And you slave out your guts in the market
While they lie in bed all the day.

I emphasize that I have changed the details; they are not a description of the family involved. I have even altered some of the details of the actual events — the boy in fact did not follow his friend into the classroom. But I think I got down the attitude accurately, and I came on this attitude a good deal in Islington. In actuality, "Joey" came to Mr. Duane, very distressed, and said "Robert's after me with a chopper." Mr. Duane left Joey in his study, found Robert and said, "Robert, give me that chopper." To his huge relief, Robert went instantly to his locker, and took out the chopper — a very competent-looking hatchet — which he laid silently in Mr. Duane's grip.

Not wanting to leave the two boys together in the school in his absence — he was due at the juvenile court where another of his boys was appearing (he always attended and did his best to explain what they had done and why) — Mr. Duane told them to jump in the car, and they talked the matter out as they went along. When he got to the court, he gave them a pound note, and said, "Spend the day out. Take a boat on the river, or go to some museums — do something you've always wanted to do and enjoy yourselves. See you at school tomorrow." When he got back to school a little while later, to his surprise he found the boys there. They were cheerfully and amiably friendly, and have remained so ever since . . . though

"Joey" when I last saw him was still anti-girl and told me that it was a girl who had knocked out "Robert's" front teeth.

That first year was the year of the gang fights. The boys of Risinghill came from Northampton, a boys' small technical school, and Gifford, a large mixed. Because the Northampton boys were older — they tended to stay on at school a year or two past the school-leaving age — they were chosen as prefects at Risinghill. Furthermore, they were well-spoken, and had always worn uniform, which meant they were different from the Gifford boys, readily identifiable, and an easy focus for anger.

The Gifford boys brought their own leaders with them — Tom, a neat, carefully dressed boy, and Sam his lieutenant, more dishevelled and hoarse, together with a close guard of four or five, and a very large and more fluctuating crowd of supporters. They must have resented going from a school where their authority was undisputed to a school where, judged most fairly, everyone was starting again equally from scratch and, judged at the worst, where other boys, prissy uniformed strangers, were given control of them. Furthermore it seems to me this group of prefects, cohering, acting together, and powerful, must have seemed to them only a rival gang, and what is more a gang unfairly and arbitrarily backed by higher powers.

The Gifford gang began to demonstrate that they were not to be treated as kids, by dropping out of lessons and, soon, out of school. There were four exits apart from unofficial ones, so disappearing, in the early days when people wanted to disappear, was always easy; at Gifford, an older building, this could never have been done. The possibilities must have appealed at once to their resentment. This demonstration went on through the first term of the school.

In the second term, things got more dangerous. The prefects, coming back to school after the summer holidays (the school actually opened in May), felt more self-confident and ready to govern. Within one day, two events twisted the tension unbearably tighter (apparently set going by "a row over a couple of girls," though this was only mentioned once, very unwillingly, to Mr. Duane by Tom). The prefects had taken over a room for themselves, which had infuriated the Gifford gang. That particular day, wielding a bicycle chain, Tom drove Mike, one of the prefects, back into the Prefects' Room and virtually kept him prisoner. The same day, a group of prefects harangued Tom and Sam threateningly, in front of a crowd of about two hundred in the school playground, telling them plainly they'd "do 'em."

This day began a series of furious incidents, which nevertheless never resulted in any *person* being seriously hurt. Bulbs were stolen, door handles unscrewed, roller towels set on fire, mirrors smashed. (Not all of this was done by the gang, and not all deliberately; some was done absent-

mindedly, by adults as well as children. Mr. Duane reported seeing a
fifteen-year-old talking earnestly and simultaneously cutting the paint off
a pillar so that it formed a pattern, and seeing an adult, similarly talking
intently, picking out the putty from the windowframes. The gang was not
responsible for all the damage that occured at this time, but they were
responsible for most of it.) Yet no human being was badly harmed . . .
even though these were children set against authority, who were even,
some of them, trained for crime by their parents (some of the Gifford
gang were on probation because they had been organized to do a job by
one of the fathers who landed himself in jail), even though their groupings
included Cypriot refugee children whose parents, brothers and sisters had
sometimes been killed before their eyes and for whom fighting was therefore murderous, even though in the neighbouring district bloody racial
riots were taking place and in their own streets swastikas were chalked on
the walls. . . . Yet these children who were constantly working themselves
into white-hot feuds never in fact hurt anyone really badly. The worst
that happened was that a boy's face was scratched — only scratched —
by a *safety* razor; and that happened one evening after school.

Going over records of these events I have wondered and been intrigued
over the way everything constantly petered out. And it seemed to me it
was because the inflammable ingredient which would normally be present
— adult provocation — was here lacking. Children are very easily pro-
voked into doing silly, sometimes dreadful things, and adults — teachers,
parents — very frequently provoke them. But all the usual adult provoca-
tions — caning, calling in the police, shouting, threatening, forcing into
corners — was not supposed to take place at Risinghill, and, as far as Mr.
Duane was able to control or choose his teachers, did not take place. (I
remember that during the period of the gang fights some of the boys of the
Gifford gang maintained with white-faced sincerity that not only did the
prefects threaten to beat them up, but that a particular teacher egged on
the prefects; Mr. Duane called a special brief staff meeting and emphasized that, however furious the teachers might find themselves growing,
"any breath of a suggestion that we contemplated or sanctioned violence,
however well-intentioned, would simply undo in a moment everything we
were trying to build up." Of course to some people this merely showed
"he did not back up his teachers."

When Tom, some time afterwards when he had left school, was asked
what broke up the gang feuds — particularly the racial fighting — he said
simply, "We needed them, to make up our football side." At one time
during this period, if asked the same question Mr. Duane would probably
have said it was the School Council that did it, for at this time the splutter-
ing flame of the School Council suddenly flared up candidly (the majority
of the staff quickly decided they preferred darkness and smothered it; but

that comes later). At the School Council, the gang fighting was discussed, and it was here that the groups pledged themselves not to fight any more but to bring all disputes to the Council. Even Sam, who was reluctant, saying disarmingly when amiably questioned, "Well, I like a punch-up!," decided finally, without pressure, to give his word. For the first time the School Council, an entirely new and alien element to these children of violence and no account, had a real issue to deal with, and it thrived on it.

But all these possible reasons for the disappearance of violence mean only one thing. The pupils had creative relationships *demonstrated* to them; they saw the value of them in action, and it made sense.

After the Council meeting, Tom exchanged his power to bring crackling chaos in an instant for the slow pleasure of affectionate cooperation. A word from him stopped a racial fight that was teetering on the edge. One day he came to Mr. Duane with a couple of hammers which he had taken from two boys who were beginning to smash up the washbasins. Tom brought them doubtfully, worriedly, almost furtively. But Mr. Duane never trumpeted abroad his new virtue, as another headmaster might easily have done, setting all nerves jangling again. He received the hammers as one receives a small gift or small service from a friend.

When Tom left school, after his one year at Risinghill, he sent his kid sister away on her school journey to Spain. The £27 she needed had been saved entirely by Tom.

One day, a woman who did domestic work in the school came to Mr. Duane, very distressed. Her basket, filled to the top with shopping, had disappeared. He instantly made an emergency announcement to the school. He explained to the children that the shopping was for her family, that she had spent all her money on it, and now her family would have to go hungry — for days, maybe — if it wasn't returned.

Two boys came to him, shamefaced, and said they had taken it.

"Where is it? We must give it her back."

"Well, we can't; we've eaten most of it."

"All right. Take this pound note. Go to the market, try and remember every single thing that was in the basket, and fill it up again. Let her have it all back as quickly as you can — she's upset. Then come back here, and we'll discuss how you're to refund me." They took three weeks to pay him back from their pocket money.

There was no anger, no contempt, no moral pressure in this solution, but only a desire to make the concern of everyone for everyone manifest, and to help children instantly to right the wrong they have done so that they can feel at one with the world. (What price the cane? One might compare this episode with an episode I heard today of a boy who was thoroughly thrashed by his headmaster, got up and said coolly, "And do you expect me to behave differently now?")

At Risinghill one began to see a developing back to the concern of one person for another that so often adults, who themselves have been warped, will over and over again warp in children. Mr. Blaize told me how once, faced with a difficult child in his class, a girl who endlessly caused trouble, he eventually threw her out. (She was a child who should have gone to a special school. A large number of children at Risinghill were waiting for places in special schools that were never forthcoming.) Then when he became calmly and fully aware of what had happened, he realized it was not the girl's behaviour that had upset the class, but his own; that the class had reacted hostilely against his own rejection of the girl, and that he would have done better to have worked with the class to help the girl.

This concern of children for each other is a wonderful power for growth; I have often wondered if teaching students are taught in training colleges to build on this natural humanity; I doubt it very much.

(Authoritarians who hate any action to be made "outside the usual channels," who hate children to move out of their desks, or — if out of doors — out of an orderly file, who hate adolescents to be "unattached," that is, not on the membership of some named club, often however do not at all like people to be genuinely *attached*, attached to each other that is, because this, they feel, takes them instantly out of the control of authoritarians. It is a very sad business.)

I remember once, when I was with about ten two- to four-year-olds, one of the little girls, Susan, started screaming. Children of this age do have fits of temper and screaming, and adults generally hit them for it. In Susan it reached an intensity of passion that I had never seen before. She was beside herself, quite out of her own control, and was screaming no longer in fury but in terror, screaming to be saved from herself; when I looked at her, I knew at once what the Bible meant when it said someone was possessed. She would do this when she was frustrated — by her own weakness, or by someone, out of friendliness, helping her. Joe, a child who loved her and whom she loved back, had done some service for her; and it was something she had intended to do herself. Her screams paralysed the whole room.

I scooped her up in my arms — very difficult to do, for she was thrashing about violently and convulsively — and managed to sit down and clutch her on my lap. "Susan is upset," I said to the amazed silent children. "We'll sing to her until she feels better." And the children gathered round and sang.

They put down everything they had been absorbed in, and came and stood by Susan. Now and then they would put out a hand and touch her back, delicately and reassuringly. At first, she would stiffen against it hysterically and the screams would get louder, and I would wonder if it was wise; but the children knew best, and they would gently do it again, singing sweetly all the time; and after a while she began to enjoy their friendship and to bask in it as if she were lying in the sunshine.

Just for a few seconds she lay on my lap, quite tranquil and quiet, and I put my cheek against hers. "There!" I said. "We've helped her feel better."

She jumped up, flashed a radiant and very shy smile at everyone, and went back to her game, humming to herself; and everybody else did the same; nothing was ever said about it. I learned a great deal from those children, not only that day but every day; and if I were running a school I would not have any adult in it who was not open to learning constantly from children.

Such growing concern for others was evident to anyone who visited Risinghill and who was open to it. Unfortunately many of the teachers and other people in positions of power were not open to it. One of the inspectors, who maintained that six of the best would cure almost anything, seeing a nuclear disarmament symbol chalked on a playground wall, was heard to exclaim furiously "I'd sooner see four-letter words [chalked on the wall] than that!" That was his angle.

A traditionalist teacher at the school was amazed to hear how friendly and helpful I found the children, later on. She despised me for it — thought I was unbalanced perhaps; she herself thought they were dreadful, but did not expect them to be anything else; she handed them religious exhortations, but she had no faith in them and did not see the grace they had. "For children like this, the world is a hard place," she said, "and the sooner they learn it the better." When I said, "But the world is not static. The world is what we make it. And these children are some of those who are going to make the world, surely, who are going to change it," she looked at me for a moment; "Yes," she conceded eventually, "the world does sometimes change." And on this note of complete passivity, we parted. Not "Yes, children do change the world." But "Yes, the world does sometimes change. . . ." Why do not religious people feel that to stamp on any of God's work, to neglect deliberately to bring it to full flowering, is blasphemy?

Some of the political governors too saw the devil in the children constantly. Partly of course they were influenced by the open site of the school, which spread out all deviations from conformity before everyone's eyes; they were public relations people, as so many politicians are nowadays; they saw votes being lost on all sides. Such governors would speak bitterly of untidy playgrounds, full bins, and running shouting children. One of them, coming into school after hours, when the cleaners were sweeping out the rubbish and putting it into boxes, looked at the boxes — empty cardboard cartons — and said sternly to the astonished women "This is what gets the school a bad name!" I cannot remember now whether it was the same one, or another, who once stood beside Mr.

Duane, looking out into the playground, and was enraged. Though Mr. Duane stared, he could not see anything dreadful happening, though the governor kept urging him to see to the matter at once. Eventually, the governor dashed into the playground, and hauled two boys out of it and into the study. "There!" It seemed that one of the boys had been swinging the other one round, helping him on his way with a foot. Mr. Duane stared at them, thinking the boys must believe he had gone out of his mind, and wondering what on earth he was supposed to do to "discipline" two children who were obviously, judging by their giggles, amiably and cheerfully disposed towards one another. "Well, Christos," he said at last, groping for words, "why were you kicking Petros?" The two boys looked at each other and laughed warmly into each other's face. "He threw clay at me in the art room," said Christos; and they poked each other in the ribs. Mr. Duane rumpled their hair and pushed them out; "All right," he said, "just see that you don't hurt one another." The governor was scandalized at such laxity, and raised the matter at the next governors' meeting, exclaiming "Why, for heaven's sake, can't they behave like children in Hampstead!"[2] (This cry, slightly varied, was to be passed like a sad beanbag from one authoritarian socialist to another. When in 1965 the L.C.C. sent spokesmen down to "tell" the parents the school would be closed, they made it clear they had expected the children of Risinghill to pull themselves together and behave like Hampstead children.)

When one did not intend to see evil in children, they could be delightful — particularly towards the end of the five years, the time when the L.C.C. closed the school down. That fifth year, in fact, was the first time one would be able to see what the school was accomplishing . . . the first time the school could have senior pupils who had been educated at Risinghill and absorbed its atmosphere, and could pass it on, unconsciously as well as consciously, towards the younger ones. When a visitor came into school at that time, a boy or girl would instantly detach himself from friends and ask, not with a cold dutifulness but with a warm friendliness, if they could help in any way. They would take you wherever you wanted to go, voluntarily; they were host and hostess and you were a privileged guest whom they were glad to welcome.

I have never met this treatment in a traditionalist secondary school, for very obvious reasons. A child there is too tied by fear, by obligations laid on him from without not from within, ever to throw everything aside and look after someone; he is always afraid he will get into trouble, he will be late for something, he won't have a "good excuse" (a typical and revealing authoritarian school phrase), he will be breaking some unknown regulation. A child at such a school is "well-mannered" — which is to say that he stands up when the head comes into the room — but never sees his own humanity in someone else. He is "polite" (according to his discretion, of course) but very cold, and lowers his eyes and sees nothing in the presence of a stranger.

A well-educated intelligent woman — she had chosen Risinghill for her children very deliberately — who was very large, and looked somewhat larger in her black cloak, told me that she came to the school to see Mr. Duane, and at once a boy and a girl detached themselves and asked her if they could help. As they escorted her to the headmaster's study, a couple of small girls said cheekily, "Ever heard of Dracula!" The elder boy, scarcely pausing in his walk, simply said, "Ever heard of good manners!" and without another word, or any feeling of embarrassment in anyone, the group went on its way

Five years later, when the L.C.C. had decided to close Risinghill School, I was in one of the art rooms — the same one, incidentally, that Mr. Sebag-Montefiore and Mrs. Townsend had by then painted as a den of vandalism. The art teacher had a book of mine he wanted to return. He looked round to see if there was a child unoccupied, and called him over. "Jimmy, would you mind doing something for me? Here's my car key. My car's a light blue Hillman. It's parked down there, on the right. I've left a book in it that I must give back to Mrs. Berg. If you can't see it on the seat, then look in all the pockets — and in my bag at the back." The boy took the key and was back almost instantly, very pleased with himself for his speed. This was in a district where the commonest children's crimes are "theft" and "taking and driving away." An authoritarian would have called the art teacher's casual trust "putting temptation in their way"; to him it was simply treating children as equal human beings, which neither the authoritarians nor the confused teachers do.

Earlier in that same period, I arrived to see Mr. Duane. He had been called away for a few minutes to a laundry up the road that had been smashed up, the laundry people said, by one of his boys. Just as he came back, out of breath, and sank into a chair, a group of little boys poked their heads into the study. "Was it Terry, sir?" they said. "No," he reassured them. "It's all right. It was Terry's brother. He doesn't go to our school." "Oh *good!*" said two of them, and a third added fervently, "I'm glad it wasn't Terry, sir. I'm glad it wasn't our school." "So am I," he said cheerfully, and waved them away. The concern in their voices, for Terry, for Mr. Duane, and for the school, was very evident, and, I thought, not only touching but remarkable.

A Risinghill teacher had said to me, telling me how she read "The Loneliness of the Long Distance Runner" to the older children, "At first they only understood why he loved running — they understood this very well — and how he felt. Only three or four could grasp at all the idea of the prestige of an institution as against individual prestige, but I think more of them began to grope after this. It's an idea that's quite alien."

Yet from the love towards individuals that had been fostered in them, and that they had been encouraged to express, they had formed a love for an entity. But I am rushing ahead. In that first year, particularly the first term when the boys and girls who had been uprooted for a pointless solitary term got their own back on a society that, to their amazement, had suddenly stopped provoking them, there was chaos.

## NOTES

1. A prostitute
2. Hampstead is a mainly rich, green, spacious, and arty district, north-west of Islington.

## SUGGESTED READINGS FOR PART THREE

### General

LITTLE, ALAN AND DENIS KALLEN
    1968    Western European secondary school systems and higher education: A warning for comparative education. *Comparative Education*, Vol. 4, no. 2:135–153.
    General discussion of problems in European school systems

### France

CAPELLE, JEAN
    1967    Tomorrow's education, the French experience. Foreword by Louis Armand. W. D. Halls (translator, editor, introduction, and notes). Oxford, N.Y.: Pergamon Press. xvi+229 pp., illustrated.
    Analysis of and comments on the French educational and social situation

CLARK, JAMES M.
    1967    Teachers and politics in France: A pressure group study of the Federation de l'Education Nationale. Syracuse: Syracuse University Press. xv+197 pp., bibliography
    Study of a primary force in French education

HALLS, W. D.
    1965    Society, schools and progress in France. London: Pergamon Press.
    Interrelationships among social, political, educational, and industrial structures are discussed.

## United Kingdom

ARMYTAGE, WALTER H. G.
1967 The American influence on English education. London: Routledge.

Discussion of the two most prominent educational models in the English-speaking world

KOERNER, JAMES D.
1968 Reform in education; England and the United States. New York: Delacorte Press. xix+332 pp., bibliographical references in "Notes".

Two different reform situations are highlighted.

WEINBERG, IAN
1967 The English public schools: The sociology of elite education. New York: Atherton Press. xix+225 pp.

Elitism, a significant factor in many parts of the world, is discussed in detail with reference to England.

It has become commonplace to observe that the "melting pot" ideal of American society is under severe strain. One of the essential ingredients of that recipe is an educational system which helps prepare the successful for either new or continued participation in the middle class. In many ways, the educational system has been remarkably effective in accomplishing that goal for a wide variety of the people from disparate backgrounds. At the same time, several segments of the American population have not been put into the cauldron in any proportion like that of European-derived citizens. The Amerindian was virtually isolated from the rest of the American population, and the Blacks were given a narrow range and depth of education and had a middle class made up largely of service professions to the Black communities: physicians (often not accepted into local units of the American Medical Association), teachers (in inferior schools and colleges), ministers (in segregated churches), funeral directors, and so forth.

*PART FOUR*

# THE UNITED STATES

Murray and Rosalie Wax are certainly among the most perceptive observers of the cultural dysfunctions in Amerindian education. Mrs. Wax's article compels any sensitive reader to reexamine the widely abused term "dropout" and, in some cases, to replace it with her far more accurate term, "pushout." The article by Dumont and Wax carefully examines what happens when an educational process with substance and methods based on a different culture and social pattern is shifted, with little or no modification, to other cultures with different social patterns.

Perhaps the most significant anthropological insight in both articles is that "cultural deprivation" and related concepts make politically and socially subordinate populations assume, in the eyes of superordinate authorities, a stance of receptive subordination in all respects, including education. An important factor in the failure of Amerindian education is its assumption of such total subordination. Many do not realize that Amerindians have great cultural and social strength with which to oppose an educational system which is not oriented to their needs as reservation-based citizens, whether the ultimate goal of that educational process is to keep the Amerindians on reservations or to enable them to move into the nation's larger, urban society. Thus, if the schools are to aid in reservation life, as Mrs. Wax shows, criteria of maleness on which young men are judged by their fellows must not be disregarded by the schools or, worse, regarded as "delinquent" behavior. If young Amerindians are to become literate, skilled, white-collar craftsmen accepted by America's middle class majority, then the schools cannot remain self-defeating in their intellectual and learning tasks. In other words, when the primary means of transmission of cultural information (and misinformation) between a donor and client culture is a one-way educational process, often in an alien language, frustration in the donor and resentment and confusion in the client result.

The education of Black citizens in the United States has become the paramount issue in recent critical discussions of American education. Included here is a selection from an autobiographical novel by a young Black who emerged from a slum backgound in New York City to go on to a university education. Claude Brown's account is not presented either as "representative" or "typical" but as common, with one exceptional quality: he escaped from the normal vicious cycle of poverty-crime-punishment-destruction.

It may seem strange to present experience in a reform school as an example of an "educational process," but actually a significant proportion of urban, Black males share such an alma mater. The same issues, such as the proper uses of authority, conflicts between prescribed goals and actual behavior, and so forth, apply to reform schools as well as to schools "on the outside," though the institutions are based on different social, cultural, and normative patterns.

There are two important similarities in the readings on Amerindians and American Blacks. First, sympathetic, strong male figures made the most meaningful contact with students of both groups. Second, the "humanness" of teachers made the critical difference between playing in a social game where both means and goals are as unclear as its rules and learning how to deal with and successfully modify life's demands.

# 14 ··················

# The Warrior Dropouts

ROSALIE H. WAX

Scattered over the prairie on the Pine Ridge reservation of South Dakota, loosely grouped into bands along the creeks and roads, live thousands of Sioux Indians. Most live in cabins, some in tents, a few in houses; most lack the conventional utilities — running water, electricity, telephone, and gas. None has a street address. They are called "country Indians," and most speak the Lakota language. They are very poor, the most impoverished people on the reservation.

For four years I have been studying the problems of the high school dropouts among these Oglala Sioux. In many ways these Indian youths are very different from slum school dropouts — Negro, Mexican-American, rural white — just as in each group individuals differ widely one from another. Yet no one who has any familiarity with their problems can avoid being struck by certain parallels, both between groups and individuals.

In slum schools and Pine Ridge schools scholastic achievement is low, and the dropout rate is high; the children's primary loyalties go to friends

Reprinted from *Trans*-action (May 1967:40–46) by permission of *Trans*-action and the author. Copyright © 1967 by *Trans*-action magazine, St. Louis, Missouri.

and peers, not schools or educators; and all of them are confronted by teachers who see them as inadequately prepared, uncultured offspring of alien and ignorant folk. They are classified as "culturally deprived." All such schools serve as the custodial, constabulary, and reformative arm of one element of society directed against another.

Otherwise well-informed people, including educators themselves, assume on the basis of spurious evidence that dropouts dislike and voluntarily reject school, that they all leave it for much the same reasons, and that they are really much alike. But dropouts leave high school under strikingly different situations and for quite different reasons.

Many explicitly state that they do not wish to leave and are really "pushouts" or "kickouts" rather than "dropouts." As a Sioux youth in our sample put it, "I quit, but I never did *want* to quit!" Perhaps the fact that educators consider all dropouts to be similar tells us more about educators and their schools than about dropouts.

## ON THE RESERVATION

The process that alienates many country Indian boys from the high schools they are obliged to attend begins early in childhood and reflects the basic Sioux social structure. Sioux boys are reared to be physically reckless and impetuous. One that does not perform an occasional brash act may be accepted as "quiet" or "bashful," but he is not considered a desirable son, brother, or sweetheart. Sioux boys are reared to be proud and feisty and are expected to resent public censure. They have some obligations to relatives; but the major social controls after infancy are exerted by their fellows — their "peer group."

From about the age of seven or eight, they spend almost the entire day without adult supervision, running or riding about with friends of their age and returning home only for food and sleep. Even we (my husband, Dr. Murray L. Wax, and I), who had lived with Indian families from other tribal groups, were startled when we heard a responsible and respected Sioux matron dismiss a lad of six or seven for the entire day with the statement, "Go play with Larry and John." Similarly, at a ceremonial gathering in a strange community with hundreds of people, boys of nine or ten often take off and stay away until late at night as a matter of course. Elders pay little attention. There is much prairie and many creeks for roaming and playing in ways that bother nobody. The only delinquencies we have heard Sioux elders complain about are chasing stock, teasing bulls, or occasionally some petty theft.

Among Sioux males this kind of peer-group raising leads to a highly efficient yet unverbalized system of intragroup discipline and powerful intragroup loyalties and dependencies. During our seven-month stay in a reservation community, we were impressed by how rarely the children quarreled with one another. This behavior was not imposed by elders but by the children themselves.

For example, our office contained some items very attractive to them, especially a typewriter. We were astonished to see how quietly they handled this prize that only one could enjoy at a time. A well-defined status system existed so that a child using the typewriter at once gave way and left the machine if one higher in the hierarchy appeared. A half-dozen of these shifts might take place within an hour; yet, all this occurred without a blow or often even a word.

Sioux boys have intense loyalties and dependencies. They almost never tattle on each other. But when forced to live with strangers, they tend to become inarticulate, psychologically disorganized, or withdrawn.

With most children the peer group reaches the zenith of its power in school. In middle class neighborhoods, independent children can usually seek and secure support from parents, teachers, or adult society as a whole. But when, as in an urban slum or Indian reservation, the teachers stay aloof from parents, and parents feel that teachers are a breed apart, the peer group may become so powerful that the children literally take over the school. Then group activities are carried on in class — jokes, notes, intrigues, teasing, mock-combat, comic book reading, courtship — all without the teacher's knowledge and often without grossly interfering with the learning process.

Competent and experienced teachers can come to terms with the peer group and manage to teach a fair amount of reading, writing, and arithmetic. But teachers who are incompetent, overwhelmed by large classes, or sometimes merely inexperienced may be faced with groups of children who refuse even to listen.

We marveled at the variety and efficiency of the devices developed by Indian children to frustrate formal learning — unanimous inattention, refusal to go to the board, writing on the board in letters less than an inch high, inarticulate responses, and whispered or pantomime teasing of victims called on to recite. In some seventh and eighth grade classes there was a withdrawal so uncompromising that no voice could be heard for hours except the teacher's, plaintively asking questions or giving instructions.

Most Sioux children insist they like school, and most Sioux parents corroborate this. Once the power and depth of their social life within the school is appreciated, it is not difficult to see why they like it. Indeed, the only unpleasant aspects of school for them are the disciplinary regulations (which they soon learn to tolerate or evade), an occasional "mean" teacher, bullies, or feuds with members of other groups. Significantly, we found that notorious truants had usually been rejected by classmates and also had no older relatives in school to protect them from bullies. But the child who has a few friends or an older brother or sister to stand by him, or who "really likes to play basketball," almost always finds school agreeable.

## DAY SCHOOL GRADUATES

By the time he has finished the eighth grade, the country Indian boy has many fine qualities: zest for life, curiosity, pride, physical courage, sensibility to human relationships, experience with the elemental facts of life, and intense group loyalty and integrity. His experiences in day school have done nothing to diminish or tarnish his ideal — the physically reckless and impetuous youth, who is admired by all.

But, on the other hand, the country Indian boy is almost completely lacking in the traits most highly valued by the school authorities: a narrow and absolute respect for "regulations," "government property," routine, discipline, and diligence. He is also deficient in other skills apparently essential to rapid and easy passage through high school and boarding school — especially the abilities to make short-term superficial social adjustments with strangers. Nor can he easily adjust to a system which demands, on the one hand, that he study competitively as an individual, and, on the other, that he live in barrack-type dormitories where this kind of study is impossible.

Finally, his English is inadequate for high school work. Despite eight or more years of formal training in reading and writing, many day school graduates cannot converse fluently in English even among themselves. In contrast, most of the students with whom they will compete in higher schools have spoken English since childhood.

To leave home and the familiar and pleasant day school for boarding life at the distant and formidable high school is a prospect both fascinating and frightening. To many young country Indians the agency town of Pine Ridge is a center of sophistication. It has blocks of Indian Bureau homes with lawns and fences, a barber shop, big grocery stores, churches, gas stations, a drive-in confectionary, and even a restaurant with a juke box. While older siblings or cousins may have reported that at high school "they make you study harder," that "they just make you move every minute," or that the "mixed-bloods" or "children of bureau employees" are "mean" or "snotty," there are the compensatory highlights of movies, basketball games, and the social (white man's) dances.

For the young men there is the chance to play high school basketball, baseball, or football; for the young women there is the increased distance from overwatchful, conservative parents. For both, there is the freedom, taken or not, to hitchhike to White Clay, with its beer joints, bowling hall, and archaic aura of Western wickedness. If, then, a young man's close friends or relatives decide to go to high school, he will usually want to go too rather than remain at home, circumscribed, "living off his folks." Also, every year, more elders coax, tease, bribe, or otherwise pressure the young men into "making a try" because "nowadays only high school graduates get the good jobs."

## THE STUDENT BODY: TOWN INDIANS, COUNTRY INDIANS

The student body of the Oglala Community High School is very varied. First, there are the children of the town dwellers, who range from well-paid white and Indian government employees who live in neat government housing developments to desperately poor people who live in tar paper shacks. Second, there is the large number of institutionalized children who have been attending the Oglala Community School as boarders for the greater part of their lives. Some are orphans, others come from isolated sections of the reservation where there are no day schools, others come from different tribal areas.

But these town dwellers and boarders share an advantage — for them entry into high school is little more than a shift from eighth to ninth grade. They possess an intimate knowledge of their classmates and a great deal of local know-how. In marked contrast, the country Indian freshman enters an alien environment. Not only is he ignorant of how to buck the rules, he doesn't even know the rules. Nor does he know anybody to put him wise.

Many country Indians drop out of high school before they have any clear idea what high school is all about. In our sample, 35 percent dropped out before the end of the ninth grade and many of these left during the first semester. Our first interviews with them were tantalizingly contradictory — about half the young men seemed to have found high school so painful they could scarcely talk about it; the other half were also laconic, but insisted that they had liked school. In time, those who had found school unbearable confided that they had left school because they were lonely or because they were abused by more experienced boarders. Only rarely did they mention that they had trouble with their studies.

The following statement, made by a mild and pleasant boy, conveys some idea of the agony of loneliness, embarrassment, and inadequacy that a country Indian newcomer may suffer when he enters high school:

> At day school it was kind of easy for me. But high school was really hard, and I can't figure out even simple questions that they ask me. . . . Besides I'm so quiet [modest and unaggressive] that the boys really took advantage of me. They borrow money from me every Sunday night and they

> don't even care to pay it back. . . . I can't talk English very good, and I'm really bashful and shy, and I get scared when I talk to white people. I usually just stay quiet in the [day school] classroom, and the teachers will leave me alone. But at boarding school they wanted me to get up and talk or say something. . . . I quit and I never went back. . . . I can't seem to get along with different people, and I'm so shy I can't even make friends. . . . [Translated from Lakota by interviewer.]

Most of the newcomers seem to have a difficult time getting along with the experienced boarders and claim that the latter not only strip them of essentials like soap, paper, and underwear, but also take the treasured gifts of proud and encouraging relatives, wrist watches and transistor radios.

> Some of the kids — especially the boarders — are really mean. All they want to do is steal — and they don't want to study. They'll steal your school work off you and they'll copy it. . . . Sometimes they'll break into our suitcase. Or if we have money in our pockets they'll take off our overalls and search our pockets and get our money. . . . So finally I just came home. If I could be a day scholar I think I'll stay in. But if they want me to board I don't want to go back. I think I'll just quit.

Interviews with the dropouts who asserted that school was "all right" — and that they had not wished to quit — suggest that many had been almost as wretched during their first weeks at high school as the bashful young men who quit because they "couldn't make friends." But they managed to find some friends and, with this peer support and protection, they were able to cope with and (probably) strike back at other boarders. In any case, the painful and degrading aspects of school became endurable. As one lad put it: "Once you *learn* to be a boarder, it's not so bad."

But for these young men, an essential part of having friends was "raising Cain" — that is, engaging in daring and defiant deeds forbidden by the school authorities. The spirit of these escapades is difficult to portray to members of a society where most people no longer seem capable of thinking about the modern equivalents of Tom Sawyer, Huckleberry Finn, or Kim, except as juvenile delinquents. We ourselves, burdened by sober professional interest in dropouts, at first found it hard to recognize that these able and engaging young men were taking pride and joy in doing exactly what the school authorities thought most reprehensible; and they were not confessing, but boasting, although their stunts had propelled them out of school.

For instance, this story from one bright lad of 15 who had run away from high school. Shortly after entering ninth grade he and his friends had appropriated a government car. (The usual pattern in such adventures is to drive off the reservation until the gas gives out.) For this offense (according to the respondent) they were restricted for the rest of the term — they were forbidden to leave the high school campus or attend any of the school recreational events, games, dances, or movies. (In effect, this meant doing nothing but going to class, performing work chores, and sitting in the dormitory.) Even then our respondent seems to have kept up with his class work and did not play hookey except in reading class:

> It was after we stole that car Mrs. Bluger [pseudonym for reading teacher] would keep asking who stole the car in class. So I just quit going there. . . . One night we were the only ones up in the older boys' dorm. We said, "Hell with this noise. We're not going to be the only ones here." So we snuck out and went over to the dining hall. I pried this one window open about this far and then it started to crack, so I let it go. . . . We heard someone so we took off. It was show that night I think. [Motion picture was being shown in school auditorium.] . . . All the rest of the guys was sneaking in and getting something. So I said I was going to get my share too. We had a case of apples and a case of oranges. Then I think it was the night watchman was coming, so we run around and hid behind those steps. He shined that light on us. So I thought right then I was going to keep on going. That was around Christmas time. We walked back to Ogala [about 15 miles] and we were eating this stuff all the way back.

This young man implied that after this escapade he simply did not have the nerve to try to return to the high school. He insisted, however, that he would like to try another high school:

> I'd like to finish [high school] and get a job some place. If I don't I'll probably just be a bum around here or something.

## YOUNG MEN WHO STAY IN SCHOOL

Roughly half the young Sioux who leave high school very early claim they left because they were unable to conform to school regulations. What happens to the country boys who remain? Do they "shape-up" and obey the regulations? Do they, even, come to "believe" in them? We found that most of these older and more experienced youths were, if anything, even *more* inclined to boast of triumphs over the rules than the younger fellows who had left. Indeed, all but one assured us that they were adept at hookey, and food and car stealing, and that they had frequent surreptitious beer parties and other outlaw enjoyments. We do not know whether they (especially the star athletes) actually disobey the school regulations as frequently and flagrantly as they claim. But there can be no doubt that most Sioux young men above 12 wish to be regarded as hellions in school. For them, it would be unmanly to have any other attitude.

At eleventh grader in good standing explained his private technique for playing hookey and added proudly: "They never caught me yet." A twelfth grader and firststring basketball player told how he and some other students "stole" a jeep from the high school machine shop and drove it all over town. When asked why, he patiently explained: "To see if we can get away with it. It's for the enjoyment . . . to see if we can take the car without getting caught." Another senior told our male staff worker: "You can always get out and booze it up."

The impulse to boast of the virile achievements of youth seems to maintain itself into middle and even into old age. Country Indians with college training zestfully told how they and a group of proctors had stolen large amounts of food from the high school kitchen and were never apprehended, or how they and their friends drank three fifths of whiskey in one night and did not pass out.

Clearly, the activities school administrators and teachers denounce as immature and delinquent are regarded as part of youthful daring, excitement, manly honor, and contests of skill and wits by the Sioux young men and many of their elders.

They are also, we suspect, an integral part of the world of competitive sports. "I like to play basketball" was one of the most frequent responses of young men to the question: "What do you like most about school?" Indeed, several ninth and tenth graders stated that the opportunity to play basketball was the main reason they kept going to school. One eighth grader who had run away several times stated:

> When I was in the seventh grade I made the B team on the basketball squad. And I made the A team when I was in the eighth grade. So I stayed and finished school without running away anymore.

The unselfconscious devotion and ardor with which many of these young men participate in sports must be witnessed to be appreciated even mildly. They cannot communicate their joy and pride in words, though one 17-year-old member of the team that won the state championship tried, by telling how a team member wearing a war bonnet "led us onto the playing floor and this really gave them a cheer."

Unfortunately, we have seen little evidence that school administrators and teachers recognize the opportunity to use sports as a bridge to school.

By the eleventh and twelfth grades many country Indians have left the reservation or gone into the armed services, and it is not always easy to tell which are actual dropouts. However, we did reach some. Their reasons for dropping out varied. One pled boredom: "I was just sitting there doing anything to pass the time." Another said he didn't know what made him quit: "I just didn't fit in anymore. . . . I just wasn't like the other guys anymore." Another refused to attend a class in which he felt the teacher had insulted Indians. When the principal told him that he must attend this class or be "restricted," he left. Significantly, his best friend dropped out with him, even though he was on the way to becoming a first-class basketball player.

Different as they appear at first, these statements have a common undertone: They are the expressions not of immature delinquents, but of relatively mature young men who find the atmosphere of the high school stultifying and childish.

## THE DILEMMA OF SIOUX YOUTH

Any intense cross-cultural study is likely to reveal as many tragi-comic situations as social scientific insights. Thus, on the Pine Ridge reservation, a majority of the young men arrive at adolescence valuing *élan,* bravery, generosity, passion, and luck, and admiring outstanding talent in athletics, singing, and dancing. While capable of wider relations and reciprocities, they function at their social best as members of small groups of peers or relatives. Yet to obtain even modest employment in the greater society, they must graduate from high school. And in order to graduate from high school, they are told that they must develop exactly opposite qualities to those they possess: a respect for humdrum diligence and routine, for "discipline" (in the sense of not smoking in toilets, not cutting classes, and not getting drunk), and for government property. In addition, they are expected to compete scholastically on a highly privatized and individualistic level, while living in large dormitories, surrounded by strangers who make privacy of any type impossible.

If we were dealing with the schools of a generation or two ago, then the situation might be bettered by democratization — involving the Sioux parents in control of the schools. This system of local control was not perfect, but it worked pretty well. Today the problem is more complicated and tricky; educators have become professionalized, and educational systems have become complex bureaucracies, inextricably involved with universities, education associations, foundations, and federal crash programs. Even suburban middle class parents, some of whom are highly educated and sophisticated, find it difficult to cope with the bureaucratic barriers and mazes of the schools their children attend. It is difficult to see how Sioux parents could accomplish much unless, in some way, their own school system were kept artificially small and isolated and accessible to their understanding and control.

## WORKING CLASS YOUTH

How does our study of the Sioux relate to the problems of city dropouts? A specific comparison of the Sioux dropouts with dropouts from the urban working class — Negroes, Puerto Ricans, or whites — would, no doubt, reveal many salient differences in cultural background and world view. Nevertheless, investigations so far undertaken suggest that the attitudes held by these peoples *toward education and the schools* are startlingly similar.

Both Sioux and working class parents wish their children to continue in school because they believe that graduating from high school is a guarantee of employment. Though some teachers would not believe it, many working class dropouts, like the Sioux dropouts, express a generally favorable attitude toward school, stating that teachers are generally fair and that the worst thing about dropping out of school is missing one's friends. Most important, many working class dropouts assert that they were pushed out of school and frequently add that the push was fairly direct. The Sioux boys put the matter more delicately, implying that the school authorities would not really welcome them back.

These similarities should not be seized on as evidence that all disprivileged children are alike and that they will respond as one to the single, ideal, educational policy. What it does mean is that the schools and their administrators are so monotonously alike that the boy brought up in a minority social or ethnic community can only look at and react to them in the same way. Despite their differences, they are all in much the same boat as they face the great monolith of middle-class society and its one-track education escalator.

An even more important — if often unrecognized — point is that not only does the school pose a dilemma for the working-class or Sioux, Negro, or Puerto Rican boy — he also poses one for the school. In many traditional or ethnic cultures boys are encouraged to be virile adolescents and become "real men." But our schools try to deprive youth of adolescence — and they demand that high school students behave like "mature people" — which, in our culture often seems to mean in a pretty dull, conformist fashion.

Those who submit and succeed in school can often fit into the bureaucratic requirements of employers, but they are also likely to lack independence of thought and creativity. The dropouts are failures — they have failed to become what the school demands. But the school has failed also — failed to offer what the boys from even the most "deprived" and "underdeveloped" peoples take as a matter of course — the opportunity to become whole men.

S. M. Miller and Ira E. Harrison, studying working class youth, assert that individuals who do poorly in school are handicapped or disfavored for the remainder of their lives, because "the schools have become the occupational gatekeepers" and "the level of education affects the kind and level of job that can be attained." On the other hand, the investigations of Edgar Z. Friedenberg and Jules Henry suggest that the youths who perform creditably in high school according to the views of the authorities are disfavored in that they emerge from this experience as permanently crippled persons or human beings.

In a curious way our researches among the Sioux may be viewed as supporting both of these contentions, for they suggest that some young people leave high school because they are too vital and independent to submit to a dehumanizing situation.[1]

## NOTES

1. In studying the adolescents on Pine Ridge we concentrated on two areas, the high school and a particular day school community with a country Indian population of about 1,000. We interviewed somewhat less than half the young people then enrolled in the high school plus a random sample of 48 young country Indians. Subsequently, we obtained basic socio-economic and educational data from all the young people who had graduated from the day school in 1961, 1962, and 1963. We interviewed 153 young people between the ages of 13 and 21, about 50 of whom were high school dropouts. We used many approaches and several types of questionnaires, but our most illuminating and reliable data were obtained from interviews conducted by Indian college students who were able to associate with the Sioux adolescents and participate in some of their activities.

   While "country Sioux" or "country Indian" might loosely be considered a synonym for "full-blood," I have avoided the latter term as connoting a traditional Indian culture which vanished long ago and whose unchanging qualities were a mythology of white observers rather than a social reality of Indian participants. In any case, I use "country Indian" to refer to the people raised and living "out on the reservation (prairie)" who participate in the social and ceremonial activities of their local rural communities, as opposed to those persons, also known as Indians, who live in Pine Ridge town and make a point of avoiding these backwoods activities.

# 15 ·················

# Cherokee School Society and the Intercultural Classroom [1]

ROBERT V. DUMONT, JR.

MURRAY L. WAX

Indian education is one of those phrases whose meaning is not the sum of its component words. Notoriously, "education" is an ambiguous word used to justify, idealize, or to criticize a variety of relationships. In the context where the pupils are members of a lower caste or ethnically subordinated group, education has come to denominate a unidirectional process by which missionaries — or others impelled by motives of duty, reform, charity, and self-sacrifice — attempt to uplift and civilize the disadvantaged and barbarian. Education then is a process imposed upon a target population in order to shape and stamp them into becoming dutiful citizens, responsible employees, or good Christians.[2]

In the modern federal and public school systems serving Indian children, there is less of the specifically religious quality; but the active

Reprinted from *Human Organization,* Vol. 28, No. 3, 1969, pp. 217–226 by permission of the publisher.

presence of the missionizing tradition, however secularized, is still felt. To appreciate this fully, we must remind ourselves that the purpose of education presented to, and often enforced upon, the American Indians has been nothing less than the transformation of their traditional cultures and the total reorganization of their societies.[3] By denominating this as *unidirectional,* we mean to emphasize that the far-reaching transformations which have been occurring spontaneously among Indian peoples are neglected in the judgments of the reforming educators.[4] As a major contemporary instance, we need but turn to the first few pages of a recent book, representing the work of a committee of a high repute. The initial paragraph states that the goal of public policy should be "making the Indian a self-respecting and useful American citizen" and that this requires "restoring his pride of origin and faith in himself," while on the following page we find that very origin being derogated and distorted with the left-handed remark that, "It would be unwise to dismiss all that is in the traditional Indian culture as being necessarily a barrier to change."[5] The mythic image of an unchanging traditional Indian culture does not bear discussion here. Rather, we direct attention to the fact that such a remark could be advanced as the theme of a contemporary book about Indians, and that this book then received favorable reviews both from liberals involved in Indian affairs and from the national Indian interest organizations. Clearly, such reviewers take it for granted that Indian education should be unidirectional — e.g., none seemed to think it noteworthy that the last chapter of the book is on "Policies Which Impede Indian Assimilation," the implication of that title being that the necessary goal is total ethnic and cultural dissolution.

An alternate way of perceiving the unidirectionality which characterizes "Indian education" is to note the curious division of labor bifurcating the process of cultural exchange with Indian peoples. That is, missionaries and educators have devoted themselves to instructing the Indians but not to learning from or being influenced by them; whereas ethnographers have devoted themselves to learning from the Indians but not to teaching or influencing them. Thus, the ethnographers valued the learning of the native languages, while the schoolmasters and missionaries only seldom bothered to learn them, even when the native language was the primary tongue of their Indian pupils and the primary domestic and ceremonial medium of the community in which they were laboring.[6]

Because Indian educational programs have been unidirectionally organized, deliberately ignoring native languages and traditions, they have had to proceed more via duress than suasion. Today the duress is in the laws of compulsory attendance, as enforced by an appropriate officer; but the climax of traditional "Indian education" was the forcible seizing or kidnapping of Indian children by agents of the U.S. government.

programs were designed to shape them within the molds of the con-
These children were then incarcerated in boarding establishments whose
quering society. Yet the irony of this crude and brutal effort was that,
while the mass of children underwent profound changes, their very
aggregation provided them with the need and opportunity to cohere and
resist. Like the inmates of any total institution, Indian pupils developed
their own norms and values, which were neither those of their Indian
elders nor those of their non-Indian instructors. This process of autonomous development has continued to distinguish much of Indian conduct
in relation to modern programs and schools, including the classroom we
will be reviewing.[7]

## TRIBAL CHEROKEE COMMUNITIES

The consequence of the various reformative and educational programs
aimed at the Indian peoples has been not to eliminate the target societies
but, paradoxically, to encourage an evolution which has sheltered an
ethnic and distinct identity, so that today there remain a relatively large
number of persons, identified as Indians, and dwelling together in en-
claved, ethnically, and culturally distinctive communities. The Tribal
Cherokee of contemporary northeastern Oklahoma are not untypical.[8]
Like other Indian communities, they have lost to federal, state, and local
agencies the greater measure of their political autonomy. Many contemporary Indian peoples do have "Tribal Governments," but these do
not correspond to traditional modes of social organization or proceed by
traditional modes of deliberation and action. In the specific case of the
Oklahoma Cherokee, for instance, the Tribal Government is a nonelected,
nonrepresentative, and self-perpetuating clique, headed by individuals
of great wealth and political power, while the Tribal Cherokee are among
the poorest denizens of a depressed region, whose indigenous associations
are denied recognition by the Bureau of Indian Affairs.

The Cherokee of Oklahoma once practiced an intensive and skilled
subsistence agriculture, which has all but disappeared as the Indians
have lost their lands and been denied the opportunity to practice traditional forms of land tenure. The rural lands are now used principally for
cattle ranching (often practiced on a very large scale) and for tourism
and a few local industries (e.g., plant nurseries, chicken processing), or
crops such as strawberries, which require a cheap and docile labor
supply. Until the recent building of dams and paved highways and the
concomitant attempt to develop the region as a vacationland, the Tribal
Cherokee were able to supplement their diet with occasional game or
fish, but they now find themselves harassed by state game and fish regulations, and subjected to the competition of weekend and vacation sports-
men.

Like the other Indian societies of North America, the Cherokee have been goaded along a continuum that led from being autonomous societies to being a "domestic dependent nation" and thence to being an ethnically subordinated people in a caste-like status. In Oklahoma there is a distinctive noncaste peculiarity, since a vast majority of the population proudly claim to be of "Indian descent" as this significes a lineage deriving from the earliest settlers. To be "of Cherokee descent" is, therefore, a mark of distinction, particularly in the northeast of Oklahoma, where this connotes such historic events as "Civilized Tribes" and the "Trail of Tears."[9] Yet, paradoxically, there exist others whose claim to Indianness is undeniable, but whose mode of life is offensive to the middle class. The term "Indian" tends to be used to denote those who are considered idle, irresponsible, uneducated, and a burden to the decent and taxpaying element of the area. Within northeastern Oklahoma, these "Indians" are the Tribal Cherokees, and their communities are marked by high rates of unemployment, pitifully low cash incomes, and a disproportionate representation on relief agency rolls. Perhaps the major respect in which the Cherokee Indians differ from groups like the Sioux of Pine Ridge is that the latter, being situated on a well-known federal reservation, are the recipients of myriads of programs from a multiplicity of federal, private, and local agencies, whereas the Cherokee are still mainly the targets of welfare workers, sheriffs, and aggressive entrepreneurs.[10]

In this essay we wish to focus on the schools attended by Indian children in the cases where they are the preponderant element of the school population. This condition is realized not only on reservations, where the federal government operates a special school system under the administration of the Bureau of Indian Affairs, but also in other regions by virtue of covert systems of segregation. As in the case of Negro/white segregation, the basis is usually ecological. Thus, in northeastern Oklahoma the rural concentrations of Tribal Cherokee along the stream beds in the hill country predispose toward a segregated system at the elementary levels. But the guiding principle is social, so that there is reverse busing of Tribal Cherokee children living in towns and of middle-class white children living in the countryside. Within the rural elementary schools, the Indian children confront educators who are ethnically and linguistically alien, even when they appear to be neighbors (of Cherokee or non-Cherokee descent) from an adjacent or similar geographic area.

Such classrooms maybe denominated as "cross-cultural," although the ingredients contributed by each party seem to be weighted against the Indian pupils. The nature and layout of the school campus, the structure and spatial divisions of the school buildings, the very chairs and their array, all these are products of the greater society and its culture — indeed, they may at first glance seem so conventional that they fail to register with the academic observer the significance of their presence within a cross-cultural transaction. Equally conventional, and almost more difficult to apprehend as significant, is the temporal structure: the school period; the school day; and the school calendar. The spatial and temporal grid by which the lives of the Indian pupils are organized is foreign to their native traditions, manifesting as it does the symbolic structure of the society which has encompassed them.

The observer thus anticipates that the classroom will be the arena for an unequal clash of cultures. Since the parental society is fenced out of the school, whatever distinctive traditions have been transmitted to their children will now be "taught out" of them; and the wealth, power, and technical supremacy of the greater society will smash and engulf these traditionalized folk. Forced to attend school, the Indian children there must face educators who derive their financial support, their training and ideology, their professional affiliation and bureaucratic status, from a complex of agencies and institutions based far outside the local Indian community. The process is designed to be unidirectional; the children are to be "educated" and the Indian communities thus to be transformed. Meanwhile, neither the educator nor the agencies for which he is a representative are presumed to be altered — at least by the learning process.

## CHEROKEES IN THE CLASSROOM

The classrooms where Indian students and a white teacher create a complex and shifting sequence of interactions exhibit as many varieties of reality and illusion as there are possible observers. One such illusion — in the eyes of the white educator — is that the Cherokee are model pupils. Within their homes they have learned that restraint and caution is the proper mode of relating to others; therefore in the classroom the teacher finds it unnecessary to enforce discipline. As early as the second grade, the children sit with perfect posture, absorbed in their readers, rarely talking — and then only in the softest of tones — and never fidgeting. Even when they are marking time, unable to understand what is occurring within the classroom, or bored by what they are able to understand, they make themselves unobtrusive while keeping one ear attuned to the educational interchange. They respect competence in scholastic work, and their voluntary activities both in and out of school are organized surprisingly often and with great intensity about such skills. Eager to learn, they devote long periods of time to their assignments, while older and more experienced students instruct their siblings in the more advanced arithmetic they will be encountering at higher grade levels.

To the alien observer (whether local teacher or otherwise), the Cherokee children seem to love to "play school." The senior author, for example, recalls talking during one recess period with an elderly white woman who had devoted many years to teaching in a one-room school situated in an isolated rural Cherokee community and who now was responsible for the intermediate grades in a more consolidated enterprise that still was predominantly Cherokee. "You just have to watch these children," she said. "If you don't pay no mind, they'll stay in all recess. They like to play school." And, as if to illustrate her point, she excused herself, went back into the school building, and returned with a straggle of children. "They told me they had work they wanted to do, but it is too nice for them to stay inside. . . . You know, I forgot how noisy students were until I went to [the County Seat] for a teacher's meeting. It's time for me to ring the bell now. If I don't, they will come around and remind me pretty soon."

Given the seeming dedication of her pupils, the naive observer might have judged this woman an exceedingly skilled and effective teacher. Yet in reality, she was a rather poor teacher, and at the time of graduation the pupils of her one-room school knew scarcely any English — a fact so well known that parents said of her, "She don't teach them anything!"

Like many of her white colleagues, this woman was interpreting Cherokee conduct from within her own culture, as is evident in her description of the intensive involvement of her pupils in learning tasks as "*playing* school." In kindred fashion, other teachers describe the silence of the students as timidity or shyness, and their control and restraint as docility. Most teachers are unable to perceive more than their own phase of the complex reality which occurs within their classrooms because they are too firmly set within their own traditions, being the products of rural towns and of small state teachers' colleges, and now working within and limited by a tightly-structured institutional context. Certainly, one benefit of teaching Indians in rural schools is that the educators are sheltered from observation and criticism. Except for their own consciences and professional ideologies, no one cares about, guides or supervises their performance, and little pressure is exerted to encourage them to enlarge their awareness of classroom realities.

Even for ourselves — who have had much experience in observing Indian classrooms — many hours of patient and careful watching were required, plus the development of some intimacy with the local community, before we began to appreciate the complexities of interaction within the Cherokee schoolroom. The shape assumed by the clash of cultures was a subtle one. At first, it could be appreciated most easily in the frustration of the teachers; the war within the classrooms was so cold that its daily battles were not evident, except at the close of the day as the teachers assessed their lack of pedagogical accomplishment. Those teachers who defined their mission as a "teaching out" of native traditions were failing to make any headway; and some of these good people had come to doubt their ability to work with such difficult and retiring children (actually, as we soon discovered, their classes contained a fair share of youngsters who were eager, alert, intelligent, and industrious). A few teachers had resigned themselves to marking time, while surrendering all notions of genuine instruction.

As these phenomena began to impress themselves upon us, we began to discern in these classrooms an active social entity that we came to call "The Cherokee School Society." Later still, we were surprised to discover in other classrooms, which we came to call "Intercultural Classrooms," that this Society remained latent and that instead the teacher and students were constructing intercultural bridges for communication and instruction (these will be discussed in the next section).

In order to comprehend the complexity of classroom interaction, we need to remind ourselves that the children who perform here as pupils have been socialized (or enculturated) within the world of the Tribal Cherokee as fully and extensively as have any children of their age in other communities. In short, we must disregard the material poverty of the Tribal Cherokee families and their lower-class status and avoid any of the cant about "cultural deprivation" or "cultural disadvantage." These children are culturally alien, and for the outsider (whether educator or social researcher) to enter into their universe is as demanding as the mastering of an utterly foreign tongue. In the compass of a brief article, we can do no more than indicate a few of the more striking evidences of this distinctive cultural background.

Even in the first grade, Cherokee children exhibit a remarkable propensity for precision and thoroughness. Asked to arrange a set of colored matchsticks into a pyramidal form, the children became so thoroughly involved in maintaining an impeccable vertical and horizontal alignment that they were oblivious to the number learning which they are supposed to acquire via this digital exercise. These six-year-olds do not resolve the task by leaving it at the level of achievement for which their physical dexterity would suffice, but continue to manipulate the sticks in a patient effort to create order beyond the limitations of the material and their own skills. As they mature, the Cherokee students continue this patient and determined ordering of the world, but as a congregate activity that is more often directed at social than physical relationships. At times, this orientation is manifested in an effort toward a precision in social affairs that is startling to witness in persons so young (here, sixth graders):

The teacher has asked about the kinds of things which early pioneers would say to each other in the evening around the campfire as they were traveling.

Jane: "Save your food."

Teacher: "That's preaching."

Jane and Sally (together): "No."

Jane: "That is just to tell you." (The tone of voice makes her sound just like a teacher.)

The teacher agrees, and his acquiescent tone makes him sound like the student. He continues, "They would get you in a room. . . ."

Jane interrupts: "Not in a room."

Teacher: "In around a campfire then." He continues by asking if everyone would be given a chance to speak or just representatives.

Dick: "That would take all night; they might forget." Jane and Sally agree that representatives would be the right way.

The foregoing is as significant for the form of the interaction, as it is revealing of the students' concern for the precise reconstruction of a historical event. The students have wrought a reversal of roles, so that *their* standards of precision and *their* notions of social intercourse emerge as normative for the discussion.

Although this kind of exchange may be rare — actually it is typical only of the Intercultural Classroom — we have cited it here, as reflecting many of the norms of Cherokee students. As healthy children, they are oriented toward the world of their elders, and they see their adult goal as participating in the Cherokee community of their parents. In this sense, the art of relating to other persons so that learning, or other cooperative efforts, may proceed fruitfully and without friction becomes more important to them than the mastery of particular scholastic tasks, whose relevance in any case may be dubious. In the matrix of the classroom they learn to sustain, order, and control the relationships of a Cherokee community; in so doing they are proceeding toward adult maturity and responsibility. According to these norms, the educational exchange is voluntary for both students and teachers and is governed by a mutual respect.

In any educational transaction, the Cherokee School Society is actively judging the competence of the teacher and allowing him a corresponding function as leader. Their collective appraisal does not tolerate the authoritarian stance assumed by some educators ("You must learn this!") but rather facilitates the emergence of a situation in which the teacher leads because he knows ("I am teaching you this because you are indicating that you wish to learn . . ."). A consequence of this configuration (or, in the eyes of an unsympathetic observer, a symptom) is that the

Cherokee students may organize themselves to resist certain categories of knowledge that the school administration has formally chosen to require of them.

We must bear in mind that within the Tribal Cherokee community, the reading or writing of English, calculating arithmetically, and even speaking English have minor employment and minimal utility. By the intermediate grades, the students perceive that, with no more than a marginal proficiency in spoken or written English, their elders are none-theless leading satisfactory lives *as Cherokees*. Attempts to exhort them toward a high standard of English proficiency and a lengthy period of time-serving in school are likely to evoke a sophisticated negative reac-tion. After one such educational sermon, a ten-year-old boy bluntly pointed out to his teacher that a Cherokee adult, greatly admired within the local community — and senior kin to many of the pupils present — had only a fifth-grade education. When the teacher attempted to evade this rebuttal by suggesting that the students would, as adults, feel inferior because they lacked a lengthy education and could not speak good English, the pupils were again able to rebut. To the teacher's challenge, "Who would you talk to?" the same boy responded, "To other Cherokee!"

Orienting themselves toward the community of their elders, the Chero-kee students respond to the pressures of the alien educators by organizing themselves as The Cherokee School Society. As the teacher molds the outer forms of class procedure, the children exploit his obtuseness as a white alien to construct the terms on which they will act as students. But, while among the Oglala Sioux this transformation is effected with a won-drous boldness and insouciance,[11] here among the Cherokee it is with an exquisite social sensibility. A gesture, an inflection in voice, a movement of the eye is as meaningful as a large volume of words would be for their white peers. By the upper elementary grades, the result is a multiple reality according to which the adolescent Cherokee appear now as quiet and shy, or again as stoical and calm, or yet again (apparent only after prolonged observation) as engaged in the most intricate web of sociable interaction. Such delicacy of intercourse, so refined a sensi-bility, reflects and requires a precision of movement, a neat and exact ordering of the universe.

Interestingly, the Cherokee School Society does not reject the curricular tasks formulated by the alien educational administrators. In fact, the pupils proceed with their usual patient intensity to labor at assignments that can have no bearing on their tradition or experience. The fact that they are unable to relate these materials meaningfully to life within the Cherokee community acts as an increasing barrier to their mastery of them. In particular, the fact that most students have acquired no more than rudimentary proficiency in spoken English means that the involved patterns of the printed language in the advanced texts are beyond their most diligent endeavors; neither the language nor the topics can be deciphered.

So far, we have emphasized that the Cherokee students are interested in learning and that, from the viewpoint of the educator, they are docile pupils. Yet the cultural differences noted, and the basic social separateness and lack of communication, ensure that conflicts will develop and become more intensive as the students mature. The school cannot proceed along the trackways established by educational authority, nor can it be switched by the students into becoming an adjunct of the rural Cherokee community. Hence, as the children mature, the tension within the schoolroom becomes more extreme. Since the participants are one adult and many children, and since the latter are imbued with a cultural standard of nonviolence and passive resistance, open confrontations do not occur. Instead, what typically happens is that, by the seventh and eighth grades the students have surrounded themselves with a wall of silence impenetrable by the outsider, while sheltering a rich emotional communion among themselves. The silence is positive, not simply negative or withdrawing, and it shelters them so that, among other things, they can pursue their scholastic interests in their own style and pace. By their silence they exercise control over the teacher and maneuver him toward a mode of participation that meets their standards, as the following instance illustrates:

Teacher: "Who was Dwight David Eisenhower?"
Silence.
Teacher: "Have you heard of him, Joan?" She moves her eyes from his stare and smiles briefly.
Very quickly, the teacher jumps to the next person. There is something in his voice that is light and not deadly serious or moralistic in the way that is customary of him. He is just having fun, and this comes through so that the kids have picked it up. They respond to the tone, not to the question, "Alice?"
Alice leans back in her chair; her blank stare into space has disappeared, and her eyes are averted. She blushes. Now, she grins.
The teacher does not wait, "Wayne?"
Wayne is sitting straight, and his face wears a cockeyed smile that says he knows something. He says nothing.
Seeing the foxy grin, the teacher shifts again, "Wayne, you know?" This is a question and that makes all the difference. There is no challenge, no game-playing, and the interrogation mark challenges Wayne's competency. But Wayne maintains the foxy grin and shakes his head, negative.
Quickly, the teacher calls on another, "Jake?" He bends his head down and grins but says nothing.

Teacher (in authoritative tone): "Nancy, tell me." But she says nothing, keeping her head lowered, although usually she answers when called upon. The teacher switches tones again, so that what he is asking of Nancy has become a command. Perhaps he catches this, for he switches again to the lighter tone, and says; "Tell, me, Debra."

The only one in the room who doesn't speak Cherokee, Debra answers in a flat voice: "President."

As soon as the answer is given, there are many covert smiles, and Alice blushes. They all knew who he was.

To most educators and observers, such an incident is perplexing. Who within that classroom really is exercising authority? Are the students deficient in their comprehension either of English or of the subject matter? Are they, perhaps, flexing their social muscles and mocking the teacher — because they don't like the lesson, they don't like him to act as he is acting, or why? For the Cherokee School Society has created within the formal confines of the institutional classroom another social edifice, their own "classroom," so that at times there appears to be not simply a clash of cultural traditions but a cold war between rival definitions of the classroom. Such tension is not proper within Cherokee tradition, since the Tribal Cherokee value harmonious social relationships and frown upon social conflict.[12] Moderate disagreement is resolved by prolonged discussion interspersed, wherever possible, by joking and jesting, while severe disagreement leads to withdrawal from the conflict-inducing situation. Given the compulsory nature of school attendance, however, the students cannot withdraw from the classroom, much as they might wish to, and the teacher can withdraw only by losing his job and his income. Thus, an unmanageable tension may develop if the teacher is unable to recognize the Cherokee pupils as his peers who, through open discussion, may share with him in the decisions as to the organizing and operating of the school.

The unresolved conflict of cultural differences typifies these classrooms. Within them, there is little pedagogy, much silence, and an atmosphere that is apprehended by Indians (or observers of kindred sensibility) as ominous with tension. The following incident, participated in by Dumont, exhibits all these features in miniature:

The classroom was small and the teacher had begun to relate a joke to Dumont. Not far away were seated four teenage Cherokee, and the teacher decided to include them within the range of his ebullience: "Boys, I want to tell you a joke. . . ." It was one of those that played upon the stoical endurance of Indians in adapting to the whimsical wishes of whites, and to narrate it in the classroom context was highly ironic. The plot and phrasing were simple, and easily apprehended by the students. But when the teacher had finished, they merely continued looking toward him, with their eyes focused, not upon him, but fixed at some point above or to the side of his eyes. As he awaited their laughter, their expressions did not alter but they continued to stare at the same fixed point and then gradually lowered their heads to their work.

The Cherokee School Society maintains a rigid law of balance that says, in effect, we will change when the teacher changes. If the teacher becomes involved in appreciating the ways of his students, then they will respond with an interest in his ways. Needless to say, the older the students become, the higher their grade-level, the less is the likelihood that this reciprocity will be initiated by their educators. There is thus a deep tragedy, for it is the students who lose and suffer the most. Yet the School Society is their technique for protecting themselves in order to endure the alien intrusiveness of the teacher and the discourtesy and barbarity of the school. Occasionally, observer and students experience a happier interlude, for some teachers are able to enter into a real intercultural exchange. Unfortunately, they are as rare as they are remarkable. And they are sometimes unaware of their truly prodigious achievements in establishing what we term the Intercultural Classroom.

## THE INTERCULTURAL CLASSROOM

Within the Intercultural Classroom, Tribal Cherokee students do such remarkable things as engaging in lengthy conversations with the teacher about academic subjects. For this to occur, the teacher must be responsive to the distinctive norms and expectations of the students; but, strikingly, he need not abide by these nor accept norms as long as he is able to persuade the students of his willingness to learn about them and to accommodate to them. This attitude places the teacher on a plane of parity such that he must learn from his students the most rudimentary Cherokee cultural prescriptions. Naturally, both parties experience conflicts in this reshuffling of teacher/learner roles. Certainly, such interaction is not what the teacher has been trained to sustain. Yet there arise structured devices for reducing these conflicts.

For instance, to bridge the social breaches that are always opening, the Cherokee students urge forward one of their members — not always the same person — to mediate and harmonize. Then if the teacher, by an unconscious presumption, disrupts the harmonious flow of class activity, it is the mediator whose deft maneuver reduces the intensity of the tension and relaxes the participants. In a sense, what the mediator does is to restore parity between teacher and students by removing the nimbus of authority from the teacher, thus allowing the students to work out with the teacher a compromise which redirects class activities and so permits them to regain their proper tempo. The teacher is freed to pursue the subject matter, but as scholastic assistant rather than classroom tyrant. With this in mind, let us examine the sequence of events which ended in a conversational repartee already quoted:

> They are reading about important men in history and have just finished with a section about adult educators.
> Teacher: (Referring to the observers.) "We have two distinguished educators here. Does this make you feel proud?"
> It is quiet for the first time in the room. It is likely that the students are all thinking, how could we be proud of educators! As observer, I am uneasy and expectant; I wonder who will break the silence and how he will handle the delicate situation.
> John: "I don't like schools myself." (!)
> Teacher: "Would you quit school if you could?" (He's asking for it!)
> John (a firm answer): "Yes."
> Teacher: "Suppose that your dad came and said you could quit, but he brought you a shovel and said, 'Dig a ditch from here to Brown's house,' since you weren't going to school."
> John: "Okay."
> Another student: "He might learn something."
> Everyone finds this humorous; the class is in good spirits and is moving along.
> John, too, is quick to reply: "Might strike gold." The topic has been discussed earlier in class. (The interaction develops and others become involved, including the more reticent students.)

Here it is John who has played, and most successfully, the role of mediator. The teacher had ventured into a delicate area that had the potential of disrupting the classroom atmosphere. The responding silence was a token of the social peril, and John, who so often among his peers had assumed the mediating role, moved forward first, boldly countering with a declaration as strong as the teacher's. As a consequence, he redefined the structure of the interaction and became the initiator of the exchange, while the teacher merely sustained it. A cultural bridge was thereby constructed, accessible alike to students and teacher; and John's "Okay" is his consent to the conditions of the structure.

The mediating role becomes less necessary as the teacher grows more attuned to the interactional norms of Indian society; it becomes more difficult (if more essential) if the teacher insists on maintaining a tyrannical control over the classroom. Yet, even as the teacher is attuned, some function is reserved for a mediator, for the teacher tends to proceed in terms of work to be done by an abstract student, while the mediator explores how the task can be redefined within the framework of the Cherokee student. His is a work of adaptation, and insofar as he is successful, the classroom becomes *intercultural* — a locus where persons of different cultural traditions can engage in mutually beneficial transactions without affront to either party.

What must the teacher do to foster the emergence of an intercultural classroom within the crosscultural situation? The answer would require another essay at least as long as the present one, but it may be helpful to quote the remarks of one teacher in the region:

> I can't follow a lesson plan, and I just go along by ear. I've taught Cherokee students for six years in high school, and this is my first [year] in elementary school." Referring, then to his experiences as a high school coach, he continued, "The thing you have to do, if you get a team, is that you got to get them to cooperate. . . .

At first glance, this appears at odds with our earlier assertions about the spontaneous emergence of the Cherokee School Society, not to mention contradictory to the conventional notions that Indians will not compete with each other. But what he is explaining is that unless the teacher chooses to recognize the social nature of the classroom and to work toward integrating his teaching with that life, he will not be able to elicit active learning experiences from his pupils. Or, to put it negatively, if the teacher does not work with his Indian students as a social group, their union will be directed toward other goals. Yet the teacher can secure their response only if he "gets them" to cooperate; he cannot "make them" do so.

## CONCLUSION

The foregoing report provides the basis for judgements and hypotheses on a variety of levels. On the practical level, it would seem that ethnic integration is not an essential precondition for satisfactory education of groups from a low socioeconomic background. The Tribal Cherokee certainly are impoverished and poorly educated. Nevertheless, we would predict that the consolidation of rural schools into larger, better-staffed, and better-equipped schools in northeastern Oklahoma may actually lead to deterioration rather than improvement of the educational condition. Given the ethos of the Tribal Cherokee, consolidation may mean the irremediable loss of many opportunities for assisting their children educationally.

On the methodological level, we are reminded of how sociologically valuable it is for researchers to focus on the frontier situation "where peoples meet."[13] The resulting accommodations, adaptations, and divisions of labor are an enlightening and fascinating phenomenon, which especially deserve to be studied as a corrective to those theoretical systems which regard the national society as an integrated social system. On the methodological level also, our study illustrates anew the value of ethnographic observations of classroom activities. Basic and simple as it may seem, and unpretentious in the face of modern testing procedures, direct observation still has much to teach us.[14]

Finally, on the substantive level, the research reported here cautions against the erosion of our conceptual armamentarium when researchers allow their research problems to be defined by educational administrators. When that happens, the educational situation of peoples such as the Indians tends to be conceived in terms of individual pupils and their "cultural deprivation." The researcher then is asked to assist the administration in raising these disadvantaged individuals to the point where they can compete in school in the same fashion as do white middle-class children. Our research is a reminder that such styles of conceptualization neglect the social nature of the classrooms and the social ties among the pupils. They also neglect the tension between teacher and pupils as a social group, and the struggles that occur when the teacher presses for individualistic achievement at the expense of group solidarity.[15]

## NOTES

1. This study is a product of the Indian Education Research Project sponsored by the University of Kansas under contract with the U.S. Office of Education according to the provisions of the Cooperative Research Act. The Principal Investigator was Murray L. Wax, and the field research on rural schools was conducted by Robert V. Dumont and Mildred Dickeman, with assistance from Lucille Proctor, Elsie Willingham, Kathryn RedCorn, Clyde and Della Warrior. Sole responsibility for this text rests with the authors.

   A paper entitled "The Intercultural Classroom," having much the same orientation but differing in details and in structure of the argument, was presented by Robert V. Dumont at a panel on Indian education at the annual meetings of the Society for Applied Anthropology, Washington, D.C., Spring, 1967.

2. *Cf.* Rosalie H. Wax and Murray L. Wax (1965), reprinted in Stuart Levine and Nancy O. Lurie (eds.), (1968), pp. 163–169.

3. For an enlightening account of the mission schools for American Indians, see the chapter, "Nurseries of Morality," in Robert F. Berkhofer, Jr. (1965), pp. 20–43.

4. Unfortunately, some of the anthropological textbooks on American Indians are guilty of the same static imagery, as they present particular tribes in "the ethnographic present." Conspicuous and happy exceptions are such books as Edward H. Spicer, *Cycles of Conquest*, University of Arizona Press, Tucson, Arizona, 1962, and Fred Eggan, *The American Indian*, Aldine Press, Chicago, Illinois, 1966. *Cf.* Murray L. Wax, "The White

Man's Burdensome 'Business;' A Review Essay on the Change and Constancy of Literature on the American Indians," *Social Problems,* Vol. 16, No. 1, 1968, pp. 106–113.

5. *The Indian: America's Unfinished Business,* compiled by William A. Brophy and Sophie D. Aberle, University of Oklahoma Press, Norman, Oklahoma, 1966, pp. 3–4.

6. While missionaries have always included a small number of individuals who have patiently tried to understand the language and culture of their alien flock, and while some few missionaries have been excellent ethnographers, the majority, particularly on the North American continent, have had quite the opposite attitude. Today, missionary activity on the world scene has become increasingly sophisticated and culturally humble (as evidenced by *Practical Anthropology*), yet it is noteworthy how slowly this has affected labors among American Indians. Despite a century (or even several!) of mission activity among some tribes, the church in many instances remains a mission, detached from tribal influence or control, and the clergyman continues to be a person who is culturally alien and socially isolated and who regards his task as preaching but not learning.

7. An excellent brief summary and bibliography of the history of research on Indian education is found in the presentation by Philleo Nash, *Proceedings of the National Research Conference on American Indian Education,* edited by Herbert A. Aurbach, Kalamazoo, Michigan, The Society for the Study of Social Problems, 1967, pp. 6–30. In order to discuss the history of Indian education research, Nash had to deal with some of the major changes of policy as well. The Conference *Proceedings* also contain a summary review by William H. Kelly of current research on Indian education and other helpful discussions and bibliographies. See also Willard W. Beatty (1956), pp. 16–49; Evelyn C. Adams (1946); Harold E. Fey and D'Arcy McNickle (1959), Chapter 12. And of course the Meriam Report included an intensive assessment of the goals and achievements of Indian education: Lewis Meriam and Associates (1928), especially pp. 346–429.

8. We take the term "Tribal Cherokee" from the research reports of Albert Wahrhaftig, which, in addition to whatever information may be inferred from the tables of the U.S. Census, constitute the best recent source on the condition of the Cherokee of Oklahoma. See, e.g., his "Social and Economic Characteristics of the Cherokee Population of Eastern Oklahoma" and "The Tribal Cherokee Population of Eastern Oklahoma," both produced under sponsorship of the Carnegie Cross-cultural Education Project of the University of Chicago, 1965 (mimeographed); and "Community and the Caretakers," *New University Thought,* Vol. 4, No. 4, 1966/67, pp. 54–76. See also, Murray L. Wax (1967) (mimeographed), and Angie Debo (1951).

9. Responding to contact and intermarriage with the European invaders, the Cherokee were one of several tribes noteworthy during the 18th century for their adoption of foreign techniques. By 1827 they had organized themselves as a Cherokee Nation, complete with an elective bicameral leg-

islature and a national superior court. Meantime, Sequoyah had been perfecting his syllabary, and in 1828 there began the publication of *The Cherokee Phoenix*, a bilingual weekly. Developments of this character led to the Cherokee and several neighboring tribes of the southeastern U.S. being called, "The Civilized Tribes;" nevertheless, this did not protect them from the greed of the white settlers, particularly in Georgia. When the Indian nations would not cede their lands peaceably, Andrew Jackson employed federal troops to herd the Indian peoples westward into the region which subsequently was to become Oklahoma. There the survivors of the terrible journey ("The Trail of Tears") incorporated themselves once again as a Cherokee Nation and remained such until dissolved by act of Congress early in the present century. Today, books, museums, and pageants commemorate these events and highlight for the tourists the high-cultural aspects of upper-status life in the Cherokee Nation. Judged by that historical standard, the life of contemporary Tribal Cherokee constitutes a blot on a record otherwise cherished by Oklahomans of Cherokee descent.

10. *Cf.* Murray L. Wax and Rosalie H. Wax (1968), pp. 101–118.

11. *Cf.* Murray L. Wax, Rosalie H. Wax, and Robert V. Dumont, Jr. (1964), Chapter 6.

12. See the discussions of "The Harmony Ethic," in John Gulick (1960), pp. 135–139 *et passim.*

13. Everett C. Hughes and Helen M. Hughes (1952).

14. Consider for example, the impact and contribution of such recent books which rely either on direct observation or participation observation of classrooms as John Holt, *How Children Fail*, Delta, New York, 1964; Harry F. Wolcott, *A Kwakiutl Village and School*, Holt, Rinehart and Winston, New York, 1967; Wax, Wax, and Dumont, *op. cit.;* Estelle Fuchs, *Pickets at the Gates*, The Free Press, New York, 1966; G. Alexander Moore, *Realities of the Urban Classroom: Observations in Elementary Schools*, Doubleday Anchor, New York, 1967; Elizabeth M. Eddy, *Walk the White Line*, Doubleday Anchor, New York, 1967.

15. Such phenomena were clearly noted by Willard Waller in his *Sociology of Teaching*, first published in 1932, reprinted by Science Editions, John Wiley, New York, 1965. It is unfortunate to see the neglect of such elementary sociological considerations in much of the more recent literature of the "sociology of education."

# 16 ................

# Manchild in the Promised Land

CLAUDE BROWN

I can't remember going to sleep that first night at Wiltwyck. I only remember lying there in a strange bed, in a strange place, for what seemed like a year-long night. I closed my eyes about a million times, hoping that I would open them and escape from that bad dream. But every time I opened my eyes, it was still there.

By the time daylight began to creep into that big old room that everybody was calling a dormitory, I had already been planning for a good two hours how I was going to get out of Wiltwyck. I couldn't run away, because I didn't know where I was and wouldn't have known which way to run. So the best way to get out was to talk that white man named Mr. Stillman into letting me go home. I decided to find Mr. Stillman as soon as I got up, and I was going to tell him that I had something real important to tell him. While Mr. Stillman was listening to me, I was going to fall down and grab my chest and start breathing real hard, like I was dying. They would probably take me to the hospital and try to find out what was wrong with me, and when they couldn't find anything wrong, they would probably kick me out of the hospital. But then I was going to stop eating, stop talking, and eat some soap powder or a lot of salt and get real sick. When they put me back in the hospital and tried to feed me I wasn't going to eat, not even if they gave me fried chicken and pear pie. And every time the doctor asked me how I felt, I was going to say, "I wanna go home." That's all I was going to say to anybody, and I wasn't going to eat anything as long as they kept me there.

I knew they would have to send me home. They wouldn't want me to die on them. I was only up there for playing hookey and stealing and stuff like that. I hadn't killed anybody, so they couldn't let me die.

When a real tall, real light-skinned man came into the dormitory, clicked on the lights, and started yelling all over the place, everything was all set in my mind. I was sure I would be back on the streets by the next week.

I was still lying in bed thinking about how I was going to get out of Wiltwyck when a voice boomed, "Let's git one!" right in my ear. Before I could turn my head to look at him, my bed started jumping up and down real fast. The bed stopped jumping all of a sudden, then the bed next to mine started jumping up and down. The light-skinned, white-looking man was shaking it and yelling, "Let's git one!" Guys were jumping out of bed and running to the bathroom, so I jumped out of bed and ran to the bathroom too. I asked a guy who was washing next to me how I could see Mr. Stillman. He told me all I had to do was go to his office. After throwing a handful of water on my face, I dashed out the door to find Mr. Stillman's office. Before I could get out of the house, I heard a voice booming out my name. Before I stopped running, I knew it was that tall, light-skinned man. And before I turned around, I knew that I didn't like that man and never would.

When I told him where I was going, he said Mr. Stillman wasn't in his office yet and that I had to make up my bed before I could go to see him. So I went back and made up my bed, then I started out to see Mr. Stillman again. Again I heard the real loud voice of the man that everybody was calling Simms. When I turned around this time, I knew that I would never like anybody named Simms as long as I lived.

The man named Simms told me that Mr. Stillman wasn't going to be in his office until after breakfast and that in the meantime someone would show me what my job in the house was. After I finished my job, which was cleaning the bathroom, and had breakfast, a bell rang. Everybody started heading for the last place I wanted to go — the school building. I started walking away from the crowd, but before I could begin to hope that I was going to get to Mr. Stillman's office, I heard the voice that I had learned to hate in just a few hours. I turned around and faced Simms. At first, I wanted to cry. Here was this big man I hated and couldn't do anything to. If I hit him, he probably would kill me. But I had to do something, because he kept fucking with me. Mr. Simms asked me where I was going. I opened my mouth to tell him, but the thing I heard myself saying — smiling to protect myself — was, "Mr. Simms, are you white or colored?" When I heard what I said, I thought, Lord, please have mercy on me.

After what seemed like a real long time, Mr. Simms smiled, real quick, and said, "C'mon, boy, you have to go to school now. Mr. Stillman will come to your class when he gets here."

I wished I had called him Mr. Red instead of asking him what I did. Not the way white people say red, but the way Dad and colored people his age say it. I should have said, "Whatcha want now, Mr. Re-e-e-d?" I'll bet he wouldn't have smiled then. He might have killed me, but he wouldn't have smiled. But I don't think he would have killed me — he would have lost his job. Then I thought, The next time he messes wit me, I'll call him that. . . . No, I'll call him yaller. Yeah, I'll say, "Whatcha want, Mr. Yaller Man?" If he wasn' so big, I'd call him yaller nigger. But if I did that, he prob'ly would kill me, job or no job.

I kept asking the teacher, who was a real pretty, light-skinned lady to let me go to see Mr. Stillman. When the teacher got tired of me asking her to let me go, she told me that Mr. Stillman wasn't at the school but that I could see Mr. Upshur, who was Mr. Stillman's assistant. I knew she was lying, but I smiled and asked the teacher to let me go to see Mr. Upshur. The teacher sent one of the guys in the class with me. The guy showed me Mr. Upshur's office and left. I went into the office and asked to see Mr. Stillman. The secretary told me that Mr. Stillman wasn't going to be in all day but that Mr. Upshur would see me as soon as he was free. I sat down and waited for a few minutes, and Mr. Upshur came in. When he said he was Mr. Upshur, I knew he couldn't help me. He was colored. What could he do for anybody?

It seemed that everybody was trying to stop me from seeing Mr. Stillman, but I was going to see him as soon as I got out of school. All I had to do was stop telling people I wanted to see him, then they couldn't stop me.

When I came out of school that first afternoon, Wiltwyck looked different from the way it had looked the day before. The sun was shining. It was real cold, and everything that wasn't moving around was covered with snow and ice. Some of the trees had little sticks stuck in them, with buckets and tin cans hanging on the end of the little sticks. Boys were sledding on a hill near the four houses that everyone lived in. Some were riding two on one sled, some were fighting over one sled, and some were crashing into trees, but everybody seemed to be having a whole lot of fun. The first thing that had caught my eye when I came out of the school building was the trees with the buckets on them. I asked Mr. Cooper, who was the counselor in charge of the sled riding, why the buckets were on the trees. Mr. Cooper told me that they were maple trees and that they were being tapped for the sap to make maple syrup. Mr. Cooper was a real funny-looking man. He was tall, thin, and kind of dark-skinned; not real dark, but a little darker than me. He was scarey-looking at first; he never smiled, and he didn't seem to like anybody. Everybody but me called him Cooper or Coop. Mr. Cooper wasn't a counselor in the house I was in, and I was glad. I didn't like being around him.

I went over to two guys who were fighting over a sled. When I asked whose sled it was, they both said, "Mine." And when I asked if I could have a ride, both of them said, "After me." A guy named Dunbaker, who was my working partner in cleaning the bathroom, came up to the guys who were fighting over the sled. He told them he would hold the sled while they fought to see who was going to get it. Dunbaker gave me the sled and said that I could have one ride but that if I gave him my beret, I could have the sled for the rest of the winter. The beret didn't mean so much to me, but I had to keep it, at least until I could find out why everybody had been trying to steal it ever since I got there. So I made a deal with Dunbaker to let him wear my beret as long as he let me ride the sled.

When I came down the hill for the third time, Dunbaker came up to me and said he wanted to ride the sled. I knew what Dunbaker wanted before he said anything, but I was busy watching a man talking to Mr. Cooper, farther down the hill. He looked like Mr. Stillman. When I got up off the sled, I saw the man coming toward me. He had the same kind of pipe that Mr. Stillman had been smoking the day before, my first day. And he was wearing the same kind of gray coat. When he got close enough for me to see his eyes, I was sure it was Mr. Stillman.

Mr. Stillman — everybody but me called him Stilly — had tiny red eyes that looked at people in a mean way from way back in his head. He must have had the only pair of eyes in the world like that. The pipe was almost as close to Stilly as his eyes. I never saw him without the pipe. I used to think that the pipe was the thing he cared about most in the world. . . . I watched Stilly coming up the slope. His look never changed. He seemed to be in his own world, just him and his pipe. I had tried to see Mr. Stillman all day. He was going to be my out; he was in charge of everything in this crazy place. He was the one who looked like and acted like he knew the most. And now here he was . . . a pair of eyes and a pipe and a big gray coat.

After asking how I was, the pipe waited a while, then it said, "You wanted to see me?"

I just asked him if I know where I could get a sled. I was in Wiltwyck, really in it.

Wiltwyck was different from the other places I had been in. Some guys had been there for years, and just about everybody had at least one real good friend or partner. When two or three guys were partners, they would share everything they got hold of — packages from home, food and fruits that their parents brought them on visiting day, things they stole, and stuff like that. It took me a long time to find a real partner, one I would share my loot and secrets with.

I knew K.B. about a year before we became ace boon coons. K.B. was the first cat I locked with up at Wiltwyck. We had three fights before we decided we couldn't beat each other, but it was a year before we got tight.

K.B. was from the Brownsville section of Brooklyn. He was a little cat with a loud mouth, big eyes, and a left hand that nobody ever saw coming at him. And like me, K.B. could beat a lot of big guys. Being so good with his hands didn't stop K.B. from being one of the nicest cats around. He would always rather argue than fight. Maybe this was because K.B. knew he was real good with his hands and was trying to learn how to be good with talk. He was always trying to get me to tell off guys he didn't like. When we first pulled tight, K.B.'s favorite saying was, "Ask Claude." I think Horse broke him out of that habit by asking him if he thought I was his father.

K.B. and I didn't get to be partners the way most of the guys did. We never said anything about being partners and sharing stuff we got. We just pulled tight and started getting in trouble together, stealing things and fighting together. One day after we became aces, we had our first fight in over a year because K.B. stole some canned apricots out of the kitchen and didn't give me any. After that, we shared everything we stole, found, were given, and even the things we bought. Because I could read and knew a lot of words, K.B. thought I was the smartest cat up at Wiltwyck and maybe in the whole world. I never told him any different.

I think K.B. must have been real shy when he came to Wiltwyck, because he used to beg me to tell him about the girls I knew. Late at night when I was sleepy and tired of lying all day and half the night, I would listen to K.B. tell me about Linda. For the six months that my bed was next to K.B.'s, I went to sleep hearing about Linda. After a week of hearing about Linda, I had to meet her just to see if she was fine as K.B. said she was. K.B. said she was real dark-skinned, had long hair, wore lipstick, had "titties, little ones, but tits just the same," had a pretty face, and was real fresh. K.B. said he had done it to her one time up on the roof, and he used to tell me about it so much and in so many different ways that it had to be a lie.

Most of the time, K.B. couldn't think about anything but girls, and anybody who could tell him a good lie about girls could get him to do things. Sometimes when I wanted K.B. to help me steal something, I would have to promise to tell him about a real pretty, real fresh girl. K.B. was always trying to jerk off, and he said he shot one time; but I didn't see it, so I didn't believe it. But about a year after K.B. and I had moved to Aggrey House, I heard K.B. come tearing down the stairs yelling as loud as he could. It was around one in the morning. He woke everybody in the first-floor dormitory. I was awake and wondering what was going on, when K.B. came running into the dormitory with his dick in his hand and yelling, "Claude, I did it! I did it!" When he reached my bed and yelled out, "Man, I shot," all the beds in the dormitory started jumping, and everybody crowded around my bed with flashlights before K.B. stopped yelling.

Some guys just said things like "Wow" or "Oh, shit," but Rickets said, "Man, that's the real stuff."

Horse said, "Man, that ain't nothin' but dog water."

K.B. said, "That ain't no dog water, man, 'cause it's slimy."

Horse, who was always talking about facts, said, "Man, that can't be scum, 'cause scum is white."

Knowing that scum was white, most of the guys said that Horse was right and that it was just dog water. I said that dog water was more than he ever made. Horse went heading for the bathroom saying he was going to show me what the real stuff looked like. Everybody followed Horse and watched and cheered him on while he tried for the real stuff. Horse only made dog water, just like K.B., but nobody paid much attention — everybody was trying to jerk off that night. It was a matter of life or death. After what seemed like hours of trying and wearing out my arm, I shot for the first time in my life. A lot of other guys did it for the first time too, but some cats just got tired arms.

After K.B. and I had been tight for a few months, a lot of guys started to get tight with us; and before we knew it, we had a gang. Our gang was always robbing the kitchen late at night, gang fighting with Windsor House, or just stealing for the fun of it.

One day in the summer of the year after I came to Wiltwyck, Simms, who had been transferred from Carver House about a year before, came into the house waving a piece of paper, grinning and shouting my name. When he came into the dormitory and saw me sitting on my bed, he ran up to me, stuck the paper in my face, and said, "Read that, Claude Brown." It was a transfer slip for me and K.B. We were going to be moved to Aggrey House, the Big "A," where all the older cats lived and where Simms was a counselor. I didn't like Simms, and I didn't like the idea of going where all those big guys were. Some of them, like Jake Adams and Stumpy Edwards, were real mean cats. I told Simms that I wasn't going to stay in Aggrey House. He just smiled and said, "Don't tell me you're scared, Claude Brown?" I told him I wasn't scared, that I just didn't want to go and wasn't going to stay.

But I really was scared of Simms. I had seen him smack big Jim Cole in the gym one day. Jim Cole was about six feet tall and weighed about 185 pounds. When Simms smacked him, the smack picked Jim up off his feet and slammed him against a wall about ten feet away. Simms was real tall, and he had long arms, big hands, and could move real fast. He would lean toward one side of a cat and hit him when the guy started moving away from him. It wasn't easy to get out of the way if he wanted to hit you. I saw a lot of guys try, but I never saw any of them make it I had only seen Simms hit one cat who didn't cry. That was Stumpy Edwards. And that was another reason I didn't want to go to Aggrey House — I didn't want to be in the same house with a cat who could be hit by Simms and not only wouldn't cry, but even looked mean.

When I told Simms for the second time that I wasn't going to Aggrey House, he showed me Stilly's name on the transfer slip and said, "Come on, boy, git your things. We're gonna see how much hell you can raise over in my house."

I ran to the linen room to get our counselor, Claiborne, and said to him, "Mr. Claiborne, Simms is here wit a piece-a paper, but I ain't goin' no-where."

Simms was right behind me. He handed Claiborne the paper. Clay read the paper and kept looking at it for a while. Then he raised his head, looked at me for a while, smiled sadly, and said, "Claude, get your ace. You gotta go."

Simms was still smiling when K.B. came running in, yelling like he always did. For once, Claiborne didn't bother to tell K.B. not to make so much noise. He just kept looking for some socks for us. K.B. looked at me as if to say, "Is it true?"

Before he could say anything, I said, "Man, I ain't goin'."

K.B. said, "Claiborne, do I have to go?"

Clay turned around. His face was trying to smile when he said, "That's what Mr. Stillman said."

Everything was real quiet in the linen room . . . and real sad too. The only one who wasn't sad was Simms. He was smiling and gloating. I had become the main problem at Wiltwyck, and Simms had been telling me for nearly a year that I would be a different boy if I were in his house. Now he was going to get a chance to prove it.

Claiborne was a strict counselor, but I had gotten used to him. I liked him even though he was always telling me he didn't trust me and always thought I had a hand in everything that went on. The moment he heard something had been stolen, he would come looking for me. But that was all right, because I was usually the one who had stolen it or had told somebody else to steal it or had stolen it from whoever had stolen it first.

Claiborne liked K.B. more than he liked anybody else in Carver House. One day K.B. made a bet with Jody that the next time Claiborne messed with him, he was going to punch Claiborne in the mouth. Jody took the bet, but he wasn't the only one who thought K.B. was lying. We all did. I hoped K.B. was lying, for his own sake. Claiborne was mean and didn't play. On the same day that K.B. made the bet with Jody, Claiborne came into the dormitory and told K.B. to get into his bed and be quiet. K.B. started talking louder than before. Claiborne walked over to K.B. and reached for him. True to his word, K.B. punched Claiborne right smack in the mouth. Claiborne was more shocked than anybody else. This kind of thing just didn't happen to Claiborne, and he didn't know how to take it. Claiborne couldn't hit K.B., since K.B. was just a kid; but he grabbed K.B.'s hand and started twisting it, and K.B. started yelling for Nick, our other counselor, to help him before Claiborne broke his arm. But Claiborne wasn't crazy. For the next two weeks, K.B. was Claiborne's yardbird. He had to go everywhere Claiborne went from morning till night. He even had to ask Claiborne when he wanted to go to the bathroom. When the other guys were playing ball or sledding or ice skating, K.B. would be there, but he had to stay with Claiborne and just watch. The one good thing about it was that everybody knew why K.B. was Clay's yardbird, and it gave him a bigger reputation as a bad cat. After that, Claiborne and K.B. became real good friends. At least the friendship was as good as it could get between counselors and boys.

The day K.B. and I were supposed to go to Aggrey House, I kept wishing Nick was around; but Nick was off. I knew Nick would have done something, because that's the way he was.

I thought Nick was an ugly cat the first time I saw him. But before long, Nick was the most beautiful cat up at Wiltwyck. He came in the door of Carver House one afternoon during the daily rest period. This was a time when everybody had to go and lie on his bed for about two hours. We used this time to bullshit and lie mostly, but sometimes somebody would really go to sleep. Nobody was sleeping when Nick walked into Carver House for the first time. He kind of leaned over when he walked, and he had a big bounce. It was hard to tell if Nick was young or old or young and old. When I first noticed him, K.B. and Jody were talking to him, feeling him out. He was standing just inside the dormitory doorway. I had heard him say, "Hi, fellas." But looking at him, it was hard for me to believe he had said that.

Nick was looking real serious while he was talking to K.B. and Jody. He was a funny-looking guy. He had real sad eyes that kept trying to smile at every cat who came up to him to ask if he was the new counselor and to size him up. His teeth all seemed to be rotten and stuck out too far. Looking at his face, I thought his hair should have had a lot of gray in it, but it was a rough black all over. I liked the way Nick looked — kind of cautious, as if he knew he was in our turf and had to be cool till we got to like him. I started to yell out to the guys on the other side of the room to stop fucking with that man and tell him where Claiborne's room was. But before I could say it, Nick was bouncing up the stairs like he knew where he was going, and K.B. and Jody were arguing about whether or not he was a nice guy. Before long, somebody in the dorm said that he was nicer than Claiborne, and nobody argued about that.

In a couple of months, Nick was running Carver House. We were all part of his gang. He would never help us rob the kitchen and stuff like that, but he used to take us on hikes around Farmer Greene's apple orchard and look the other way sometimes. He was more like one of the guys because he liked a lot of the things we liked. He would play the dozens, have rock fights, and curse us out. But I think we liked Nick mostly because he was fair to everybody. Nick never liked to see anybody getting bullied, but he was always ready to see a fair fight. I liked the way Nick was always lying to us. Everybody knew he was lying most of the time, but we didn't care, because he used to tell such good lies. Nick was a real big cat, even bigger than Simms, and he was from Texas; and some of the lies he used to tell were bigger than him and Texas.

Nick was much better to have as a counselor than Simms. Nick didn't get excited real quick the way Simms did, and Nick had sense. I wasn't so sure about Simms. I was always getting into fights with Nick, since I knew I wouldn't lose too bad. When Nick hit me, I would just hit back and keep swinging. But somehow I just couldn't see myself taking Simms on and living afterwards.

Within six months after I had moved into Aggrey House, most of the guys who had been in Carver House with me had been transferred to Aggrey. I had my old gang from Carver and some bigger cats who were already in Aggrey when I got there. I was raising twice the hell that I had raised in Carver House, and Simms wasn't smiling now. Some of the counselors were starting to say that nothing could be done with me and that I should be sent to Warwick. But there was a new man, Papanek, in charge of everything at Wiltwyck, and he didn't feel that I should be sent to Warwick or anyplace like that. Papanek had the last word on everything about Wiltwyck. Even Stilly had to listen to him, like it or not. At first, most of the cats up at Wiltwyck thought Papanek was kind of crazy. And I think some of the counselors felt that way too. But Papanek wasn't anything like crazy. He was probably the smartest and the deepest cat I had ever met. Before long, we all found out that Papanek was the best thing that ever happened to Wiltwyck and maybe one of the best things that could ever happen to any boy who got into trouble and was lucky enough to meet him.

I remember the first day Papanek came to Wiltwyck. Everybody was told to come to the auditorium that afternoon. For a long time, we had heard rumors about getting a new director, and it seemed that this was the day. The counselors usually had a lot of trouble getting guys to go to the auditorium for anything other than a movie. But the day Papanek showed, it was different. Everybody, boys and counselors, was real anxious to see what this cat looked like, if he knew anything, if he was big or small, mean or kind, colored or white, young or old. We wanted to know what kind of changes were in store for us . . . for Wiltwyck. Every boy and every counselor knew that the man we were going to meet that afternoon would be the one to handle all our troubles at Wiltwyck for a long time to come. Just the thought of a cat being able to do that was enough to make us really wonder about him. Some of us wanted to know mainly if he was as mean as the outgoing director. All I ever knew about that cat was that he was mean as hell, and I think that's all a lot of cats ever knew about him. He looked like one of those mean old preachers who would think nothing of killing somebody in the name of the Lord. I hated to be around the cat. He never smiled, and he was too quick to take off his belt and beat your ass.

After Stilly told us that the new director was going to introduce himself to us and say a few words, most of us were still looking for the cat when he started talking. I remember Papanek saying, "My name is Ernst Papanek." I just watched him. He wasn't tall or short, and he was real straight with a bald head and a kindly face. He didn't look real bold, but the seemed to have a whole lot of confidence, as if he knew he could handle Wiltwyck. Like everybody else, I was more interested in him than in what he was talking about. To me, he just didn't look like the kind of cat who could handle Wiltwyck. The poor guy looked like somebody even the counselors could run over. After a while, Papanek stopped talking and asked if there were any questions. After the first question, it seemed that Papanek was talking *with* everybody, not *to* us.

As we left the auditorium after hearing Papanek tell us who he was, where he was from, and what he wanted to do at Wiltwyck, I had the feeling that the rule of the staff was over. It was a good feeling. I knew that the boys were going to run Wiltwyck now. And I was going to be the one in charge. I was going to be the director of Wiltwyck, thanks to that poor old nice Mr. Papanek.

I tried to joke about Papanek's accent with K.B. and Horse, but they seemed to be kind of lost. Tito said, "Man, he sure can't talk." J.J. said something about how shiny Papanek's bald head was. A few guys tried to laugh, but I could tell they were faking. Some of the counselors were trying to make fun of Papanek, but they were faking it too. I couldn't understand this. I started talking to everybody about the new director, counselors and boys; everybody was lying and trying to hide it, but I could tell that they liked him and thought he was a nice guy. I got kind of scared of this guy Papanek. He had come to Wiltwyck and talked for a little while. And in that little while, with just talk, he had won every living ass in the place — just took over everything with a few words that we couldn't even understand too well. No, I didn't like this cat. He was slick . . . real slick. Papanek was so slick that he didn't have to be mean. He could take anyplace right on over in less than a day and never fire a shot. I had never met anybody that slick before. He scared me a little bit, but I had to get to know this cat and find out just how smart he was.

I went looking for Papanek. I had to talk to him and find out about him. I saw him coming out of the dining room, talking with a couple of kids. He had his arm around their shoulders, and a lot of guys were crowding around him and walking with him. I wondered if he thought he was Jesus or some fucking body like that. Papanek stopped and started answering questions asked by some of the cats crowding around him. He was leaning forward with his neck stuck out and his hands folded behind his back. I used to be afraid of people who kept their hands behind their backs, because I once had a teacher who used to slap me right after she put her hands behind her back.

When I came up to Papanek and his crowd, I just stood on the outside and listened for a while. I don't know if I was scared or just wanted to get a better idea of what I was up against before I declared war. Floyd Saks was telling Papanek about all his ills and troubles. Papanek was listening, but he seemed to know that Floyd was a little crazy and just liked to fuck with people by talking a lot of nonsense for a long time. Papanek knew Floyd had him, but he didn't seem to know how to get away. He kept looking over the crowd and all around him, as if hoping to see somebody who would call him and save him from Floyd. Every time Papanek would look away, Floyd would call his name and make him pay attention to what he was saying, crazy though it was. I think too many people were trying to pick Papanek's pocket at the same time, so nobody was getting anything. But it didn't really matter, because they would have just given whatever they took back to him. They liked this cat.

I didn't say anything to Papanek that first day, but after he took over, we were warring until I went home for good. After I got to know Papanek, I found out how to really bother him; but I had to keep finding new ways, because the cat was slicker than anybody else at Wiltwyck. It was hard to bother him the same way twice. Papanek brought a whole new way of doing things to Wiltwyck. He made a rule that boys were not to be beaten or even slapped by counselors any more. I expected Stilly to leave the day that Papanek passed that rule, but he didn't. He stayed on for nearly a year. Then I guess he just couldn't take it any more.

Papanek might have been a little crazy, but he meant all the crazy things he said to the boys and counselors. This was one of the things that made Papanek so hard to fight. I could never catch him in a lie, and he would never hit anybody. And as time went by, nobody could make him mad. At least he never showed it. He would look real sad sometimes, but he wouldn't get mad. But you could always tell when he got excited, because his accent would get stronger but his words would be real clear. I had never met anybody before who never got mad, and I had never met anybody who was always telling the truth like Papanek. But that's the way he was. If you asked him the hard Wiltwyck questions like, "When am I going home?" or, "Why are you keeping me here so long?" and Papanek couldn't tell you, he wouldn't lie about it. He would tell you something that left you knowing no more than before you asked him the question, but you would feel kind of satisfied about it. Sometimes he would have you talking about something else altogether different from what you asked him, and most of the time you would never know it. He was smarter than social workers, that was for sure, because he knew how to answer the hard questions without lying. So nobody could ever be mad at him for lying to them. And even though cats up at Wiltwyck lied a whole lot, like me, we didn't like grown-ups to lie to us about important things like the hard questions. Sometimes I use to get real tired of all that damn truth Papanek was telling, but I couldn't get mad at him for it.

For the next year or more, I tried to make life real sad for Papanek. This became harder and harder as time went by, because I grew to like him more and more, just like everybody else.

## SUGGESTED READINGS FOR PART FOUR

### American Indians

1969   A wide range of basic articles, analyses, and testimony is available in a series of volumes issued by the Subcommittee on Indian Education of the Committee on Labor and Public Welfare, United States Senate, Ninety-First Congress. The title is *Indian Education* (1969). Senator Edward Kennedy heads this subcommittee which his brother, Senator Robert Kennedy, formerly headed.

### American Black Population

Many relevant books are now being published. Two moving personal accounts are Herbert Kohl's *36 Children* (1967: Signet Q3684) and Jonathan Kozol's *Death at an Early Age* (1967: Houghton Mifflin). Elliot Liebow's *Tally's Corner: A Study of Negro Streetcorner Men* (1967: Little, Brown and Company) provides an illuminating portrait of Black males who eke out an existence at the periphery of an increasingly education-oriented society. A comparison of Liebow's views with those of Rosalie Wax, Murray Wax, et al. is especially interesting.

# Bibliography

ADAMS, EVELYN C.
1946    American Indian education. New York, Kings Crown Press.

BANTON, MICHAEL P.
1960    West African city. London, Oxford University Press.

BEATTY, WILLARD W.
1956    Twenty years of Indian education. *In* The Indian in modern America, David A. Baerreis, ed. Madison, State Historical Society of Wisconsin.

BERKHOFER, ROBERT F., JR.
1965    Salvation and the savage: An analysis of Protestant missions and American Indian response, 1787–1862. Lexington, University of Kentucky Press.

BROPHY, WILLIAM A. AND SOPHIE D. ABERLE (COMPS.)
1966    The Indian: America's unfinished business. Norman, University of Oklahoma Press.

CLIGNET, REMI AND PHILIP FOSTER
1964    Potential elites in Ghana and the Ivory Coast: A preliminary comparison. American Journal of Sociology LXX (3):349–362.

COMMITTEE ON HIGHER EDUCATION
1963    The demand for places in higher education. Higher Education (appendix II). London, H.M.S.O.

DEBO, ANGIE
1951    The five civilized tribes of Oklahoma: Report on social and economic conditions. Philadelphia, Indian Rights Association.

DUBOIS, VICTOR
1965    The student-government conflict in the Ivory Coast, American Universities Field Staff Reports, West Africa series, VIII(1).

EDDY, ELIZABETH M.
1967    Walk the white line. New York, Doubleday Anchor.

EGGAN, FRED
1966    The American Indian. Chicago, Aldine.

FEY, HAROLD E. AND D'ARCY MCNICKLE
1959    Indians and other Americans. New York, Harper

FOSTER, PHILIP
1965    Education and social change in Ghana. Chicago, University of Chicago Press.

247

FUCHS, ESTELLE
1966     Pickets at the gates. New York, Free Press.

GOLDTHORPE, J. E.
1961     Educated Africans: Some conceptual and terminological problems. *In* Social change in modern Africa, A. Southall, ed. London, Oxford University Press.

GULICK, JOHN
1960     Cherokees at the cross-roads. Chapel Hill, Institute for Research in Social Science, the University of North Carolina.

HOLT, JOHN
1964     How children fail. New York, Delta.

HUGHES, EVERETT C. AND HELEN M. HUGHES
1952     Where peoples meet: Ethnic and racial frontiers. Glencoe Free Press.

IWAO, GOTOO
1949     Zooho atarashii kyooikuhoo.

KOHL, HERBERT
1967     Thirty-six children. New York, World.

KOZOL, JONATHAN
1967     Death at an early age. Boston, Houghton Mifflin.

KUPER, LEO
1965     An African bourgeoisie. New Haven, Yale University Press.

LE LIVRE DES INSTITUTEURS
1948     19ᵉ édition. Paris, Le Soudier.

LEVINE, STUART AND NANCY O. LURIE (EDS.)
1968     The American Indian today. Delano, Florida, Everett Edwards, Inc.

LIEBOW, ELLIOT
1967     Tally's corner: A study of Negro streetcorner men. Boston, Little, Brown.

MERIAM, LEWIS AND ASSOCIATES
1928     The problem of Indian administration. Baltimore, Johns Hopkins Press.

MOLEMA, S. M.
1920     The Bantu past and present. Edinburgh, Green.

MOORE, G. ALEXANDER
1967     Realities of the urban classroom: Observations in elementary schools. New York, Doubleday Anchor.

NASH, PHILLEO
1967     Proceedings of the national research conference on American Indian education, Herbert A. Aurback, ed. Kalamazoo, Michigan, The Society for the Study of Social Problems.

NGUBANE, JORDAN
1963     An African explains apartheid. New York, Praeger.

NYUUSU, SHUPPAN
1951     Shuppan nenkan.

REPORT OF THE FORT HARE COMMISSION
1955    Lovedale, Lovedale Press.

SOKOLSKI, ALAN
1965    The establishment of manufacturing in Nigeria. New York, Frederick Praeger.

SPICER, EDWARD H.
1962    Cycles of conquest. Tucson, University of Arizona Press.

TAMOTSU, TAKATA
1952    Daini burari-hyootan.

WALLER, WILLARD
1932    Sociology of teaching. New York, John Wiley (Science Editions).
(1965)

WARHAFTIG, ALBERT
1965a   Social and economic characteristics of the Cherokee population of eastern Oklahoma. Chicago, Carnegie Cross-Cultural Education Project of the University of Chicago (mimeo.).
1965b   The tribal Cherokee population of eastern Oklahoma. Chicago, Carnegie Cross-Cultural Education Project of the University of Chicago (mimeo.).
1966    Community and the caretakers. New University Thought IV (4):54–76.

WAX, MURRAY L.
1967    Ecology, economy, and educational achievement. Lawrence, Indian Research Project of the University of Kansas (mimeo.).
1968    The white man's burdensome "business": A review essay on the change and consistency of literature on the American Indians. Social Problems, Vol. 16, No. 1, 1968, pp. 106–113.

WAX, MURRAY L. AND ROSALIE H. WAX
1968    The enemies of the people. *In* Institutions and the person: Essays presented to Everett C. Hughes, Howard S. Becker, *et al.*, eds. Chicago, Aldine Press.

WAX, ROSALIE H. AND MURRAY L. WAX
1965    American Indian education for what? Midcontinent American Studies Journal VI (2):164–170.

WAX, MURRAY L., ROSALIE H. WAX AND ROBERT V. DUMONT, JR.
1964    Formal education in an American Indian community. Kalamazoo, Michigan, The Society for the Study of Social Problems.

WILSON, GORDON
1961    Mombasa: A modern colonial municipality. *In* Social change in modern Africa, A. Southall, ed. London, Oxford University Press.

WOLCOTT, HARRY F.
1967    A Kwakiutl village and school. New York, Holt, Rinehart & Winston.

ZAY, JEAN
1938    Enseignement du premier degré. instructions relatives à l'application des arrêtés du 23 mars 1938 et du 11 juillet 1938. *In* Journal officiel, Annexe, 24 septembre.